THE NEW
INVESTMENT
FRONTIER

THE NEW INVESTMENT FRONTIER

A Guide to Exchange Traded Funds for Canadians

Howard J. Atkinson
with Donna Green

INSOMNIAC PRESS

Edited and designed by Mike O'Connor
Copy-edited by Jan Barbieri

National Library of Canada Cataloguing in Publication Data

Atkinson, Howard J., 1958–

    The New Investment Frontier: A Guide to Exchange Traded Funds for Canadians

ISBN 1-894663-14-4

    1. Exchange traded funds. 2. Stock index futures. I. Green, Donna M. II. Title.

HG6043.A85 2001   332.63'228   C2001-902143-7

The publisher and the author gratefully acknowledge the support of the Canada Council, the Ontario Arts Council and the Department of Canadian Heritage through the Book Publishing Industry Development Program.

Printed and bound in Canada.

Insomniac Press, 192 Spadina Avenue, Suite 403,
Toronto, Ontario, Canada, M5T 2C2
www.insomniacpress.com

THE CANADA COUNCIL | LE CONSEIL DES ARTS
FOR THE ARTS | DU CANADA
SINCE 1957 | DEPUIS 1957

ONTARIO ARTS COUNCIL
CONSEIL DES ARTS DE L'ONTARIO

For my parents, who continue to make the investment of a lifetime.

Acknowledgements

The biggest challenge in writing this book was laying hands on data. Thanks go to Norman Rothery of *www.stingyinvestor.com* for his invaluable research and number crunching, and to Morningstar Canada's J. Stephen Burnie for making Morningstar's extensive mutual fund data available and putting it in a useful form.

I also want to thank all the people who agreed to be end-of-chapter interviews: Nate Most, Bill Fouse, John Bogle, Duff Young, Steve Rive, Paul Mazzilli, Gavin Quill. Special thanks to Dan Hallett, who also contributed throughout the book and read the entire manuscript.

There were many others who also gave generously of their time. I'd like to thank Peter Haynes at TD Newcrest for his explanation of the ETF market making activity and his tour of TD's ETF trading area; Janice Russell, investment tax specialist with PricewaterhouseCoopers for reviewing the tax-related information and explaining the intricacies of Canadian tax legislation; Mark Rubinstein, the unrecognized inventor of ETFs, who went well out of his way to explain the history of modern financial markets; Eric Kirzner who was a help in the early history of TIPS, along with Gord Walker and Bruce Thompson.

Thanks go to Lea Hill, closed-end fund specialist, for some statistics; Glenn Doody at S&P Canada and Jim Nevler at Dow Jones Indexes in New Jersey for explaining the technical aspects of indices; and thanks to Rudy Luukko for rummaging through his basement one glorious weekend on a fruitless quest for some hard-to-find numbers.

A number of financial advisors volunteered information on the way they work with ETFs: John De Goey, Keith Matthews and John Hood. Paul Morse at Charles Schwab Canada and Craig Ellis, Portfolio Manager, took a good part of their days to explain their Core and Explore approach in Canada.

Much of the information on U.S. ETFs was drawn from the excellent ETF research reports written by Morgan Stanley, Goldman Sachs and Salomon Smith Barney. I salute their hardworking ETF analysts. Sarah Thompson and John Mountain at Investment Funds Institute of Canada answered more than their share of questions.

Steve Geist and Stephen Hoffman at TD Financial Group read some of the manuscript and promptly responded to questions and requests for information. Jean Dumoulin and Louis Basque at State Street Global Advisors were similarly helpful.

A very special thanks to the team at Barclays Global Investors Canada

Limited (BGI)—Gerry Rocchi, Steve Rive, Linda Brillante, Warren Collier, Ruby Velji, Barb Clapman and Ed Hughes—for their support on this project.

I am indebted to Brad Zigler, Adam Gebler and Jeannie Somsen from BGI's head office in San Francisco, for ensuring that this work continued no matter which side of the border I was on.

Erica O'Keeffe, assistant extraordinaire, has been and continues to be invaluable in holding even projects like this together. I am grateful a hundred times over for her untiring help.

I hope Deb, who painstakingly reviewed the manuscript, and my three children, Sydney, Garrett and Olivia (who think that ETF stands for "Extremely Tardy Father"), realize that a few missed dinners and fatherless baseball games don't mean I love them any less.

And finally, my sincerest appreciation to Donna Green. Without her tireless effort and forgiving nature, these words would not have made it to paper.

The night is late and I hope that if there is anyone I have inadvertently left out they know that it isn't due to a shortcoming of gratitude, but only to the feebleness of memory.

Howard J. Atkinson
Oakville
July 2001

My warmest thanks to Howard Atkinson whose vision made this book possible and whose generosity and good nature sustained the effort. Thanks to Anne Papmehl for suggesting me to Howard; Tim Whitehead for starting me on this path in the first place; and to Jane Sembera, in keeping with a very old promise and in gratitude for an even older friendship that showed itself again on a long gloomy night of revisions. Love and thanks to my unceasingly supportive husband, Arthur, and my very understanding children.

Donna Green
Oakville
July 2001

Table of Contents

Author's Foreword

Exchange traded funds (ETFs) are the most exciting investment vehicle to come along since mutual funds, and I'm thrilled to be involved in bringing these useful tools to Canadian investors. ETFs allow you to invest the way you do now, only better.

At the risk of sounding like a pessimist, I think we are all slowly coming to the realization that the terrific returns of the last ten years are not likely to be repeated in the next ten years. Markets will almost certainly revert to their historic norms, and when they do, we're all going to be scrutinizing how much of the far-more parsimonious pie investment costs and taxes are eating up.

Fortunately, there is an investment alternative: ETFs are enviously tax efficient and refreshingly low cost. It's about time something that has been tremendously popular with institutional money managers on Bay Street and Wall Street should gain popularity on Main Street, too. Institutional investors have long embraced ETFs. Today, about 75% of ETF assets are held in institutional accounts. ETFs are "the funds the fund managers use," but there's no reason why you and I shouldn't be in on the secret.

Knowledge really is power, and the Internet has given us the information and the confidence to become impatient with investment products that are unneccesarily complicated. We want simplicity. We want to know exactly where our investment dollars are going, unbundled from fees and costs. We want value for money. ETFs are simple to use, unbundled in costs and available in real time.

As of July 2001, there were 150 ETFs trading globally. Nine years ago there were only two. Other recent developments continue to underscore the momentum ETFs are gaining. The American retail indexing giant, Vanguard Group, has done an about-face and marched into the arena by offering their own ETFs. The New York Stock Exchange has broken a century-old gentlemen's agreement among the major exchanges by trading three ETFs that were and still are listed on the American Stock Exchange. Finally, the venerable *Wall Street Journal* has created a permanent, separate listing section for all ETFs entitled, "Exchange Traded Portfolios." These moves are all in response to the popularity and promise of these full-flavoured, low-calorie index investments.

How to Use This Book

The New Investment Frontier is divided into four sections. Part One explains what ETFs are and how they work, and explores the concept of indexing and the alternatives to ETFs for implementing an indexing approach. Part Two explores investment strategies using ETFs, their tax implications and tax saving strategies, and how to use ETFs with an advisor. Part Three looks to the past and future of ETFs: where did they come from and what will they evolve into? Mutual funds are going to rise to the competitive threat and you'll be best equipped to understand the new products that will inevitably spring forth by knowing a little bit of history and stealing a peek at the future. Part Four is an aggregation of vital statistics on ETFs, their universe and related information sources. The appendices in Part Four alone comprise an invaluable ETF resources centre. Feel free to skip around to the chapters that most interest you. Both the material in this book and ETFs themselves can be used to complement existing investment strategies or help to develop new ones, whether you invest on your own or with the aid of an advisor.

It's easy to forget that financial products are invented and run by people, people who often face obstacles in making their products come alive. To capture this human dimension, there's an interview at the end of each chapter with product pioneers or industry experts intimately in touch with the birth pangs of the new investment frontier. Among them are men like Bill Fouse, who invested the first index fund and whose patriotism was questioned for doing so; and John Bogle, the founder of the world's largest index fund company, who has made it his mission to challenge the fund industry to justify its management costs. This is an unusual element in a personal finance book, but one I'm particularly proud of.

When you close the cover of this book, the story will be far from over. As I write, many more ETFs are in developmen, and the prospect of a new breed of (actively managed) ETFs seems very close. ETFs will continue to evolve and so should our consciousness of their benefits. May you reach your goals, and if ETFs can help get you there, this book should be of service.

Disclaimer

The author is National Marketing Manager for iUnits in Canada and a principal with Barclays Global Investors Canada Limited.

The opinions expressed in this book are exclusively his and do not necessarily reflect those of Barclays Global Investors.

While every effort was made to ensure the accuracy of the information herein, the author and the publisher assume no responsibility for errors, omissions or inconsistencies, and they disclaim any liability arising from the use of information in this book. Every investor's situation is different and it is always prudent to consult qualified financial professionals.

Part One
The Powerful Case for ETFs

Chapter 1

What Are ETFs? How Are They Different From Mutual Funds?

Exchange traded funds (ETFs) are the investment world's equivalent of a nectarine—part mutual fund, part stock, but a marvellous improvement over both. Canada went from having one ETF to fourteen in two years, and at least one more is slated for launch in fall 2001. Globally, the number of new ETF products is exploding, even against the backdrop of uncertain markets. In April 2000 there were 30 ETFs trading on American stock exchanges worth $36.5 billion. A year later there were over 100 listed globally with assets exceeding US$75 billion, and nearly another hundred awaiting launch. Boston-based Financial Research Corporation predicts that total ETF assets will reach somewhere around $500 billion in the U.S. alone by 2007. Conventional mutual funds can only envy this growth and likely suspect their glory days are over.

In this chapter we'll explore the differences between ETFs and conventional mutual funds. ETFs have a lot in common with mutual funds, but the differences are significant because they can have a big effect on the overall cost of your investments, and as a result, your returns. What follows is a brief rundown of the similarities and differences between mutual funds and the more delectable hybrid, ETFs.

An Exchange Traded Fund Is a Portfolio of Securities that Trades on a Stock Exchange

An exchange traded fund is a mutual fund that trades like a stock. It may not seem like much of an innovation, but this feature gives ETFs several advantages including greater tax efficiency and better price transparency. Lets look at conventional mutual funds for a moment, in order to better understand the advantages of ETFs.

A mutual fund is a basket of securities owned by a number of investors but managed by a professional money manager. It's a bit like an office gift pool, where everybody throws in some money and one person buys the gift. Only in the case of funds, the person buying the gift isn't giving up her lunch hour. She's a professional money manager shopping for securities— and getting paid handsomely for it, too.

Because the fund holds a basket of different investments, you spread your risk among a plentiful number of bets. Broad, diversified investments and professional management have propelled mutual funds into the behemoths they are today, managing $403 billion—more than all the money in savings accounts in Canada.[1]

Once a day, after the close of trading, a mutual fund's stocks and bonds are priced and the fund is given its daily value. When the fund has been priced, all fund unit buy and sell orders that have been queuing up throughout the day are transacted by the mutual fund. This pricing arrangement doesn't allow you to know beforehand what price you are going to get when you place an order to buy or sell a mutual fund.[2]

ETFs, on the other hand, trade on a stock exchange exactly like a stock: they are priced continuously and can be bought and sold any time the market is open. This means you can know exactly what will end up going into or coming out of your pocket. It also means that all the devices used for stock trading can be applied to trading ETFs: price limit orders, stop loss orders, short selling, margining, and in some cases, even option strategies.

Unlike mutual funds, a brokerage commission applies up front on the sale or purchase of ETFs because they trade on an exchange. While most mutual funds usually have no transaction costs on a sale or purchase, there can be "loads" triggered. A "load" is a sales commission payable to an advisor and his company. Front-end load funds pay the sales commission on purchase of the fund directly from your investment money. Back-end load funds ding you for a sales commission on the sale of the fund if you redeem before some specified holding period—usually six or seven years.

Both conventional mutual funds and ETFs enjoy the single biggest advantage of funds—their broad diversification—but ETFs have the added advantage of being traded like a stock. It seems investors are warming to the unique benefits of the ETF. Canadian ETFs have so far racked up $5 billion in assets—about 1.5% the size of Canada's $354.5 billion mutual fund assets—not including moneymarket funds.[3] In the U.S., ETFs account for $73 billion—1% the size of the $7 trillion invested in U.S. mutual funds and related fund products—and growing 128% a year.[4] ETF sponsors in Canada expect proportional growth. But acceptance of this next generation of mutual fund, at least for the time being, will depend on the popularity of indexing.

Most ETFs Mirror a Stock Index

An index is a collection of stocks or bonds intended to reflect the movement of a broader market. The S&P/TSE 60 Index, for instance, is a collection of 60 of Canada's largest and most widely traded stocks. The movement of those 60 stocks is indicative of the broader Canadian market as a whole—or at least the larger companies that make it up.

A conventional mutual fund uses a manager to select the fund's investments. The manager actively buys and sell securities hoping to outperform the market. The sad truth is that most fund managers don't often surpass benchmark indices, especially over the long haul. This sticky little fact has prompted many investors to turn to a passive style of management, in which a fund manager simply replicates the market she's in with the more modest ambition of merely keeping pace with the market—which passively managed funds do reasonably well.

Cost Advantages

When you consider that the cost of running an actively managed fund is often considerably more than double the cost of maintaining an index fund, it's surprising more fund managers don't just pack up their laptops and move to Vegas. The management expense ratio (MER) is a standard measure of fund costs. It is an annualized figure that captures a fund's operating expenses and management fees, stated as a percentage of the fund's assets. The bigger this number, the less of the fund's return you see. An average Canadian (load) equity fund carries an MER of 2.34% (234 basis points). About 40 of the basis points goes to paying the manager for investment research and decisions. A much larger portion of the MER is used to finance sales and distribution. Index funds, free from the burden of active management, though not always entirely free of paying sales commission, typically shoulder a much lighter .75% MER or less because all they've got to do is hold on to an index.5 ETFs also have an MER but it is even smaller than a load equity fund or an index fund. Canada's most popular ETF, the i60 Fund, has a sporty MER of .17%. And coming in at the incredible bantam weight of a mere .08% is State Street Global Advisor's Dow Jones Canada 40 ETF.

Index fund managers generally buy the same stocks in the same proportion as the index they are tracking, put their head in their hands and watch it work. Good index funds will mimic the performance of their index—minus the cost of the fund's MER.

Most of the ETFs available now work in roughly the same way as an index fund. Each ETF tracks a specific index, domestic or foreign, but does it even more cheaply than an index fund. Canadian-based ETF MERs range from .08% to .55%, a fairly ascetic lot.

If you don't think saving 1% or 2% in MERs over the lifetime of your investments is anything to worry about, consider the chart below. It shows the difference a few percentage points can make on what you get to keep of your own returns. It's chilling.

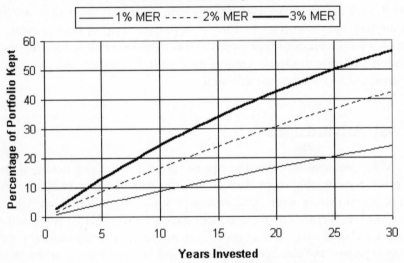

What Funds Keep (fig. 1)

Source: Norman Rothery, www.stingyinvestor.com

Your financial advisor's commission on a back-end load fund (otherwise known as a "deferred sales charge fund," or DSC) is around 5% of the value of your investment; and on equity funds, the fee for providing ongoing service is typically another .5%. The charge is not paid directly by you, but is financed through your fund's MER. The economics work because the MERs are high enough to make it work, and if you should have to redeem your fund before your declining sales charge schedule has run its course, you'll find that ETFs, even with their trading commission costs, are a real bargain.

As long as you hold a back-end load fund for the full course of its DSC schedule (usually about seven years), you don't pay any sales charge on redemption. Most fund companies do allow free 10% annual redemptions and free switches among funds in the same fund company, but if you should happen to want to move your money out of the fund company altogether before the DSC schedule has run its inexorable course, you pay a back-end load that starts as high as 7% of your investment and declines over the schedule.

Compare the percent of your assets charge to the flat fee cost of selling an ETF at a discount broker for $29 a trade:

A $10,000 ETF sale with a commission of $29 = .29% (or 29 basis points).
A $10,000 mutual fund redemption with a load of 3%* = 3% (or 300 basis points).
Therefore, $300 - $29 = $271.00 savings.
*insert any number from 0 to 7 here depending on holding period

You can escape a back-end charge by purchasing front-end load funds. These are the second most popular commission option through full service and discount brokers. Under the front-load arrangement, your advisor's sales commission comes immediately and directly out of your invested dollars. You can often negotiate around this charge especially for large accounts, but the MER doesn't budge; and front-end load fund MERs are little different from their back-end twins. Why are the MERs so high when there is no advisor commission? Well, front-end load equity funds are paying out a sweet 1% annual trailer to your advisor. So with either the front-end or back-end option, one percentage point of your MER is going to pay advisor compensation in one form or another.

It's up to you to decide if you are receiving value commensurate with the cost. Once you understand the impact these charges have on your returns over time, it's hard to feel indifferent to them.

Canadian Equity Fund vs. Index Fund vs. Index (fig. 2)

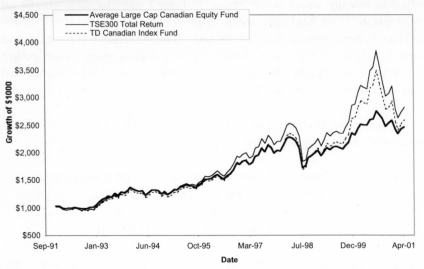

Source: Norman Rothery

Note: 2.3% MER on Cdn large cap fund, .85% MER on TD Canadian Index Fund.

Tax Advantages

Index investing with either index mutual funds or ETFs has some tax advantages over conventional actively managed funds because active managers generate capital gains when they sell securities at a profit, which is their job after all. Where an active fund manager might turn over 80% of a portfolio in a year on average, the S&P/TSE 60 Index turns over its holdings on average about 8% a year.[6] All these changes often generate capital gains that must be passed on annually to the fund investor. The unhappy consequence of this is not only a tax bill, but sometimes you can find yourself paying tax on gains the fund made before you even owned it.

The less a portfolio trades, the fewer capital gains are realized and ultimately distributed. Since an index manager is most often sitting passively on her portfolio, doing little more than trying to keep it as similar to the target index as possible, index funds tend to be more tax efficient than actively managed funds. Sure, a change to the underlying index will trigger a buy or sell within the fund, but these changes are seldom momentous.

This isn't to say that index mutual funds and ETFs have the same potential tax liabilities, because they don't; the difference is in how they deal with redemptions. Imagine a popular index suffering a severe and prolonged downturn, like Nasdaq. Push your imagination even further—if you owned a Nasdaq linked investment in 2000, you needn't push your imagination into overdrive. Suppose that Nasdaq index fund investors decided to flee to safer ground, redeeming their units in droves. The index fund manager would be forced to liquidate some portfolio holdings to get the cash to buy back the redeemed units. This move could lead to some unwanted capital gains distributions for the remaining loyal unitholders who went on to see the value of their holdings diminish as the bear market continued to maul their index and fund manager. A tax bill on top of a disastrous year could make these besotted investors wish the bear had simply left them for dead.

ETF investors don't have to stay up late worrying about redemption runs because retail investors can't redeem their shares; they can only buy and sell them to other parties. These transactions on the secondary market don't affect the underlying portfolio and thus have no tax consequences to other fund investors. This is the main reason ETFs should be more tax-efficient than index mutual funds: U.S.-based ETFs are decidedly more tax efficient than U.S.-based index funds. In Canada the jury is still out because up until recently there hasn't been an ETF to compare to an index fund tracking the same index.

There's reason to believe, though, that the tax efficiency difference in Canada may not be as pronounced as it is for U.S. products. As we'll discuss later, institutional clients can cash in large ETF positions for their underlying securities. In the U.S. this redemption does not trigger tax calculations; but in Canada it does.

Nevertheless, in general, ETF index investors have greater control over their own tax liabilities than their counterparts have with mutual funds. Actively managed fund unitholders are at the mercy of the manager's selling activity. Index mutual fund owners are at the mercy of the redeeming millions.

Managing the cash within a mutual fund to anticipate those redemptions is always a fine balancing act. Too little cash and the fund may not be able to meet redemptions, have to sell positions and possibly trigger tax. Since ETFs don't redeem shares for cash, they don't have this problem. Nor do they share with mutual funds the opposite problem of having too much cash. Any mutual fund can underperform in a rising market when it has too much money in cash and not enough invested. This can happen when there is a swift influx of new money into the fund or when a market surge catches a manager off guard. The resulting effect on fund returns is known as "cash drag." ETFs have some cash drag from dividends accumulated from underlying securities, but they don't have a problem with uninvested cash. ETF units are created by designated brokers in discrete units with a fixed number of securities. This means there is never any cash in an ETF portfolio waiting to be invested in more of the underlying securities, as is the case with conventional mutual funds.

What Mutual Funds Have that ETFs Don't

Mutual funds do have some attractive features that ETFs don't share. For one thing, mutual funds can be bought with small minimum invest-ments—often as little as $500—and it is easy to arrange small regular monthly purchases commonly known as pre-authorized chequing plans (PACs). ETFs, in contrast, are generally bought and sold in lots of 100 shares. In spring 2001, i60s were trading around $43 a share. Based on 100 shares (a "board lot"), that's a $4,300 minimum investment plus brokerage commission. Of course, it is possible to buy less than 100 shares (an "odd lot"), but the brokerage commission isn't reduced for these smaller orders, which makes them less cost effective than a board lot purchase.

While ETFs have a trading commission associated with them, there is usually no transaction cost to buy or sell a mutual fund. The mutual fund company executes these transactions for free. Remember, of course, that mutual funds often have front or back-end loads.

Another nice feature of a mutual fund is the ease with which dividends can be reinvested. Mutual fund owners can elect to have their dividends and other distributions either sent to them in cash or reinvested into units of the fund automatically. ETF investors have to take the cash unless their brokerage house has a private dividend reinvestment plan in place. At the time of printing, only one brokerage firm in Canada, RBC Investments, was offering the dividend reinvestment option, but don't be surprised to see other firms follow suit in the future.

Keep in mind that ETF distributors do not issue certificates. Your ETF holding is noted electronically and no physical certificate is required or produced. Most mutual fund companies, on the other hand, will provide share certificates upon request and for a small fee. The certificate permits you to hold the investments in a safety deposit box. But even without a cer-tificate, you can still pledge your ETFs at a bank for a loan.

The Varieties of ETFs

ETFs are easy to use and make it simple to gain exposure to just about any geographical area, economic sector or market segment. The sheer number of ETFs currently trading or awaiting launch testify to this attractive feature. As of July, 2001 there were 114 ETFs trading in North America: 101 in the U.S. and 13 in Canada.

Most of the ETFs traded in North America are related to an index. There's no shortage of financial indices and subindices, so as you might expect, ETFs show a similar and related proliferation. There's an ETF for all the major indices: S&P 500, the Dow Jones Industrial Average, Nasdaq 100, TSE 300, S&P/TSE 60, and as of August 2001, MSCI EAFE (Europe, Australasia and the Far East.) Then there are ETFs for just about every industry sector known to analysts: Financial, Industrial, Technology, Utilities, Internet, Business-to-Business Internet, Biotechnology, Pharmaceuticals, Regional Banks, you name it. (For a complete list of ETFs and their indices see Appendix B.)

And if sectors aren't enough, there are ETFs to suit your taste in investment style and/or market capitalization. State Street Global Advisors in the U.S. offers a series based on the Dow Jones Index broken down according to a combination of capitalization and investment style: DJ U.S. Large Cap Value is one such example.

There are also ETFs for a broad swath of developed and developing countries from humble Malaysia to languorous Brazil. There are 21 country ETFs in all, each one trying to track their respective country's broad market. There are even ETFs that track the movement of large, actively traded U.S. real estate investment trusts (REITs).

In Canada, the RRSP rules that limit foreign content to 30% has spurred the development of two 100% RRSP eligible ETFs based on foreign indices. These should give chase to the clone mutual funds that were the rage in early 2000. Clone funds track a foreign market by buying complicated derivative contracts on the targeted market and investing the majority of the fund's money in Government of Canada Treasury Bills (T-bills).7 Because most of the fund is in T-bills and similar instruments, the fund is considered 100% RRSP eligible even though it gives full investment exposure to foreign markets. Thus, Canadian investors can have unlimited exposure to foreign markets within their RRSPs without violating the foreign content rules. Trouble is, these mutual fund Dollies are fat with fees. Fortunately, there are now 100% RRSP eligible foreign index ETF counterparts to clone funds, and their relatively low MER makes these ETFs look positively athletic in comparison.

This brief survey might lead you to think ETFs are restricted to indexing, but the ETF structure and concept lends itself easily to other investments. Two Canadian ETFs, for instance, hold bonds—well, one bond each, to be exact. Barclays Global Investors (BGI) Canada Limited's iG5 Fund holds one Government of Canada five-year bond, which changes periodically to maintain a five-year maturity. Similarly, BGI's iG10 Fund invests in one Government of Canada ten-year bond. So far Canada is the only country to have a fixed income ETF, but this distinction will not hold for long: both Chicago-based Nuveen Investments and BGI plans to launch the first exchange traded funds that track U.S. Treasury Indexes.

Beyond indices and bonds you find actively managed ETFs. These are exchange traded baskets of investments, the contents of which are actively bought and sold by a fund manager. This type of ETF is handled exactly like a conventional actively managed mutual fund, but it trades on an exchange like a stock. Australia and Germany already have actively managed ETFs, and while there aren't any in North America now, they're likely to appear within the next few years. When they do come to North America, the whole mutual fund industry will be looking over its shoulder, if it's not already.

What's in a Name?

For all their conceptual elegance, exchange traded funds have a nomenclature that's easy to confuse with a spoonful of vegetable soup. Take, for example, streetTRACKS DJ U.S. Small Cap Value, or even the simpler i60C Fund. Generally, a letter or word in the name indicates the company that constructs and administers the fund. That company is known as the fund sponsor. For example, "streetTRACKS" is the general product name for a number of ETFs offered by State Street Global Advisors, a U.S. investment firm. The rest of the name identifies the particular index the ETF is associated with. In the example, the ETF is associated with the Dow Jones U.S. Small Cap Value Index, an index that consists of stocks in companies with small market capitalization, which are considered undervalued and longer-term holds.

The i60C Fund has a similar name structure. The "i" stands for "index" and is the distinctive indicator of "iUnits," the brand name for all of BGI Canada's ETFs (iShares are a Barclays' U.S. and global product). The "60" refers to the S&P/TSE 60 Index consisting of Canada's biggest and most frequently traded companies. The "C" stands for "capped." A capped index sets limits on how large a percentage any one stock in an index can obtain—typically no more than 10%, which is the case with the i60C Fund. It's important not to confuse "capped" with "cap," which is a short form of "market capitalization." There are small, mid and large cap ETFs, all of which have "cap" in their name but are not necessarily "capped" in terms of their investment weightings. "Cap" refers to the size of companies that make up the fund's core holdings or emphasis. Market capitalization is determined by multiplying the number of a company's shares outstanding by the market price per share.

TD Asset Management has an ETF based on a capped index, as well: TD TSE 300 Capped Fund. Capped indices became respectable when Nortel Networks Corporation made up a third of the TSE 100 in early 2000. So great was its concentration on the index that it was said when Nortel sneezed, the whole index shivered. Well, Nortel caught pneumonia and investors realized the appeal of limiting index concentrations as they were carried off to portfolio clinics, gasping for air.

The following is a list of all Canadian ETFs as of July 2001, and their sponsors.

Canadian-based Exchange Traded Funds

Fund	Description	Symbol	Sponsor
i60	Oldest and biggest ETF in Canada. TIPS35 and TIPS 100 merged with i60s in 03/00. Based on S&P/TSE 60 Index.	XIU	BGI Canada
iG5	5-year Government of Canada Bond	XGV	BGI Canada
iG10	10-year Government of Canada Bond	XGX	BGI Canada
i60C	Based on S&P/TSE 60 Capped Index (weights capped at 10%).	XIC	BGI Canada
iMidCap	Based on S&P/TSE MidCap Index (The next 60 companies by market cap after the i60 companies).	XMD	BGI Canada
iEnergy, iIT, iGold iFinancial	Four funds: Energy, Information Technology, Gold Financials. Based on respective S&P/TSE indices	XEG XIT, XGD XFN	BGI Canada
i500R	Based on S&P 500 Index 100% RRSP eligible.	XSP	BGI Canada
SSgA Dow Jones Canada 40	Based on Dow Jones Canada 40 Index	DJF	SSgA
TD TSE 300	Based on the TSE 300 Index	TTF	TDAM
TD TSE 300 Capped	Based on the TSE 300 Capped Index (weightings limited to 10%)	TCF	TDAM

BGI Canada: Barclays Global Investors Canada Ltd.; TDAM: TD Asset Management Inc.; SSgA: State Street Global Advisors

Popular U.S.-based Exchange Traded Funds

Fund	Description	Ticker	Sponsor
Standard & Poor's Depositary Receipt	Abbreviated as SPDR (Spider) Based on the S&P 500 Index. Oldest and biggest US ETF.	SPY	SSgA
Nasdaq 100	Often called "Qubes." Nasdaq 100 Index. Most heavily traded U.S. ETF.	QQQ	BoNY
MidCap SPDR	S&P MidCap 400 Index	MDY	BoNY
IShares S&P 500	Based on S&P 500 Index	IVV	BGI
Diamonds	Dow Jones Industrial Average	DIA	SSgA

BGI: Barclays Global Investors Ltd.; BoNY: Bank of New York; SSgA: State Street Global Advisors

To avoid confusion, please note that in Canada mutual funds and ETFs are sold in "units," while in the U.S, they are sold in "shares." We'll be using the terms similarly in this book.

Sponsors, Index Providers and Distributors

Index products, be they index mutual funds or ETFs, correspond to a specific index and must gain permission from the index provider to use that index. The i60 Fund, for instance, uses the S&P/TSE 60 Index which is administered by Standard & Poor's (S&P), the index provider. Money changes hands in these arrangements as the index provider charges a licensing fee to the fund manufacturer, otherwise known as the fund sponsor. For example, BGI Canada, the originator and sponsor of the i60 Fund, must pay Standard & Poor's for the use of its index. (As you might expect fights over licensing fees have kept a number of ETFs from market—especially the long awaited S&P 500 VIPER from U.S. index fund giant, Vanguard Group.)

And just to make things complicated, in the U.S., the company that sponsors or manufactures the ETF is not the same company that distributes it. BGI manufactures the iShares series but they are distributed by a separate company, SEI Investment Distribution Co. Ltd.

This isn't terribly relevant for ETFs in Canada but knowing this can avoid some confusion when you're looking at U.S. ETFs.

ETFs and Closed-end Funds

The idea of a basket of securities trading on a stock exchange is not new. Closed-end funds have been around for a long time. Like all funds, they are composed of a group of securities, but the fund is "closed" because it issues a fixed number of shares that stay constant in number. These shares trade either on a stock exchange or over-the-counter. Unlike a conventional mutual fund, which is open-ended because it will continually issue and redeem shares, closed-end funds do not issue or redeem shares after the initial offering. Therefore, investors in closed-end funds must find someone else to buy their shares when they wish to sell, just as they would for a stock.

Closed-end funds sound like a good idea, but in practice they have one stiff disadvantage: they frequently trade at less than the value of their underlying assets. This is called trading at a discount. (If they were to trade at more than their net asset value, they would be trading at a premium.) The average discount for closed-end funds in Canada is about 5%.[8] It's not entirely clear why there is a discount and why it is of this magnitude. Some have suggested that closed-end fund managers are not as aggressively profit-oriented as conventional fund managers because the shares cannot be redeemed. Others have suggested that discounts arise because of a worry about liquidity, or the ease with which the investment can be sold.

In any event, despite certain similarities, ETFs have none of the familiar disadvantages of closed-end funds. Like a closed-end investor, the typical retail ETF investor must buy and sell ETFs on the secondary market; in other words, the transaction must take place with another buyer or seller. However, with a sufficiently large holding, ETFs can be redeemed for their underlying securities. This requisite chunk is called a "creation unit" and generally consists of around 50,000 shares (the exact number varies from ETF to ETF). In the normal course of business, closed-end funds do not redeem their shares no matter how many are tendered. Open-end mutual funds usually don't redeem their underlying securities; they sell and redeem their shares daily for cash.

The first closed-end fund in Canada was Economic Investment Trust, launched in 1928. In the 73 years since, closed-end funds have gathered $6.7 billion in assets.[9] ETFs have been around for only 11 years, but at $5 billion and counting, they will certainly soon surpass their closed-end counterparts in assets. You'll often see closed-end funds grouped with ETFs and referred to as exchange traded funds. The contemporary crop of ETFs is then distinguished by the fetching term "index-linked." Closed-end funds might like to think of themselves as ETFs, but they're a generation behind, and even now not all contemporary ETFs are index-linked.

Fund Structure Comparison

Features	Index-Linked ETFs	Closed-Ended Funds	Open-Ended Funds
Management Style	Passive	Actively Managed	Passive/Active
Management Fees	Very Low	Low	Moderate to High
Pricing	Intraday	Intraday	End of Day
Restrictions on Investments in illiquid securities	No	No	Yes
Ability to Leverage	No	Yes	No
Premium/Discount Risk	Low	High	None
Tax Efficiency	High	Moderate	Moderate
Redemption Feature	Yes	No	Yes
Can Be Shorted	Yes	Yes	No
Transparency of Portfolio	Yes	No	No
Marginable	Yes	Yes	No
Can Place Limit Orders	Yes	Yes	No

Why ETFs Trade Close to the Value of Their Underlying Securities

Simply having some way to convert ETF shares to the underlying investments, and vice versa, means that ETFs almost always trade very close to the full value of their assets. Unlike close-end funds, ETFs seldom suffer much of a discount or a premium over their net asset value. That's because of a useful thing called "arbitrage." Here's how arbitrage works for ETFs.

If the market price for an ETF share is cheaper than the proportional portfolio value, an investor with enough shares to form a creation unit, typically an institutional investor, can redeem the shares for the underlying securities. Since the securities are worth more than the ETF share, the investor then sells the individual securities and pockets the profit. That's basic arbitrage and it works in reverse just as well. Should the ETF shares be selling for more than the value of the underlying portfolio, an investor can independently buy up the individual securities and hand them over to the ETF administrator, who will issue shares in the ETF. The investor can turn a profit by immediately selling those ETF shares.

So arbitrage in simple terms is buying cheap and simultaneously selling what's dear, and pocketing the difference after your costs. If you are arbitraging identical or nearly identical investments, there is little risk to this strategy, provided you can execute your orders instantaneously.

Arbitrage Mechanism Results in Low Premium/Discount (fig. 3)

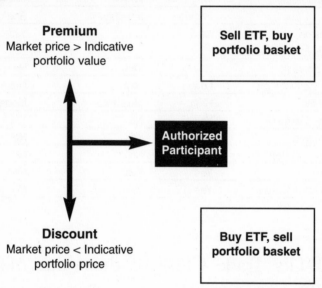

Premium
Market price > Indicative portfolio value

Sell ETF, buy portfolio basket

Authorized Participant

Discount
Market price < Indicative portfolio price

Buy ETF, sell portfolio basket

Source: Salomon Smith Barney

As a retail investor you'll never have to do this type of arbitrage; the fact that somebody else can keeps the price of the ETF shares cozily close to the value of the underlying investments. And that's what really matters.[10]

"I've never seen a product as good at tracking their bogey as this one," says Steve Elgee, Executive Managing Director, Equity Derivative Products, with BMO Nesbitt Burns, Inc., referring to the i60 Fund. Nesbitt Burns is one of the designated brokers for the i60, and as such, is responsible for ensuring an efficient, liquid and orderly market for iUnits. "There's a lot of eyes on this. We are always watching for price discrepancies greater than a dime because that presents arbitrage opportunities."

Arbitrage is made possible by two important features of ETF's: transparency and interchangeability. ETFs are transparent because their portfolio holdings are known at all times. (Conscientious mutual fund holders, particularly those who are interested in social investments, know how hard it is to get current positions in a conventional mutual fund portfolio. The information is, at best, a month old by the time it is public or because the law permits it, as old as six months. With average actively managed portfolio turnover of 80% a year, almost half the portfolio can be different from the six-month-old snapshot. To those who would prefer to know exactly what they're buying, this is an abysmal state of affairs.)

ETFs are also interchangeable with their underlying securities and vice versa. You will sometimes see ETFs referred to as "fungible," another way of saying they are interchangeable. It's the creation/redemption mechanism that makes this possible.

Even with this creation/redemption mechanism, however, ETFs do sometimes experience a premium or discount—most often towards the very end of the trading day. The price discrepancies are generally minor; nevertheless, it's best to trade ETFs while the market for their underlying securities is open. In the U.S., it means avoiding that tempting period from 4:00 p.m. to 4:15 p.m., when many ETFs still trade. For ETFs pegged to foreign markets, it means coordinating your trades with time zone considerations.

How can you be sure you are getting a fair price? With U.S. ETFs it's easy since the American Stock Exchange (AMEX), where almost all U.S. ETFs trade, calculates the value of the underlying portfolio of securities every 15 seconds. The AMEX also supplies real time quotes for ETFs themselves. The Toronto Stock Exchange doesn't have a similar net asset value (NAV) calculator (so if you're inclined, get your calculator ready for Chapter 7, where we'll lift the hood and take a good look at how ETFs run and how they're priced).

In any event, there's an important case to be made for the usefulness and effectiveness of ETFs in a portfolio. Since so many ETFs are index-related, we'll start off by exploring the arguments for and against indexing. Then we'll go on to compare the different indexing products you can buy, ETFs among them. Part Two will lead you through portfolio construction methods and investment strategies using ETFs, including a look at taxation. The more technical details of ETF operation will follow with a survey of the past and future for clues about what's to come in the ETF universe. Part Four is a reference guide for the numerable ETFs in the world and the indices they're associated with, and with detailed fact sheets for all Canadian ETFs.

What follows is an interview with the man who is most responsible for bringing the first and biggest ETF to American investors, Nathan Most.

The Father of "Spiders":
An Interview with Nathan Most

A man who earned a living trading coconut oil in the 1960s was the driving force behind the first successful ETF in the U.S., the now famous Spiders (SPDRs). Nathan Most, now 87, had been responsible for the international trading of coconut and palm oil for a San Francisco company, Pacific Vegetable Oil.

When the company closed because of a falling out between the owners, Most was approached by the Bank of America to start up a futures exchange in San Francisco to trade western commodities. It opened in 1970, and as Most says with disarming casualness, he "finally ended up running it."

According to Most, there was a worldwide draught in 1974 that sent the price of coconut oil soaring.

"Our principal contract was trading coconut oil from the Philippines. The price went from $.13 a pound to $.56 a pound in six months, and I had a lot of millionaires on my trading floor who thought they knew something about coconut oil.

"When the crop began to come back in we got a market reversal that wiped out half my trading floor. Then the brokerage houses that were clearing for my floor traders said they weren't going to clear it anymore, so I had to shut it down."

That was in early 1976. Before he could dust off a pair of bell-bottomed jeans he was invited to Washington as technical assistant to the first chairman of the Commodities Futures Trading Commission.

Very soon thereafter, however, the American Stock Exchange (AMEX) asked him to help them put together a futures exchange, the AMEX Commodities Exchange. This was subsequently sold to the New York Stock Exchange and now runs as the New York Futures Exchange.

Most stayed on with AMEX, however, as head of new products. It was a splashy title but Most admits he "pretty much made it [up] as I went." His job was to build AMEX's then languishing trading volume, and his first thought was to get mutual funds to trade on the exchange.

He approached Jack Bogle, founder of Vanguard Group, and famed advocate for low-cost index funds. Bogle didn't have any interest in putting his funds on an exchange. He believed the resultant trading in and out of the fund would drive up fund costs. Most was aware of other attempts to trade baskets of securities, but he liked best an idea hearkening back to his commodities days: a warehouse receipt. With such a receipt, commodities are bought and sold innumerable times without ever leaving the warehouse and with no additional expenses. Most applied that principle to a basket of securities, namely those in the S&P 500 Index—hence Standard & Poor's Depositary Receipts (SPDRs). To actually implement them, Most created an investment company as a modified Unit Investment Trust and then spent three years and a million dollars of AMEX's money in legal expenses to break down the regulatory barriers.

Standard & Poor's Depositary Receipts, more affectionately known as Spiders, launched in January 1993. What was originally just a way to build trading volume has become an internationally popular investment vehicle.

Asked if the launch of Spiders was a particularly gratifying personal moment, Most says, "When you work on something that long, it is sort of an anticlimax." But Most, still in the game as Chairman and President for iShares Trust for Barclays Global Investors, says the gratification is coming now. "Looking where it's gone it is almost unbelievable. It is spreading around the world very rapidly. It is just incredible."

Notes

1) According to the 2000 Canadian Banker's Association annual survey published in "Canadian Bank Facts," and the Investment Funds Institute of Canada's (IFIC) monthly funds asset survey (3/2001).

2) With mutual funds, the price you buy or sell at is determined only at the end of the trading day and after you've placed your buy or sell order. The exception is with moneymarket funds; their value stays constant at one dollar per unit.

3) Canadian mutual fund assets minus moneymarket funds as of March 31, 2001 from the IFIC's monthly statistical report (*www.ific.ca*).

4) U.S. fund data from Investment Company Institute as of April 30, 2001 at *www.ici.org*. A 128% average compounded rate, according to Financial Research Corp., as reported by *www.plansponsor.com*, June 5, 2001.

5) MERs in the U.S. are considerably lower than in Canada. According to *www.Morningstar.com*, the average actively managed U.S. equity fund had an MER of 1.44% as of March 31, 2001. The two most popular ETFs in the U.S., Spiders and Qubes, have a small MER of .12% and 18% respectively. The average MER for Canadian equity index funds was provided by Morningstar Canada, PALTrak as of March 31, 2001. Average Canadian equity fund MER number came from IFIC.

6) An article in *Canadian Investment Review* by Michael Thorfinnson and Jason Kiss, Fall, 1996, pp. 17–21, cites 80% as a best guess for the average Canadian equity mutual fund turnover. The 8.2% for the TSE 300 turnover was based on their historical research.

7) There are two ways of cloning. The one described uses index futures and options to track the performance of an index without fully investing the cash in those indices. An other way to clone involves buying foreign fund swaps.

8) As per Lea Hill, closed-end fund specialist, CIBC World Markets in Toronto, April 2001.

9) Ibid.

10) This is how arbitraging works in principle. In actual practice, however, ETF arbitraging in Canada benefits from additional tools without redeeming fund units. What regularly happens by sophisticated players is arbitraging between the i60 and an index future on the S&P/TSE 60 Index. When the future is cheaper, arbitrageurs will buy the future and sell the corresponding ETF, and vice versa. Since both investments have claim to the identical assets, the S&P/TSE 60 Index, it is an easy and fairly risk-free way to make money and help the market keep the price of the i60 in line with its underlying asset value.

Chapter 2
Why Index?

Most exchange traded funds are related to an index. You've got to be convinced tracking the market is a good and noble pursuit, or ETFs in their current incarnation will have little appeal. Fortunately the argument for indexing is very easy to make. The stark and simple truth is that for most asset classes, indexing gives better investment returns over the long run than active management; but somehow the perverse gambler in us all urges us to forsake the certain for the extraordinary. Here's why you shouldn't.

It's Too Hard to Pick this Year's Top Funds

Ask yourself just how many times you've had one of the 25 top-performing mutual funds of the year, the year they were in the top. If you're like most, chasing yesterday's star means making a bed for today's tired dog.

A study done in 2001 by Financial Research Corporation (FRC) found that on average funds do about 20% better than most fund investors in those very same funds. How is that possible? It's the phenomenon of chasing returns. Most investors jump into a fund after it has made most of its gains, so a fund can have, say, a 15% annualized rate of return yet most of its investors will see only a 12% annual gain or less. It's long been known that investors don't hold their funds long enough, and have a nasty habit of investing just after a fund's top performing quarter, when most of the gains have been made. The FRC study found on a three-year rolling return basis from January 1990 to March 2000 the average U.S. mutual fund's mean three-year return was 10.9%, while the average invested dollar gained only 8.7%. FRC also reports that American fund investors hold their funds for a fraction under three years. Four years ago their patience lasted five and a half years.[1] There's no reason to think the Canadian experience is much different.

"Investors [in aggregate] have poor timing and tend to *underperform* the very funds in which they are invested," says Dan Hallett, a mutual funds analyst based in Windsor, Ontario, in a 1999 report he wrote for FundMonitor.com Corp., a financial advisory support company based in Toronto.[2] Hallett's study looked at two popular specialty funds with big sales and redemptions, AIC Advantage I and AIC Advantage II. He tracked the money going in and out of them and timed these cash flows to the fund's actual performance. Combining the figures for these two funds together, nearly 70% of the money in the funds at the end of September 1999 was invested in just the 36 months before. During these 36 months, Hallett says, "investors earned an aggregate annualized return less than one-seventh of the fund's own published performance numbers." This means that most of the money came into the funds after the funds had already made their gains and left before the funds got back on track.

Jumping around among funds is a form of market timing. It's ironic that mutual funds should have this problem since one reason investors have flocked to them is in acknowledgement that they can't time the market, yet investors continually try to time their mutual fund purchases. Clearly, market timing is just as difficult to do with mutual funds as it is with stocks. (If you're going to try to time the market, the best way is to invest in the market itself, and ETFs are absolutely the best way to do that. But more on that later.)

Winners Don't Stay Winners

Even if you are lucky enough to have picked a winner just before its glory, only a small fraction of today's stars stay in the top quartile of funds the next year. After three years, your chances of still having a fund in the top quartile are wispy. In 1995 there were 45 Canadian equity funds in the top performance quartile. Of those winners, only one was left in the top quartile in 1998. By 2000 not a single one was still a top quartile performer. The funds don't just quietly slip down into the second quartile either. In 1997, 17 of them (37%) had tumbled into the fourth quartile.[3]

Durability of Performance (fig. 4)

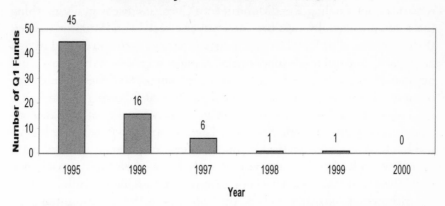

First Quartile Funds in 1995 that Remain First Quartile in Subsequent Years

Source: Norman Rothery

Where the First Quartile 1995 Funds Landed in 1997 (fig. 5)

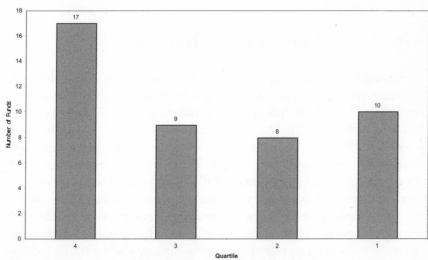

Only six funds were in the first quartile in '95, '96 and '97.
Ten funds were in the first quartile in '95 and '97 but were not in the first quartile '96.

Source: Norman Rothery

Furthermore, the more outstanding the fund, the worse its chances of remaining outstanding. FundMonitor.com Corp. has discovered something the company playfully calls the "newspaper effect." FundMonitor tracked the performance of funds from the first time they were advertised in one newspaper's mutual funds supplement. A staggering 92% of these funds did not match their advertised three-year record, and 45% of these funds went on to do at least 10 percentage points less the year following the ad.4

This is called "reversion to the mean," and the reality of it is as unattractive as the phrase itself. Sooner or later, returns gravitate to the historical levels of their asset class. Of course, a few exceptionally brilliant managers have index-breaking ten-year records, but as their funds grow larger, their chances of continued success seem to diminish all the faster.

Although it's possible to beat the index, even over a substantial period—it is unlikely, and it is even more unlikely that you are going to be fortunate enough to own the fund that does it. What you need to ask yourself, to use Dirty Harry's famous words, is "Do you feel lucky?" Do you think your luck will steer you to the winning active manager this year and the year after, and the year after that, until retirement? Chances are your funds will have more mediocre than exceptional years, and a mediocre year with an actively managed mutual fund usually means getting returns below the benchmark index.

After Tax, Where's the Advantage?

Having an excelling fund does not necessarily mean it beat the index, especially after taxes. Fund returns are always quoted after management expenses are deducted, but take no consideration of the after-tax return. Because the average Canadian equity fund sells 80% of its holding in any given year, which is a normal portfolio turnover rate for actively managed funds, there are usually taxes to pay. Too few investors scrutinize their after-tax returns. If they did, they'd realize holding a hot fund outside a registered account can be, if not a pyrrhic victory, sometimes an uncomfortable one. Of course, everyone would prefer to pay tax if it meant they were making money. The trouble comes when the outperforming fund becomes just a mediocre fund and its old, formerly winning trading habits continue kicking out tax liabilities.

Using their proprietary software, PALTrak, Morningstar Canada surveyed a broad range of mutual fund categories to show the impact of taxation on average fund returns. Their chart is an eye-opener. An abbreviated version is reproduced

IMPACT OF TAXATION ON FUND RETURNS
Period Ending May 31/2001

1 YEAR

IFSC Category	# Funds	Total Assets $Millions	Avg Return	Avg After-tax Return	Percentage Lost to Tax	% of Returns Lost to Tax
CdnBal	133	30,044.20	4.0	2.8	-1.2	30.0
CdnBond	124	23,748.00	6.3	3.9	-2.4	37.5
CdnDivdnd	39	15,521.50	15.8	13.8	-2.1	13.0
CdnEquity	110	52,753.50	5.0	4.0	-1.0	19.8
CdnLgCap	36	10,128.00	4.6	3.4	-1.2	25.9
CdnSmMdCap	68	9,828.10	2.0	0.9	-1.1	52.5
CdnTAA	24	9,743.40	5.5	4.0	-1.5	27.6
GlobalEq	126	59,061.80	-7.1	-7.6	-0.5*	7.1
Sci&Tech	71	10,691.50	-26.1	-26.6	-0.5*	2.0
USEquity	122	20,198.40	-5.5	-6.1	-0.6*	10.0

5 YEAR

IFSC Category	# Funds	Total Assets $Millions	Avg Return	Avg After-tax Return	Percentage Lost to Tax	% of Returns Lost to Tax
CdnBal	91	46,147.10	8.3	6.2	-2.1	25.5
CdnBond	72	20,777.90	6.6	3.8	-2.9	43.2
CdnDivdnd	28	14,065.40	12.7	10.8	-1.9	14.9
CdnEquity	74	56,042.90	10.5	9.1	-1.4	13.0
CdnLgCap	38	14,839.30	10.8	9.0	-1.8	16.3
CdnSmMdCap	36	9,198.90	8.0	6.9	-1.0	13.0
CdnTAA	25	16,655.80	8.3	6.4	-1.9	22.4
GlobalEq	59	54,795.30	9.7	7.7	-2.0	20.4
Sci&Tech	10	4,527.00	11.5	9.4	-2.2	18.9
USEquity	67	21,059.70	13.1	11.0	-2.1	15.7

Source: Morningstar Canada

* Even in negative year money was lost to tax.
Assumed tax rates: interest 50%, capital gains 25%, Canadian dividends 34%.

here. Keep in mind that their universe included index funds and the i6os, which would tend to make the average after-tax returns a little better.

Taxes can take a big bite out of the returns you're paying a manager to get for you.

A seminal paper in *Canadian Investment Review* calculated the perform-ance penalty due to taxes on a Canadian equity portfolio with 80% turnover at a painful 4 percentage points.[5] Since that study, tax rates have gone down, and although the calculations haven't been redone, it's reason-able to estimate the tax bite now closer to 2 percentage points of return. To overcome the taxes you must pay on an actively managed fund with average portfolio turnover, your mutual fund will have to outperform an index by 2 percentage points after management fees every single year you own the fund. Just how likely do you think that is? That's why high turnover mutual funds, the ones that inevitably generate capital gains, should, at the very least, be held in a tax-sheltered account like an RRSP.

After Tax Returns (fig. 6)

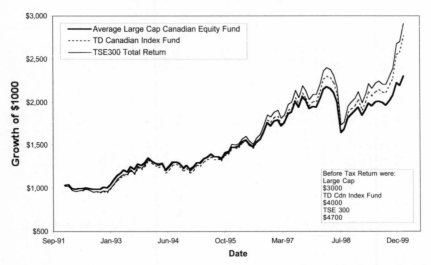

Source: *Morningstar Canada*

Capital Gains Tax: 25% and Dividend Tax: 37.5%

Management Fees Are Corrosive

If all your money is safely tucked away from the worrying touch of Canada Customs and Revenue, and you're reasonably content with consistent but not stellar funds, why should you consider indexing? For one thing, you'll still make more money in the long run with an indexing strategy, because the large fees required to keep an actively managed fund going are corrosive. Over time these fees will eat into your returns as surely as battery acid on aluminum.

No doubt fees played a big part in keeping two-thirds of U.S. active equity managers from surpassing their benchmark in the ten years between 1990 and 2000.

Active Managers vs. Their Benchmarks

Percent of actively managed funds in the U.S. that outperformed their benchmark index from 1990 to 2000.*

	Large Cap	Mid Cap	Small Cap
Growth	32%	38%	79%
Blend	21%	15%	42%
Value	27%	23%	22%

Source: BGI analysis of Morningstar (U.S.) data

Benchmarks: S&P 500, Barra LargeCap Growth, Barra LargeCap Value, S&P MidCap 400, Barra MidCap Growth, Barra MidCap Value, Russell 2000, Russell 2000 Growth, Russell 2000 Value.
*Ten-year data through June 30, 2000 except for MidCap Growth and MidCap Value, which use five-year data.

Except for the small cap growth sector, active U.S. equity managers struggled and mostly failed to outwit the index in those ten years. That's the battery acid at work, not a lack of skill.

The Canadian long-term experience is hardly different. In the race for returns, the index wins the marathon mostly because fund management fees are a big obstacle for even the most talented fund managers to consistently overcome. Where an average MER for an actively managed Canadian equity fund is 2.34%, the average MER for a Canadian equity index mutual fund is .75% [6] The MER on a Canadian equity index-based ETF is .25% or less. Those little numbers make a big difference.

Not only does the average fund underperform the index over long stretches, but so do the majority of funds. Of the 33 large cap Canadian equity funds existing from May 31, 1991 to May 31, 2001, only two beat the S&P/TSE 60 Total Return Index (backrun), and only one beat the S&P/TSE 60 Capped Total Return Index. With regard to Canadian equity funds in general, and including index funds, only 33 out of 77 (43%) beat the TSE 300's total return of 11.06%. Only 15 funds (19%) beat the TSE 300 capped total return of 12.6%.[7] That's a remarkable indictment of active management when you think that all those funds struggling behind the Canadian index had up to 20% foreign stocks in their holdings—a benefit the indices don't have.[8]

The miracle of compounding ensures that the longer these fees eat away at your returns, the greater the damage will be. The Ontario Securities Commission has a mutual fund fee-impact calculator that shows the compounding effect of MERs on returns (go to *www.osc.gov.on.ca*; located under "tools.") Let's look at just one example.

An MER of 2.34% in a no-load mutual fund held for 20 years and earning an annual return of 10% will eat up 15% of your total returns. Over the years, the absence of that money ends up costing 24.8% in foregone earnings so that your final return is only 60% of what it would have been without any MER at all. At a 7% annual return, you end up with only 56% of what should have been the total return. The smaller the returns, the more proportional damage the fees do, so every bit of return counts—as does every bit of MER.

Distribution of Returns and Cost, 7% annual return (fig. 7)

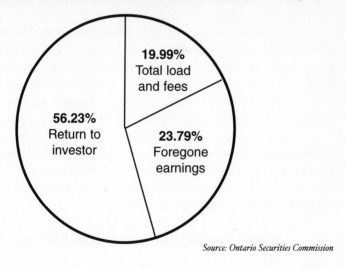

Source: Ontario Securities Commission

Distribution of Returns and Cost, 10% annual return (fig. 8)

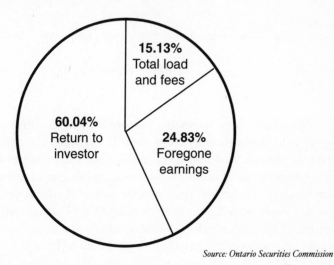

Source: Ontario Securities Commission

Are Actively Managed Funds Better in a Down Market?

The long-term superiority of indexing doesn't mean there aren't bursts when active managers come into the fore. Last year was a prime example: in 2000, the median Canadian equity fund manager beat the TSE 300 by a handsome 5.4%. Her counterpart in U.S. equities underperformed the S&P 500 by .88%.[9] By historical standards, 2000 was an exceptional year for professional money managers. The market was also busy tanking.

No accident, you might say, because active funds protect against a falling market. At least, that is the popular belief, but it isn't supported by history. Yes, active funds did protect investors from the precipitous fall of the major markets in 2000, but they haven't always and there's not much reason to think they will do so with any more consistency in the future.

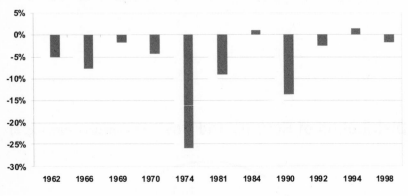

What Protection in a Down Market? (fig. 9)

Market ▪ **Median Manager**   *Source: BGI Canada*, 2001

The chart above shows the performance of institutional money managers in 11 down markets from 1962. If anything, the collective performance of pension fund managers and the like will be better than the collective performance of mutual fund managers because their management fees are much lower. As you can see, these active managers did better than the market in six periods, but in most cases they eked out only a minor differential. In five periods they did substantially worse. It's often said that the cash component of an actively managed fund will pad the fall of a bad market. In fact, active managers seldom have the prescience to throw a sizable chunk of money into cash at the right time.

Ted Cadsby, one of Canada's foremost indexing advocates, took a look at cash levels in actively managed mutual funds during the 1998 bear market in his book, *The Power of Index Funds* (revised edition). He found barely a difference in cash holdings throughout that dreadful year when the TSE dropped a painful 25%. In fact, the average Canadian equity fund went into the '98 bear market with less cash than it started with, though not by much (9.5% versus 10.2%), which shows the managers didn't see what was coming. Overall, the percentage of Canadian equity funds with 15% or more in cash *decreased* immediately before the downturn (from 19.4% to 18.2%). Clearly, fund managers can't see into the future any better than you or me.

In 2000 it wasn't cash that saved fund managers' bacon, it was legal fund restrictions that saved them from themselves. At the beginning of 2000, Nortel Networks' huge price run up had rocketed Nortel to 36% of the TSE 300. But because Canadian equity fund managers are not permitted to buy a position that costs more than 10% of their assets, Nortel and its stunning growth was under-represented in Canadian equity fund portfolios. Managers were banging on security regulator doors to increase or eliminate the threshold because they were getting creamed by the TSE 300.

Regulators did not acquiesce for actively managed funds, though they did allow funds to exceed 10% in cases of spin-offs, and they did loosen the threshold for index funds. As you might expect, when Nortel plummeted later in 2000, the actively managed funds suddenly looked pretty smart in spite of themselves (though it didn't salvage their ten-year records).

It wasn't active management that served investors well in 2000, it was securities regulation. But one good benefit of the Nortel experience was the general acceptance of capped indices, both as benchmarks for mutual funds and as indices for investment products like index funds and ETFs. Investors who want to index, but still see the prudence of moderation, can now buy a capped index product in which no single component of the index exceeds 10%.

You might think the amount of cash managers have in their portfolios would say something about their market outlook—a bearish outlook leading to more cash and a bullish outlook resulting in less cash—but it seems cash levels are mostly just a reflection of money coming into or going out of a fund. In actual practice a mutual fund's cash levels are more a function of investor behaviour than manager savvy. Cash often results from an influx of new money into a fund that can't be invested fast enough; or it can indicate that the manager is expecting a rush of redemptions.

You also have to wonder why you'd want to pay a manager a high MER to manage your portfolio's cash position. Frequently, managers plow excess cash into an ETF so not to be handicapped by low interest rates, this means cash may not stay cash for long. Determining your cash allocation is

basic and critical asset allocation decision *you* should be making, not defer-
ring to a portfolio manager who knows nothing of your overall portfolio,
investment objectives or risk tolerance. Cash, too, is notoriously easy to
manage at little or no cost, so why have a pricey equities portfolio manager managing it?

Indexing Provides Better Portfolio Diversification

One of the biggest advantages of mutual funds is their diversification.
Owning a great number of stocks diminishes the investment risk of a few
stocks getting into trouble. In actively managed funds, the fund manager
selects a limited number of those stocks he prefers. Investors can only hope
the fund manager's wisdom isn't flawed. In general, index funds and ETFs are
more diversified than actively managed funds because they hold more stocks
and are in proportion to an index—not in proportion to the manager's
favourites. With index funds and ETFs, there's more portfolio diversification
and less active manager risk than with actively managed funds.

Asset Allocation

The equity component of a well constructed mutual fund portfolio will
be diversified according to investment styles, capitalization, industry sectors, geographical regions, countries and so on. Trouble is, mutual funds
don't always stay true to their original colours, and this throws off prudently assembled portfolios.

Active managers come and go but funds often remain. With each
change of fund manager, the fund can undergo a change of investment
style. It doesn't happen all the time, but it is common. A large cap fund can
start taking on more small cap, for instance, or a fund that is predominantly value-oriented can start getting more aggressively growth-oriented.
Even a continuing manager can feel pressure to adjust his style to prevailing market conditions in order to enhance performance. This change in
investment style is called "style drift," and it was common during the tech
run up, when value got left in the dirt and Warren Buffett was being called
yesterday's man. Plenty of value-style funds bought Nortel Networks the
prototypical growth play in 2000, just so not to be left out of the party.

The issue of style purity is particularly complicated by the fact that
mutual fund investors rarely know current portfolio holdings. Fund managers disclose their entire portfolio only semi-annually, and even that dis-

closure can be dated before it is made public. Looking for style drift or manager signature in an actively managed mutual fund portfolio is an almost impossible task.

Style purity is never an issue with an index product. With a portfolio of index investments, your asset allocation will be affected by only one thing: the changing proportional values of the indices themselves. The S&P/TSE 60 may go up relative to the S&P 500 and require you to rebalance your portfolio, but you'll never have to worry that your large cap index is slipping into small cap territory, or that your value index is slowly letting in more growth plays.

A Zero Sum Game

Perhaps the simplest argument for indexing is William F. Sharpe's famous argument from logical first principles. Sharpe is Professor of Finance at the Stanford University Graduate School of Business and a Nobel Laureate. He argues that the average actively managed dollar will equal the return on the average passively managed dollar, but after costs, the return on the average actively managed dollar will be less than that of the average passively managed dollar.

He begins with the self-evident observation that the market return will be a weighted average of the returns on all the securities within the market. Since each passive manager will obtain the market return (before costs), then it follows that the return on the average actively managed dollar must equal the market return. The market is a closed system, thus

Before Costs
Average passive return = market return
Average active return = market return

Therefore: the average passive return must equal the average active return (before costs).

If the average active dollar outstripped that passive dollar, then the total market return would be increased, and this isn't the case because it is a closed system. The market return is unchanged whether active or passive managers are plying their trade. Therefore, collectively, active managers cannot beat out passive managers.

However, our returns in the real world are after costs. Since active management costs are higher than passive management costs, then,

After Costs
Average passive return > Average active return

Sharpe acknowledges that some active managers do beat the market sometime (even after costs) but the trick, of course, is to find them just before they do it. Despite the great difficulty identifying the stars, most people still place the majority of their money on active managers. One reason for the common active managers preference is because of the shamelessly self-serving practice mutual funds have of comparing themselves to each other rather than to a index benchmark. Standard Canadian fund comparisons rank funds by their peer group performance—all large cap Canadian equities, for instance, or mid cap U.S. equities, or balanced funds. If none of the funds managed to trounce their relevant index, being first among a group of under-performers is like graduating top of the class of a remedial program. It is better than nothing, but do you want your money there? As of early 2001, Canadian securities regulators have required mutual funds to identify every fund's benchmark index so investors can compare the fund's returns with that of an appropriate index. This is a good first step, but appropriate benchmarking still has a long way to go. Nevertheless, once it is understood that the real prize is not to get the best fund out of all funds, rather it is to get the best return relative to the proper index, indexing will seem less a counsel of despair and more a strategy of choice.

Ultimately there's only two ways for a fund manager to beat his benchmark index. The first is to buy investments that aren't in the benchmark index. The second is to overweight or underweight benchmark positions. If you find a manager who has successfully outperformed using the latter method and you believe it will continue, you should own that manager. Don't tell anyone else about it either, lest money rush into the fund and handicap your manager's performance. In mutual funds, success really can lead to an embarrassment of riches—for the manager.

As CIBC's Ted Cadsby says, the decision to index is a trade-off. You trade off "the low *possibility* of doing better than the index, for the high *probability* of doing better than most other funds."[10] If the evidence has any sway, the probability of the index outperforming your active manager is a lot greater than your possibility of picking a winning fund. Add to that the tax burden of so many actively managed funds, and it seems anything but an index play is a gambler's folly. Overall, indexing is cheaper, more tax efficient, less risky, better suited for fine-tuning asset allocation, and it gives more consistent returns than actively managed mutual funds. It's hard to do much better than that.

The Origin of Indexing and the Efficient Markets Hypothesis

You might think indexing as an investment strategy would be as old as the invention of a stock index, but indexing is actually a latecomer. The first stock index was invented by Charles Henry Dow in 1884 and was originally computed by adding up the price of 11 big U.S. stocks (most of them railroads) and dividing them by the number of companies. The index was revised to 12 stocks on May 26, 1896 for an average of 40.94. Today the Dow includes 30 blue chip companies like Wal-Mart and General Electric (the only remaining original Dow component), with an average over 10,000. Of course many more indices have followed, almost all of them weighted by market capitalization rather than the straight price average of Mr. Dow.[11]

For a long time, indices were used simply as a gauge for broader market movement, rather like how a windsock indicates the direction and strength of the prevailing wind. Then, in the 1940s, the academic Harry Markowtiz began to scrutinize index returns for what they could reveal about the risk/return trade-off among asset classes. His paper in 1952 lead to what is called "Modern Portfolio Theory," and the now widely accepted practice of asset allocation.

It's Modern Portfolio Theory (MPT) that says investors should pay more attention to getting their asset allocation right for their desired level of risk, leaving market timing and individual security selection as secondary considerations. An ideal asset allocation gives an investor the optimal mix of investments that have the potential to get the desired return with the least fluctuation in the total value of their portfolio. This is achieved by mixing together asset classes that react to market conditions in different ways. Asset classes whose performances diverge under similar market conditions have what's known as "low correlation" with each other. Real estate, for instance, goes up during periods of high inflation. Bonds, on the other hand, tend to wither away under those conditions. This kind of counterbalancing of risk and return through asset classes diversification (especially those with low correlations) is the hallmark of asset allocation. According to MPT, diversification has a far greater impact on portfolio returns than smart investment selection or psychic market timing, and this wisdom is the foundation of all portfolio management today. Dr. Markowitz subsequently took home a Nobel Prize for his MPT insights.

Around the time Modern Portfolio Theory was being propounded in the early 1960s, another market theory was taking hold, the Efficient

Markets Hypothesis (EMH). EMH says that stock prices reflect all past and present public information about a stock. In other words, the market is perfectly efficient and immediately factors into a stock price all relevant information. As a result, you cannot *expect* extraordinary returns from a stock. You may get extraordinary returns, but if you do, it is purely a fluke. Don't bother doing detailed fundamental analysis, it won't pay; at least according to EMH.

There are three versions of EMH: wea,; semi-strong and strong. The weak version says you can't predict future stock price moves by studying past movements, thus technical analysis is pointless. Likewise, the semi-strong version also puts the kibosh on fundamental analysis. It says that the current market price of a stock reflects all publicly available information about a stock and that scrutinizing annual reports, financial statements and economic forecasts will not lead to any consistently superior returns. The strong form of EMH holds that the market price of a stock reflects absolutely all information, including insider information. This means that even those trading on insider information will not be able to make superior returns.

Despite market regulators' skepticism about EMH, the weaker forms of EMH had some popularity for a number of years and together were one of the philosophical foundations of indexing. If the market is as perfectly efficient as the theory purports, there's not much point in trying to beat it—you might just as well join it by indexing.

There have been, however, a number of demonstrated, perfectly legal, contradictions to the weaker forms of EMH, such as the Value Line stock selection system, the January Effect and the tendency of low price-to-earnings (P/E) multiple stocks to do better than expected. It seems, then, that no markets are perfectly efficient.

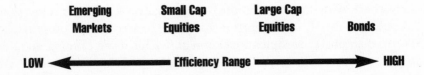

Relative Market Efficiency
Asset Class

| Emerging
Markets | Small Cap
Equities | Large Cap
Equities | Bonds |

LOW ◄————————— Efficiency Range ————————► HIGH

Indexing: Is It Just for Efficient Markets?

It's often said that indexing works best in efficient markets, and active management works best in inefficient markets. That may be true. At least it makes sense from first principles. Those poor, beleaguered active managers do have a better track record outpacing certain international indices and Canadian and U.S. small cap indices. Small caps and emerging market stocks trade within a wider band of fair market value than more actively followed stocks like large cap blue chips. This wider margin gives active managers an opportunity to add value.

Still, it is devilishly hard for the majority of managers in these less dense waters to overleap their respective indices. A quick look at *www.globefund.com* reveals that only 164 Canadian global managers beat the Morgan Stanley Capital International World Index (MSCI) out of 476 funds trying for one year to the end of June 2001. In international equity, 59 managers out of 171 funds surpassed the MSCI Europe, Australasia and the Far East Index (EAFE) for one year to the end of June, and in the U.S. mid cap and small cap sectors, an embarrassing 12 out of 71 managers topped the Russell 2000 Index.

The five-year record for funds in this sector is much better: 10 out of 19 managers beat the Russell, but global Canadian managers over the long run don't have too much to crow about. The median international equity manager lagged the MSCI EAFE index by 1.3 percentage points on a compounded annual return basis in the 15 years ending December 31, 2000.[12]

Markets are not inherently efficient, and what efficiency they get is owed to an army of bright analysts identifying and acting on any mispricings. As markets continue to develop through regulation, increased competition among investment managers and robust security analysis, this opportunity to extract value diminishes. It reaches the point where the research costs start plundering any value that is added. The market may still be inefficient, but the inefficiency can't be exploited without self-defeating costs. It isn't easy to know when inefficiencies will become difficult to exploit in any given market, though the proliferation of large, actively managed funds in any one market might be a harbinger.

The EAFE index was long considered easy to beat, but the proliferation of funds, increased competition among fund managers and better index methodologies by index designers has made EAFE less of a pushover now.

A skilled manager stays skilled long enough to capture the inefficiencies, and as long as that happens, active funds should have a place in even a predominantly indexed portfolio. Actively managed funds aren't all bad, they're just a lot less useful than you've probably been led to think.

Meanwhile in the next chapter we'll look at the various ways you can do indexing—with ETFs, index mutual funds, index-linked GICs and futures.

Although indexing seems as though it should have sprung up with the introduction of an index, in fact, it took almost 90 years and some determined personal conviction to bring the first index fund into existence; and as we'll see in the following interview, Bill Fouse is the man who did it.

The Inventor of Passive Investing:
An Interview with Bill Fouse

Back in the early days of indexing, William Fouse's advocacy put even his patriotism into question. The Leuthold Group, an investment research company, played on the famous "Uncle Sam Wants You" posters producing posters reading "Indexing is un-American."

"They sent these posters out everywhere and most trading rooms in money management organizations had one of those posters over the Marilyn Monroe poster," recalls Fouse.

He laugh now, but in the early 1970s it was a much more serious insinuation." It was just like an atheist trying to set up an operation in Baptist country," Fouse commented on his attempts to introduce the notion of passive investing. "It was emotionally charged."

His boss at Mellon Bank in Pittsburgh, where Fouse had worked for 18 years, was positively hostile to Fouse's suggestion that they start an index fund. His boss' reaction was just the first of many similar responses in the industry.

"It's an anti-establishment product," says Fouse, "because it doesn't square with the beliefs, intuitions and emotions of either the majority of plan sponsors or the investment bankers, brokers, traditional analysts and portfolio managers. It attacks their fantasy system."

In 1970 Fouse found a more receptive employer and moved camp to Wells Fargo Bank in San Francisco. There he started a quantitative group, and in July 1971, he gained the pension account for the luggage manufacturer Samsonite Corporation. That was, by all accounts, the first passive portfolio to be implemented. Fouse characterized it as an above-average risk index account replicating an equal weighted New York Stock Exchange (NYSE) Index. He says it had about a 10% higher risk than the NYSE capitalization-weighted index, and between 1972 and 1973 it did just what it was supposed to do: it lost money like the rest of the market.

In 1972 Wells Fargo started an S&P 500 index fund, originally funded by the bank's own pension fund. The next year they got their second client, Illinois Bell Telephone Company, an account they still retain. Together the two accounts totalled $10 million.

Eventually, Samsonite switched to the less volatile S&P product, too.

Fouse's study of market pricing and the efficacy of analysts recommendations confirmed his conviction that returns were random and that indexing was the surest way to consistently good performance. Thirty years later, a lot of people agree with him, though he complains that the pension management consulting community still gives little more than lip service to indexing.

"It is certainly inimical to their interests. Through luck, or through skill, they've been able to classify indexing as a style, and logically, you wouldn't put all your money in one style, would you?" In Fouse's mind, indexing simultaneously rises above all styles and encompasses them all. Fouse remarks that the investment community can't very well say, "'Put all your money in an index fund and go fishing and then you don't have to pay us any more.'"

Asked why investors should put money into index products in a bear market, Fouse replies, "Historically, active managers have usually done worse in falling markets than the index funds. Where they have done better by raising cash, for example, they typically miss the market when it recovers. So there is no hard evidence that you're protected in a market decline by being with an active manager. I would say the only protection you can conjure up is a valid tactical asset allocation approach where you take a look at the alternative values in the marketplace between stocks, bonds and cash."

The company Fouse co-founded, San Francisco-based Mellon Capital Management, does just that for over US$30 billion. At 73, the man who graduated in 1952 from the University of Kentucky with an MBA in Industrial Administration says he wouldn't hire himself today. It's a good thing Wells Fargo did because Fouse and other indexing pioneers revolutionized modern investing. Far from being un-American, Fouse says, "It's Yankee ingenuity to take advantage of all the hard work and effort expended by others to make the market efficient and get a free ride."

Mellon Capital still has the Samsonite account. Barclays Global Investors bought Wells Fargo Investment Advisers in 1995.

Notes

1) FRC study as reported in *www.advisor.ca*, "Mutual Fund Investors Lose the Performance Chase: Study," by Jim MacDonald, April 30, 2001.

2) Dan Hallett is now Senior Investment Analyst with Sterling Mutuals, Inc. in Windsor, Ontario. His paper is entitled "Distributions and the CGRM" and it was published on *www.fundmonitor.com* on November 17, 1999. See also "Buy High, Sell Low: Timing Errors in Mutual Fund Allocations," by Stephen L. Nesbitt, *Journal of Portfolio Management*, Fall 1995, pp. 57–60.

3) This finding based on a study commissioned for this book and done by Norman Rothery using Fund Data information to the end of May, 2001.

4) Duff Young, CEO of FundMonitor.com Corp. reported this finding in the *Globe and Mail*, May 9, 1998. It is available at *www.fundmonitor.com* under articles sorted by date.

5) The 80% turnover figure comes from "The Overlooked Piranha," by Michael Thorfinnson and Jason Kiss, *Canadian Investment Review*, Fall, 1996, pp. 17–21.

6) Average index fund from PALTrak to March 31, 2001 as per Dan Hallett. Not including segregated funds, .75% is for Canadian equity index funds. Excludes CIBC Protected Index funds (since no longer available) and iUnits.

7) As per *www.globefund.com* as of May 31, 2001. The fund universe was selected out of all funds existing for the ten-year period with returns greater than zero. The index return numbers provided by TD Newcrest who regularly backrun S&P/TSE 60 return figures and capped indices— both of which didn't exist over the ten-year period.

8) Federal government regulations allowed foreign content limitations in RRSP accounts to increase by 2% every year, from 1989 (10%) to 1993 (18% of book value). In 1999 the foreign content limit was increased to 20%; in 2000 it was increased to 25%, and in 2001 to 30%. Mutual funds, to be fully RRSP eligible, must not exceed the foreign content limit threshold and almost all take advantage of it to boost their returns.

9) As per Norman Rothery based on Fundata information.

10) Ted Cadsby, *The Power of Index Funds* (revised edition) Stoddart Publishing Co., Limited, Toronto, 2001, p.113. Emphasis is Mr. Cadsby's.

11) A capitalization weighted index is one whose constituents are weighted according to the total market value of their outstanding shares. These indices will move in keeping with the price changes of the underlying stocks. The Dow Jones Industrial Average is a price weighted index. Higher priced stocks have a greater percentage impact on the index than

lower priced stocks. Dow historical information from Dow Jones Web site, *www.dowjones.com*.

12) The 15-year historical data from *www.bylo.org/15yr4q00.html*. A very interesting site maintained by a private, but very knowledgeable Canadian investor.

Chapter 3
Index Products: Which One Is Best for You?

If you're now convinced that indexing will speed your way to a yacht in the Bahamas, what, then, is the best way to index?

Hulking institutional accounts can simply replicate the index by buying everything in the index in the right proportions. Done. The rest of us have to rely on index products, of which there are many. However it's easy to narrow down the field pretty quickly. A number of index-linked products require a degree of sophistication few of us desire to cultivate, for instance index futures and index-linked equity notes. On the opposite end of the spectrum, index-linked GICs are just barely an index product at all. For most investors, index mutual funds and ETFs are the most accessible and practical way to index. I'd like to say unequivocally that ETFs are always the best choice, but in fact, like most things, it depends on your circumstances. It depends most critically on how much money you want to give over to passive investments; but it also depends on the product features that are most important to you.

If you've already made up your mind that indexing is the way to go, this chapter will help you decide what index product is best for you, comparing index mutual funds to ETFs and touching briefly on index-linked GICs, index futures and index-linked notes.

Any index product should trigger the following questions.

•Does it track the index you need?
•How closely does it track that index? (What's its tracking error?)
•How much does it cost in management fees and other costs?
•What are the tax implications?
•Is it easy to sell?
•What is the minimum investment?

•How are dividends handled?
•How do redemptions/sales affect the product?
•Is it efficient to invest and withdraw small dollar amounts?
•Is it best for short-term or long-term positions?
•Is it restricted in an RRSP?

It's important to know the answers to these questions because buying an inappropriate product can cost you in returns, taxes and aggravation. By the end of this chapter you should have the answers easily in hand for most of the index products available today.

Index Mutual Funds vs. ETFs

Chapter 1 discussed the differences between actively managed mutual funds and ETFs. Because index mutual funds are passively managed, much of that ETF versus mutual fund comparison doesn't apply to index funds. Where an active manager is buying and selling positions in the fund regularly in order to boost returns, a passive manager simply positions a portfolio to replicate the movement of a target index. That requires a lot less buying and selling in a passive fund, and when trades do occur, they are not for the purpose of making gains or preventing loses; they are made to better track the index. This difference in management approach makes index funds considerably different from their actively managed confreres, and more comparable to ETFs, but with some notable differences.

Index Tracking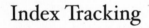

The biggest errors typically are due to the MER's and the fees charged by the planners - not to mention the brokerage costs of buying & selling the ETF or Fund!

An index mutual fund, like an ETF, is designed to track a target index. The best performing index product is one that most closely tracks its index. Any deviation either above or below the index return is a tracking error. Of course nothing will perfectly track a target index.

Indices are abstract constructs. They don't live and breathe in the real world where trading costs add up. It's important to realize that an index is calculated, but not actually implemented, by the index sponsor. That means an index and its returns are blissfully unaffected by trading costs or price run-ups when its securities are changed. Index mutual funds and ETFs are, however, real things with real costs. Take for example the addition of Fluor Corp. to the S&P 500 Index in late December 2000. The stock went up $4 on the day from indexers scrambling to buy the stock in order to match the completely theoretical S&P 500.[1] That's some real-world pressure at work. Index managers aren't exactly as idle as the Maytag repairman.

Tracking Methods

There are three different ways to track an index and both index funds and ETFs take advantage of all of them. The most straightforward tracking method is to completely copy the index by buying all the securities in proportion to their weighting in the index. This is called, obviously enough, "replication."

Alternately, a fund could buy a representative sampling of the index's securities. This is known as "sampling" or "optimizing." Managers resort to this because of restrictions on portfolio concentrations or as a way of coping with thinly-traded stocks on some indices. Markets in which many listed securities lack liquidity creates a problem for those trying to manage a replicated index in real time. Managers try to avoid this problem by carefully selecting liquid securities representative of the market they are trying to track without actually owning everything in the index. This solution is never perfect, which is one reason why developing country index products have greater tracking errors than similar products in more efficient markets. Optimizing can also result from an attempt to save fund costs. It can be a bet that the securities being left out have too minor an impact on the index to make much difference, while including them increases transaction costs.

Finally, a fund can itself buy other index products, such as derivatives or ETFs. Fully RRSP eligible foreign index funds, for instance, typically buy forward contracts or futures on their target indices and put the lion's share of the portfolio into staid Canadian T-bills. This approach allows the funds to be fully RRSP eligible despite giving full foreign exposure, and is known as a "derivatives indexing strategy."

Not all tracking strategies work equally well. Portfolios that do not perfectly reproduce their index have a bigger chance of running afoul of the index returns than replicated funds. Indexing strategy, then, plays a part in tracking error.

Concentration Limits

Securities regulation also impacts tracking. Mutual fund regulators stay up at night worrying about excessive concentration in mutual fund portfolios, because diversification is one of the biggest benefits of mutual fund investing. Conventional mutual funds (that is non-index mutual funds) may not purchase a security if, after the purchase, the fund would have more than 10% of its net assets (at current market value) invested in the securities of any issuer. Regulators relaxed this restriction for index funds first by capping them at 25% and then, as of May 2001, eliminating the concentration restriction altogether. This serves index funds well because any portfolio restriction always has the risk of throwing off tracking.

ETFs in Canada have no regulatory restrictions on concentration (although Barclay Global Investors Canada's sector funds have a 25% cap on the weight of any single security, which reflects the cap set by the sector indices themselves). U.S.-based ETFs are not so lucky, because they're restricted by law from holding a position in any single issuer worth more than 25% of the ETF's assets. Other restrictions apply as well. Securities that have a weighting of 5% or more within the fund cannot collectively add up to more than 50% of the fund's assets. Sector ETFs can run up against this restriction easily. Take, for example, iShares Dow Jones U.S. Energy Sector Index Fund whose index had a 38% weighting in ExxonMobil in February 2001. The fund had to optimize its positions by buying other oil and gas producers with a high market correlation to Exxon's stock.[2] It's not perfect, but it's the best that can be done.

Cash Flow

Cash flow is another reason index tracking can derail. The more cash in an index portfolio, the less well that fund will track its index. That's called "cash drag" and in a down market, it can buffer the fund from a precipitous market crash. In a rising market, cash holds the fund back from the market highs. Index mutual funds can be particularly hobbled by cash flow effects. Mutual funds take in and give out cash on a daily basis. A large rush of money into or out of a fund can create a pile of cash not tied to the index—always a risky situation.

ETFs don't have a similar cash flow problem. The reason is quite simple. ETFs don't have any cash (except what comes from dividends). ETFs don't redeem their units for cash, nor do they take in cash from new unit sales the way mutual funds do. Instead, what's called an "authorized participant," or in Canada an "underwriter," uses its own capital to put together the stocks needed to constitute a creation unit. This basket of stocks is turned into an ETF unit in advance of market demand, so there are always new ETF units available and no cash standing idly by.

Dividends

Stocks within an ETF portfolio do sometimes spit out dividends, so ETFs are not entirely without cash drag. Some ETFs can reinvest the dividends into the portfolio immediately upon receiving the dividend; others must segregate the cash for quarterly distribution. Which method is used depends on the structure of the ETF, and unfortunately, there are different structures. We'll talk more about the differences in ETF structures in Chapter 7, where we'll look at Canadian and U.S. ETF structures. For now it's enough to know that ETFs that can reinvest dividend cash have better tracking than those that have to coddle the cash separately. Even with today's low dividend rates, the distinction in treatment can make a difference. For instance, in 2000, i60s had $5.8 billion in assets and received $65.8 million in dividends. That's more than 1% of the fund's assets, a discrepancy which is not insignificant in the least.

Index mutual funds get dividends just like ETFs, but index funds can immediately reinvest the dividends in the fund when they are received. So, dividend cash is less of a tracking problem for index mutual funds than for ETFs.

Index Adjustments

Index funds and ETFs show their difference markedly when there is an index change that involves a large addition to the index. Both index funds and ETFs sell the stock leaving the index (triggering gains, if any), and both buy the stock entering the index. But if the purchase is more than the sale, the index fund sells more of the other stocks in the index thereby triggering more gains. The ETF, in contrast, issues more units to the underwriters to finance the additional purchases. The ETF does not need to sell as much stock and so ends up triggering fewer gains.

This isn't significant all the time, but big index changes will make the difference apparent.

Management Expense Ratio

With all the noted impediments to tracking you may wonder how any product manages to keep hold of an index. It's not as easy as it may look, and we haven't even come to the most important, inescapable tracking impediment of all: the management expense ratio. The MER pulls on an index strategy like an undertow. Even if a manager could perfectly manage cash flow, avoid concentration restrictions and fully replicate the target index, the fund would still fall short of the index's return exactly by the amount of the fund's MER. There are some mitigating circumstances, though, that may find an index fund occasionally squeaking out a better performance than its index. Sometimes fund managers can make (or lose) a little money relative to the index by trading the index changes. And sometimes cash flow even comes to their rescue.

To see how well an index fund has tracked its index, go to *www.globefund.com*, select a specific index fund or all index funds generally and in "charts" you can compare their performance one by one to their respective index. You can do the same for all of BGI Canada's ETFs offerings, though at this book's printing neither State Street Global Advisors nor TD Asset Management's ETFs were listed on Globefund.com. BGI's U.S. site, *www.ishares.com*, also allows you to compare an iShare to its respective index, as will BGI's Canadian site, *www.iunits.com*, in the future. The American Stock Exchange is said to be working on a similar project for all its listed ETFs. Unless it is what is called an "enhanced fund," the closer the fund's returns are to its target index return (after costs), the better the indexing strategy is working.

In general, ETFs have better tracking records than index mutual funds mainly because the new kid on the block has moved in with a lot less baggage; namely, much smaller MERs. MERs on U.S.-based ETFs range from .12% to .99%.[3] Canadian MERs run from a rock-bottom .08% to .55%. Contrast that with .75% for an average index fund in Canada and you can see why less onerous MERs mean ETFs can track their indices more closely.

Below is an example of how a good Canadian equity index fund with a long track record has tracked its target index.

Compare the above information with how well TIPS, the predecessor of the i60, tracked the Toronto 35 Index from TIPS' inception to its merger with the i60. There are four lines in the graph below, but if you see only three it's because the TIPS and the TSE 35 lines are so close they are indistinguishable. Just beneath the TIPS and TSE 35 lines, we've manipulated the tracking a lit-

TSE 300 vs. Index Fund (fig. 10)

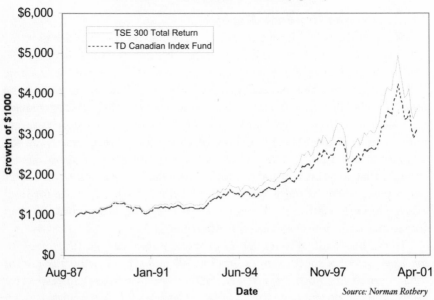

Source: Norman Rothery

tle to show the marvellous symmetry of TIPS tracking. Not coincidentally, TIPS had an expense ratio of .04%. (To see how other Canadian ETFs have tracked their indices, refer to the Appendix A and look at the fact sheets on each Canadian ETF. A tracking graph is included in each.)

How Do All These Causes for Tracking Error Add Up?

According to a Salomon Smith Barney research report from February 2001, "In most cases tracking error is extremely small, many times no greater than the management fee."

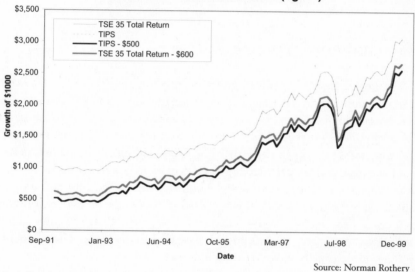

TIPS vs. TSE 35 Index (fig. 11)

Source: Norman Rothery

The average weekly return differential between Spiders and the S&P 500 Index in 2000 was .0016%. The iShares S&P 500 Index Fund from its introduction in May 2000 to the end of the year was .0013%. Optimized ETFs don't do quite as well. The iShares Dow Jones Energy Sector Index Fund for 2000 had an average weekly return differential of .037%. You're unlikely to lose any sleep over those tracking errors.

Enhanced Indexing

Enhanced index mutual funds (there are as yet no enhanced ETFs) try to second-guess the market by overweighting certain securities within the index in the hope of enhancing returns. If it works, the fund will beat the market. If it doesn't, it will underperform the market more than other index funds. It's almost a contradiction of the idea of indexing, but hope springs eternal in the hearts of some fund managers. National Bank's American Index Plus Fund is a good example of an enhanced fund. In April 2001 it had about 70% in Spiders, the remainder in individual stocks. In three years to the end of April it did 6.60% compared to the S&P 500 Composite Index return of 7.83%. The difference in returns would be even more alarming if you included the decline in the value of the Canadian dollar during that period, something that would have only helped the fund. At an MER of 1.39%, this fund was no bargain. Clearly, enhanced funds should be treated with appropriate skepticism.

Management Expense Ratios

Because of their enormous impact on tracking, MERs deserve a little bit more examination. From an investor's standpoint, management fees are a necessary evil: funds cost money to run, and the manager has to get paid. The companies that record the securities and their transactions must get paid, too, and so on down the costly line. These administrative costs come out of the fund and are calculated as a ratio of expenses to assets, hence the name, "management expense ratio." The MERs on index mutual funds in Canada range from .31% for a few of TDs Index eFunds, to an eye-popping 3.15% for a fully RRSP eligible guaranteed (segregated) U.S. equity index fund. Most non-segregated retail index mutual funds have MERs around .77% and most usually have MERs under 1%.

These MERs may sound like a bargain when you compare them to actively managed funds, but they're still bloated compared to the MERs on ETFs. MERs on ETFs in Canada range from a slender .08% to .55%. This is one very important aspect in which ETFs shine.

Management fees represent money slipping from your account into the pockets of fund managers. Of course, there's nothing wrong with that, especially if you have a fond relative in the fund business, but most of us would prefer to keep our gains to ourselves. The longer management fees and ancillary fund expenses erode your investment, the more damage they'll do. On the face of it, 1% either way doesn't seem too much to be paying for management, but you'd hardly be blamed for being resentful once you see how harmful it is to your long-term returns. Saving even 1% in management fees increases your returns by an astounding amount over the long haul. Saving 1% over 15 years will mean a 16% improvement in total returns. Thanks to the miracle of compounding, that shoots to 22%

after 20 years, 25% in 30 years and an astounding 49% in 40 years.4

Obviously, the bigger the MER, the less well the fund will track its market. In the indexing world, you get what you *don't* pay for. The more you pay in management fees and expenses, the less you get in returns. Period. Always scrutinize MERs. The lower the MER, the more money you'll make. All other things being equal, select an index product with the lowest MER.

Expenses

You might think the MER gives the full cost of running the fund. It doesn't, and to my mind, regulators have abetted the mutual fund industry in this misleading practice. In fact, the MER doesn't tell the whole story. Trading costs (the commissions the fund must pay to brokerage houses for transacting trades) aren't included in any MER calculation. This means your actual costs of holding a fund are always going to be higher than the posted MER and will adversely affect the fund's net return. The more active the manager, the more the costs pile up. In extreme cases, trading costs have been known to be double the fund's MER.5 Gratefully, an index product normally has so little buying and selling that the trading costs are usually miniscule in comparison with the size of the portfolio. As it happens, the i60s, a 5.8-billion-dollar fund, paid no trading commissions in 2000 because of favourable arrangement with a brokerage. Usually though, you can expect some very small trading commission costs with ETFs.

Taxes and How Redemptions Affect the Fund

Index mutual funds and ETFs are very tax efficient because they are passive investments. With so little selling going on inside a passive portfolio, very few realized capital gains are generated. That's good because index funds and ETFs, all mutual funds in fact, distribute their capital gains at least annually to unit holders who then must pay tax on those gains. The bottom line is, the longer you put off paying tax on capital gains, the better.

There's another good tax feature of index mutual funds and ETFs. The distributions from Canadian ETFs and Canadian-index mutual funds retain their tax character, which means dividends from Canadian corporations are eligible for the dividend tax credit, and capital gains retain their tax-advantaged status. (Canada Customs and Revenue Agency is not favourably disposed to dividends or capital gains from U.S.-based ETFs. All their distributions are dinged as income, but more on this and other tax-related matters in Chapter 6.)

But even in a tax-lean passive environment, ETFs have an advantage over index mutual funds. ETFs have something of a buffer from the onslaught of redemptions from retail investors. A redemption run on an index fund could force the manager to sell profitable positions in order to raise the cash to pay out the redemptions. This could impose capital gains tax liability on the remaining fund investors—ouch. Retail ETF investors, in contrast, sell their units for cash on the open market which has no implications whatsoever for the underlying fund.

Now, ETFs can be redeemed for their underlying shares, but only institutional accounts would own a large enough position to form a redemption unit. Even for institutional accounts, selling an ETF is cheaper and easier than redeeming it. However, when a redemption does occur and the fund surrenders the underlying securities in exchange for its own units, Canadian tax rules view this as a deemed disposition, a sale of sorts, which triggers capital gains reckoning. (This is not the case with U.S.-based ETFs.) Canadian ETFs, then, do not entirely escape the redemption tax problems of index mutual funds. However, redemptions at the fund level are not all that common in Canada. TD hasn't had one redemption since its two funds were launched early in 2001. According to Linda Brillante, Senior Portfolio Manager with BGI Canada in Toronto, only about seven redemptions have occurred since the launch of the i60s in September 1999, but these, along with some index reconstitution, were significant enough to cause the fund to pay out $1.67 per unit in capital gains in 2000. Fund level redemptions may not be common, but when they happen, they are in weighty amounts of 50,000 units and more.

Looking at the difference between ETF capital gains distributions and index funds distributions, you can surmise just how much redeeming is going on because the capital gains from the underlying portfolio readjustments will be fairly similar (even though the underlying indices are not identical). However, a comparison of the capital gains distributions in 2000 for some popular index funds and the i60 isn't a hands-down win for the i60. Its $1.67 capital gain distribution in 2000 represented 3.1% of the i60's unit value. A number of index mutual funds didn't distribute any capital gains at all that year, though the TSE 300 index funds at CIBC, Royal Bank, and TD Asset Management all had capital gains distributions in 2000—two of them were around 1.5% of the unit value. To get a true sense of tax efficiency you have to compare the distribution histories over a longer period, and unfortunately, with most index funds popping onto the scene in 1998 or later, there just isn't much of a history to report right now. It is expected that the i60's will have lower capital gains distributions in the future. Stephen Rive, General Manager for iUnits comments on the sizable distribution: "We had an unusual year last year. Generally the activity in the fund is quite low."

In the U.S., fund level redemptions don't trigger any kind of capital gains liability, so U.S. ETFs have minute capital gains distributions. From 1993 to the end of 2000, while appreciating from US$45 to over US$125 a share, Spiders distributed total capital gains of $.09 a share. From 1998 to the end of 2000, Diamonds distributed no capital gains at all. (Historical distribution information for all US ETFs is available on *www.amextrader.com*.) As a species, ETFs are just about the most tax efficient pooled investment you can get.

Is It Easy to Sell?

The ability to buy and sell an investment at a competitive price, its liquidity, should be a big consideration in an investment decision. All mutual funds score high on ease of buying and selling, but when you think of it, it's a little surprising that the mutual fund industry has grown so successful with a product whose price cannot be determined when it is bought or sold. Investors buy and sell mutual funds without ever knowing beforehand at what price those trades are going to be executed. Imagine buying a car or a house, or doing your grocery shopping like that?

This strange arrangement stems from the way mutual funds are priced. At the end of each trading day, a mutual fund company tallies up the value of all the fund's constituents, establishes a net asset value (NAV) and transacts all the buy and sell orders that have come in that day at that NAV. The pricing process is completely controlled by the mutual fund company without any market scrutiny because, remember, the actual portfolio holdings are not known on a daily basis. All this might sound rather sinister, but in fact, the mutual fund industry has a sterling record of fair dealings and has earned the trust of investors. Mutual funds have great liquidity because the mutual fund companies themselves buy and sell the units and are committed to ensuring the liquidity of their product and the integrity of their pricing. Nevertheless, this arrangement is in contrast to the ETF's, whose prices are posted in real time and subject to the scrutiny of the market as a whole.

Index mutual funds in Canada are almost exclusively no load funds which means they can be bought or sold without commission. To discourage short-term trading, however, many fund companies impose a minimum holding period or charge a short-term trading fee. Altamira, for instance, charges a 2% penalty on many funds held less than 90 days. CIBC, the bank with the widest selection of index funds, does the same. There is no such restriction on ETFs. If anything, the more ETFs trade, the better: the more trading, the better the liquidity, and the more money stock exchanges make.

ETFs are as easy to buy and sell as a large and frequently traded stock, because that's what they are. ETFs such as Spiders, Diamonds and Qubes are regularly among the most heavily traded securities on AMEX. In Canada the i60s were the fifth most actively traded security on the TSE last year. They have enormous liquidity. Even U.S. ETFs that have low trading volumes are perfectly liquid, as long as their underlying securities are liquid.

As with all stocks, you have to have a brokerage account and pay brokerage commissions on an ETF transaction. This runs $29 at TD Waterhouse, $58 for a round-trip buy and sell. It's a cost you don't have with an index mutual fund, but it's a small, fixed, non-recurring cost that is very quickly surpassed by a pricey MER. And if you do your ETF trading within a fee-based account, you may escape commission charges all together.

The virtue of stock trading is that it brings with it complete price transparency and prompt, if not nearly instant, order execution. All the normal stock trading mechanisms are available for ETF transactions, too. In the U.S. you can short sell ETFs without waiting for an uptick. You can also buy ETFs on margin, trade them with stop loss orders or limit orders, and when available, even write options on them. Prompt execution is more valuable than you might suspect. Remember that mutual funds are transacted only at the end of day, after market close. The U.S. market as measured by the S&P 500, fluctuates on average 1.4% a day, which translates into a possible 1.4% average loss each time you have to wait a trading day to execute your order.

How Much Do You Need?

Mutual funds have become hugely popular, in good part because they require a very small minimum investment. You can buy a mutual fund for as little as $500 in one shot or for $25 a month with no fees or penalties. Many people invest regularly with a fund company by arranging a monthly pre-authorized chequing plan (PAC). Mutual funds make it is easy to withdraw large or small amounts from mutual fund positions regularly or on demand. There are no trading fees imposed, and with no load funds, there are no redemption fees unless you trigger a short-term trading penalty. It's also easy to automatically reinvest your dividends. Since almost all index mutual funds are no-loads, an index mutual fund investment is singularly flexible in letting you into the game with a small amount of money.

ETFs, on the other hand, are generally bought in board lots of 100 units, though it is equally easy to buy less than 100 shares of an ETF, but trading commissions aren't reduced proportionately. If you intend to actively trade your ETFs, it is most cost effective to stick to board lots. For practical purposes then, the minimum investment in an ETF can be relatively steep. One hundred units of i6os in the spring of 2001 would run you $4,710. One hundred Spiders would set you back more than CDN $18,000, and a number of popular ETFs like Diamonds and MidCap Spiders regularly trade around US$100 per share. The cheapest Canadian ETF was the spring 2001 iUnits' S&P/TSE Canadian Information Technology ETF trading around $11. Even that's a considerable amount more than the minimum $500 for a mutual fund purchase.

Any addition or withdrawal from an ETF position requires a buy or sell order and an associated trading commission. This makes reinvesting the quarterly dividends from equity ETFs impractical and a bit of a nuisance. (Canadian bond ETFs distribute their interest income semi-annually.) Only RBC Investments in Canada has a dividend reinvestment plan for i6os, but perhaps with increased investor demand, more investment houses will catch on. Until then you can stash those dividend cheques into a money-market fund or treat them like birthday money from a kindly aunt, taxable as they are. In 2000, i6os gave its unitholders $2.34 for every unit—with a board lot that's a generous aunt.

Short-term or Long-term Plays?

The mutual fund industry has gotten blue in the face advising clients that mutual funds are long-term investments. Not many investors seem to believe that information when they purchase their funds because the average holding period for fund investors keeps declining and is now under three years.[6] But investor behaviour aside, the longer you hold a mutual fund, the longer the MER compounds to corrode your returns. For the long term, there's no question the index product with the lowest MER is preferable.

For one or two years and an investment of around $10,000 or less, an index mutual fund is probably your best bet, says Steve Geist, Senior Vice President with TD Asset Management. The calculation goes something like this:

Over the short term there may not always be a cost advantage to an ETF over an index mutual fund, but the comparison with a conventional (load) mutual fund is unequivocal.

Cost Comparison: ETFs vs. Index Fund

Investment	$6,000		$10,000		$10,000	
Time Horizon	2 Years		1 Year		2 Years	
	ETF	Index Fund	ETF	Index Fund	ETF	Index Fund
Commission (in and out)	$58	$0	$58	$0	$58	$0
MER Cost	$42	$96	$35	$80	$70	$160
Total Cost	$100	$96	$93	$80	$128	$160

Assumes ETF MER of .35% and index mutual fund MER of .8%, trading commissions at $29

RRSP Eligibility

Another attraction of index mutual funds is the selection they offer of fully RRSP eligible foreign indices. This allows investors to build a diversified indexing strategy completely within their RRSPs without having to compromise on foreign exposure due to foreign content restrictions. (These index mutual funds are usually distinguished from their counterparts by using "RRSP" in their name, like CIBC's International Index RRSP that's linked to the MSCI EAFE Index.)

So far there is only one ETF linked to foreign indices that is fully RRSP eligible and it's a very recent invention. BGI Canada launched a 100% RRSP eligible ETF based on the S&P 500 Index in May. They expect to follow that up later this year with a product that tracks the MSCI EAFE Index.

Choice of Indices

Currently, Canadian ETFs fall short on fully RRSP eligible funds, but mutual funds can't match the extraordinarily broad range of indices ETFs track. You can find an ETF for just about any index you can think of. The breadth of U.S. ETF offerings makes it easy to gain exposure to just about any geographical area, economic sector, market segment, country or major investment style. This diversity proves very useful in portfolio construction as we'll see when we put together some model portfolios later in this book.

With 160 index mutual funds at last count, Canadians still don't have a huge selection of foreign indices to select from—and that's with all the major banks, insurance companies and no-load fund companies falling all over themselves to provide an index product. It's not hard to find a TSE fund or one using the S&P 500, Nasdaq, the Dow, MSCI EAFE or the Wilshire 5000. But the huge selection of style and capitalization indices available in the U.S., like the Russell value/growth indices, and the large, mid and small cap indices, have not spilled over into the Canadian mutual fund industry. This can be a problem for those wishing to use index mutual funds to add, for instance, a small cap index to their overall index strategy, or a value index to capture the growth of a whole investment style.

Frustrated Canadian investors can only press their faces to the glass and look longingly at the tantalizing selection of low cost index funds sponsored by Vanguard Group, one of the largest mutual fund companies in the U.S. Canadians are prohibited from buying U.S. mutual funds, but the whole universe of over 100 U.S. ETFs (and counting) is open to us.

Where the Smart Money Goes

Canada got its first index mutual fund for the retail investor two years after the Vanguard Group gave all Americans the first shot at index investing in 1976. National Trust's TSE 300 Index Fund was launched in 1978.7 Twenty years later, index funds finally seem to have come into their own. Their ranks have swelled from five funds in 1996 with a hardly noticeable $618 million, to over 220 funds duking it out in 2001 with $16 billion in assets.[8]

In 2001, however, index mutual funds have seen an uncomfortable decline in assets as investors have yanked their money out in fear of uncertain markets. They've gone from $18.4 billion in January to $16 billion in May. ETFs have not gone entirely unscathed either. Canada's biggest ETF, the i60, went from $6.2 billion in January 2001 to $5 billion in May of the same year. These fair-weather indexers will almost certainly miss the best part of the inevitable market rebound, as do most mutual fund investors who cannot help themselves from chasing last year's winners. Index mutual funds are, unfortunately, well suited to those who have little commitment to the indexing philosophy. The same might prove true of ETFs, but at least the behaviour of one investor doesn't affect the tax liability of the next investor.

Index-linked GICs

Index-linked GICs are designed for those taking their first timid steps towards indexing. These products are offered by banks and credit unions to appeal to regular GIC investors who are disappointed with low interest rates but aren't ready to take the plunge into index mutual funds. The GIC's principal is fully guaranteed, but its return is linked to the performance of an index or set of indices. This sounds like an easy enough concept, but its implementation can be complicated.

Let's look at TD Bank's index-linked offering as an example. They have three index-linked GICs, one linked to the S&P/TSE 60 Index, one to the S&P 500 and one based on an assortment of global indices. Each GIC comes in three-year or five-year maturities. The returns are calculated by subtracting the closing value of the index at maturity from the value of the index when the GIC was purchased. (Technically, most index-linked GICs use the index values a day or two after purchase and a day or two before maturity.) You'd be excused for thinking that if the index goes up 40% over three years, your GIC would show a similar 40% return for that period. It doesn't work that way.

All index-linked GICs have either a cap or a participation rate that affects your gains. In TD's case the three-year GICs are capped at a 25–30% return depending on what index is involved. Capping limits how much you can earn on your GIC. A 25% cap means that your GIC will not earn more than 25% over the maturity of the GIC, no matter how well the index does over that period. CIBC also offers an assortment of index-linked GICs. They have no cap, but they do have a participation rate of 55% or 65% which means that the investor gets only 55–65% of the index's gain over the investment period. CIBC's product also has a small guaranteed interest component.

A few years back these products used to be horrifically complicated because the growth on the index would be averaged and each institution, it seemed, had its own way of doing that average. Some averaged the index's movement monthly from the first month; others averaged only the last twelve or six months, or maybe did the averaging only quarterly in the last year to maturity. As the period of averaging increases, the index's gains will always decrease, so averaging in an up market is disadvantageous. Remember, too, that the participation rate and the cap were both based on this average. Royal Bank averages the monthly level of the index over the last year of the term. Some credit unions also average, but thankfully averaging is getting less common with index-linked GICs and the product is becoming far more straightforward.

Index-linked GICs are fully RRSP eligible—even the ones linked to foreign indices—and they can be bought in $500 to $1,000 minimums. Your principal is fully guaranteed, and if you hit the market at the right time, you can make considerably more than the ordinary GIC interest rate. Of course, you can also make nothing if markets turn miserable and there are no dividend payments; and you're also locked in until the GICs mature. You cannot cash in these GICs (except for death and hardship) and all the gains are taxed as interest income at your highest marginal tax rate.

Moshe Milevsky, a finance professor at York University and author of *Money Logic: Financial Strategies for the Smart Investor*, says that the insurance on a five-year GIC (in the form of a principal guarantee) probably isn't advantageous enough to put up with the cap. Markets tend to go up, especially over five years, so he'd buy a three-year product on the most volatile market he could find, and that way, get the biggest advantage from the product's insurance. He doesn't like averaging and always looks for the highest cap available, but fundamentally, he'd rather buy an ETF with a put option. A "put" is a contract that allows you to sell the index at a prearranged price some time in the future. That arrangement automatically limits your downside risk while giving you full scope to soar with the index. It's not exactly a simple strategy or something you can buy at the bank, but for folks with $10,000 or more to invest in index-linked GICs, it is a better overall approach, aeven though it may be a big stretch psychologically for habitual GIC investors.

Futures

Instead of buying your target index through a mutual fund or an ETF, you can get the same benefit by buying a futures contract on your index of choice. It takes some sophistication, serious assets and a special trading account, but for those determined to squeeze the last nickel out of their investment costs, it shouldn't be overlooked.

A futures contract is a legal obligation to buy or sell a very specific commodity or financial instrument at a specific price at a specific time in the future. These contracts are traded on a futures exchange which sets all the terms of the contract except for the price. Each day the accounts of the two parties to the contract—the one who must sell and the other who must buy—are marked to market. That means the exchange tallies up the (symmetrical) loss or gain on both sides: when one party makes money, the other party loses exactly the same amount.

Marking to market is one of the things that distinguishes futures from options. An option gives you the right but not the obligation, to buy or sell at a fixed price in the future. You can exercise an option or let it expire, and there is no daily marking of profits and loses.

Suppose you figure the S&P 500 is going to go up in the next month. (Future contracts can go out as far as a year, but one-month contracts are the most heavily traded.) You can buy one contract (expiring on the third Thursday in your target month) for 250 times the current value of the index. On July 31, 2001 the S&P 500 was 1222. One September contract would cost 250 x 1222 = US$305,500. Before you faint, know that much of that cost can be borrowed from the brokerage firm doing your trade. One of the big attractions of futures is that they can be done on margin. In the example above a broker would require only about US$24,000 in a futures margin account to cover the September contract purchase. So for 10% or less of the contract price down, you execute your trade and watch your account daily for either profits or margin calls, if you're losing money. And you pay commission only when you get out of the contract. In the case above, that commission is US$90. A discount broker might charge as little as US$35.

In Canada, futures (and options) trade on the Montréal Exchange. Canadian futures contracts exist on the S&P/TSE 60 Index and are planned for the four S&P/TSE sector indices: Information Technology, Financials, Energy, and Gold. There is also an option on the i60 ETF itself.

What Index?

The most commonly used financial futures contracts in Canada are contracts on the S&P/TSE 60 Index. On U.S. exchanges the most popular are futures contracts on the S&P 500, Nasdaq 100, the Dow Jones Industrial Average, the Russell 2000, S&P MidCap 400 and the Fortune e-50 Index. For the more ambitious, other contracts can be arranged.

Tracking and Management Fees

Futures track an index as smoothly as the Montréal Métro hugs its rails from day to day, though intraday, the contracts can anticipate the market and trade rich or cheap. Marking to market generally means your contract's value will go up and down daily in exact proportion with the index. There are no management fees and transaction costs are limited to the small brokerage commission for the contract. Since you sell or reverse contracts before they mature, little of your money is consumed by the actual cost of the contracts, which further improves your tracking. And don't forget that these contracts are done on margin. You get enormous exposure to a market index with very little of your own money tied up.

You do have to foot money to open a futures/margin account which requires some capitalization, but the nice thing is that T-bills are acceptable. You're not even losing money on the money tied up to support the margin account.

Taxes

Profits from futures contracts are fully taxed as income. You cannot elect to have them treated as on capital account (see Chapter 6 for more on taxes). Losses from futures contracts are fully deductible from income. You cannot hold futures in your RRSP.

Short-term or Long-term Plays?

A study by an analyst at UBS Warburg in New York concluded that futures are a cheaper way to get short-term exposure to financial markets but that long-term ETFs are better. That analyst believed the "roll costs" of contracts over time had more of an effect on costs than the MER on Spiders. The analyst also pointed out that the minimum investment for futures trading was much higher than 100 shares of an ETF, and that ETFs are often linked to sectors where no futures contracts are available.

It seems, however, that whether you opt for ETFs or index futures is a matter of debate. Another analyst, Jon Maier, who has looked at this question, doesn't agree. He thinks ETFs are always cheaper when you take into account mispricing risk and market impact of the futures contract itself. Maier's Salomon Smith Barney report on exchange traded funds released in February 2001 calculates all costs of an ETF purchase at 23.16 basis points (.23%). An identical calculation for a three-month futures contract would cost 60.14 basis points (.60%) by his calculation, and the longer the hold, the better ETFs look, according to Maier. The biggest advantage he reports with futures is the ease with which they can be leveraged. ETFs can be margined but you can borrow only up to 50% of their value; 70% if they're optionable. Futures will let you get away with borrowing up to 90% of the contracts' value.[9]

Leverage, of course, is a very sharp double-edged sword. Most investors would rather not. Hillary Clinton is said to have made a tidy sum on cattle futures. Maybe by the time she's running for president there will be a livestock ETF. Until then it's likely most of us will content ourselves with relatively simple ETFs and leave futures to those who don't mind margin calls.

Index mutual funds, ETFs or futures—you've got to decide which product best suits your situation, a decision that in part depends on how much money you want to give over to passive investing and for how long. The longer the hold period, the more you should favour ETFs for their parsimonious MERs. As you'll see in Chapter 4, there's a wealth of investment strategies suited for ETFs. Some of these strategies would not be possible to replicate with index funds because the index selection is no where near as broad as the buffet offered by ETFs, and of course, index funds are hard pressed to come anywhere close to matching ETFs in rock-bottom cover charge.

You might be surprised to discover that John Bogle, the American investment pioneer and outspoken advocate for low cost index investing, has kind words to say about ETFs, without actually liking them.

ETFs Or Index Mutual Funds?:
An Interview with John Bogle

John Bogle is founder of the Vanguard Group, the largest index mutual fund company in the world. He's an active advocate of low cost mutual funds, but not a great fan of ETFs despite the fact that Vanguard is the first U.S. mutual fund company to come out with an ETF, the VIPER series. (Mr. Bogle is retired from the day-to-day management of Vanguard.) As you read this keep in mind that Mr. Bogle is speaking from an American perspective, where the difference in annual costs between his hugely popular index funds and ETFs is quite small. The MER on Vanguard's S&P Index Fund is .18% versus the S&P 500 ETF (the Spider) with an MER of .12%. In Canada the disparity between index fund MERs and comparable ETFs can be much wider.* Here's what Mr. Bogle had to say in an interview dated June 19, 2001.

John Bogle: ETFs are a truly great product badly used. There's no reason not to use an ETF for long-term holdings. I'd call it a flip of the coin for long-term investors. That says they're a very, very good product because the index fund is the killer app[lication]. There's no way to improve on it for the market as a whole. It gives you virtually 100% of the market's return, and in the long run, probably 1% of all managers can give you 100% of the market's returns over 50 years and there aren't very good odds. Why would somebody take a 1% chance when they're guaranteed to get the market's return in an index fund?

Now what is the reality with ETFs? The turnover rate of all stocks in the U.S. is about 100% a year. Spider's is 1800%. The average holding is 12 days. That's a misuse of a big aggregated index. Turnover for Qubes is 3500% a year. It's a speculative medium [in which] shares are held for a fraction over two days on average. It's a great way to trade the Nasdaq, but why would anybody in their right mind think they can make any money trading the Nasdaq? Trading is a loser's game.

I contrast it with a great Purdey shotgun. It's a perfect

instrument for hunting and for suicide. I think many more investors are using these ETFs to commit financial suicide than they are to hunt for long-term returns. Anything that persuades people to trade more is against their best long-term investing interest.

We came out with VIPERs because we want to be competitive in the marketplace. If everybody else is doing it, we want to do it too. There are some potential tax advantages for our existing shareholders [because] we can move very low cost stocks into the VIPER class without a tax impact to the fund. [VIPERs will also be helpful in] getting traders who are now in our funds out of our funds into the trading shares.

I'm not madly in love with it. People have argued that we should not let people trade our funds: slap'em down. We've tried to be fairly good at that. [We allow] one round trip every six months—very tough trading restrictions. Maybe we could do that a little better, but in any event, we've elected to go the other way. It may not be a decision I would have made but it's not a decision that's unrespectable.

An ETF is an index fund. If you buy and hold it for your investment lifetime of 50 years, it's completely indifferent as to whether you've owned a mutual fund or an ETF if it's a broad index. It's a distinction without a difference. What matters is how these funds get used. The evidence is overpowering that they're both marketed to traders and used by traders. All market mutual funds are boredom personified. ETFs are excitement personified. It's like sailing: hours of complete boredom punctuated by moments of sheer terror.

The ETF is great with the right long-term perspective because they keep costs and taxes low, and those are crucial factors. And that's good, but if they're used for trading, they're just another stock, maybe a little less risky one because of their diversification.

*The lowest cost Canadian index ETF is SSgA's Dow Jones Canada 40 Index with an MER of .08%. Contrast that with the lowest cost publicly available Canadian equity index fund, TD's Canadian Index eFund, with an MER at .31% covering the TSE 300 Index. TD's TSE 300 ETF has an MER of .25%. Altamira's Precision Canadian Index, which is pegged to the S&P/TSE 60 Index charges .50% versus the i60's MER of .17%. (MERs from www.globefund.com.)

Notes

1) Salomon Smith Barney research report on exchange traded funds, Feb. 6, 2001, p.16.

2) Ibid.

3) The iShares MSCI series (formerly the country share "WEBS") carry MERs of .84% for developed markets and .99% for emerging markets; otherwise, U.S. ETF MERs tend to be .60% or less.

4) This point is made graphically at *www.bylo.org* in an article entitled "Performance of Indexed vs. Actively Managed Portfolios (CARs for the 15 years ending Dec. 31, 2001)."

The article compares the returns of median mutual funds to median index funds over 15 years and calculates how profoundly the MER differential affects long-term returns. See also *www.osc.gov.on.ca* for an MER impact calculator, *www.stingyinvestor.com/SI/articles/0401.shtml* and another article on that site, "Active Funds vs. Indexing."

5) For a more detailed discussion of the MER calculation and what it leaves out, see *MoneySense* magazine, "Ask MoneySense," by Donna Green, October 2000, online at *www.moneysense.ca* (searching on "MER").

6) The author was not able to find Canadian data on holding periods, but there's no reason to think the Canadian holding period is that much different from that in the U.S. Two-and-a-half year U.S. holding information from John Bogle, President of Bogle Financial Markets Research Center, founder and past chairman of the Vanguard Group, "Mutual Fund Directors: The Dog that Didn't Bark," Jan. 29, 2001 speech. Available on *www.vanguard.com*. Bogle's speeches, *www.vanguard.com/bogle_site/january282001.html*. See also FRC study cited in Chapter 2 for 2.9 year holding period.

7) As per Eric Kirzner reported in "Passive Investors' Choices Expand," *Globe and Mail*, May 2, 2001.

8) Numbers from PALTrak as of May 31, 2001 with $5 billion subtracted for iUnits which are included in PALTrak's computation. Thanks to Stephen Burnie at *www.morningstar.ca*.

9) SalomonSmithBarney research report on exchange traded funds, Feb. 6, 2001, p.18, and UBS Warburg report by Jon Maier, March 13, 2001.

Part Two
Making ETFs Work for You

Chapter 4
Investment Strategies Using ETFs

Staking your money on an index among the countless number of them out there seems to require either strong opinions or impressive self-confidence. Where do you begin when there are over 100-plus ETFs available? Well, in truth, the choices get narrowed down remarkably fast because you want to establish two main goals in your overall portfolio: prudent diversification and intelligent asset allocation.

When investment gurus contemplate portfolios, they chant "diversification." Diversification lowers the blood pressure just as surely as yoga meditation, and is the uncomplicated essence of good portfolio management.

Part of good diversification is another mantra: asset allocation. You've likely heard more times than you care to remember that asset allocation is responsible for 93.6% of your portfolio returns. That is possibly the most widely quoted false statistic in all of Christendom. The study, done by Gary Brinson in 1986, actually says, "Data from 91 large U.S. pension plans indicate that investment policy dominates investment strategy (market timing and security selection), explaining on average 93.6% of the variation in total plan return."[1] In other words, asset allocation explained, on average, 93.6% of the variation in the portfolios studied. Variation, or variance, is a measure of the risk of the asset. So what the study is actually saying is that asset allocation is the predominant factor in controlling the riskiness of the portfolio. Perhaps it is not the profound conclusion of the misquotes, but an important observation anyway. Evening the peaks and valleys of your returns will give you a better opportunity to put compounding to good long-term benefit. Compounding works more quickly on consistent gains rather than an equivalent return spread over years of losses and gold strikes.

Because the Brinson study has been wildly misunderstood, it has been revisited a number of times. A more recent paper looks at this study, adds some more empirical evidence and wrings a more meaningful conclusion from it all. Roger G. Ibbotson and Paul D. Kaplan, in their article, "Does Asset Allocation Policy Explain 40, 90 or 100 Percent of Performance?" say

In summary, the impact of asset allocation on returns depends on an individual's investing style. For the long-term, passive investor, the asset allocation decision is by far the most important. For the short-term investor who trades more frequently, invests in individual securities and practices market timing, asset allocation has less of an impact on returns. The impact of asset allocation on performance is directly correlated with investment style.[2]

So if you're going to be a buy-and-hold investor, your asset allocation should be your foremost consideration; and the key to an effective asset allocation is diversification.

Diversification means not putting all your eggs in one basket; in other words, not buying one stock when you can buy a number of different stocks to hedge your risk. Ditto for bonds and any other investment vehicle. Asset allocation is simply the process of extending the principle of diversification across asset classes. Holding 12 different stocks may mean you're diversified across equities (if you've selected stocks from different industries), but you're still exposed to the vagaries of the stock market without the backstop of bonds, cash, real estate, precious metals, et cetera.

Mutual funds make diversification and asset allocation quite easy. There's a mutual fund for any asset class you can think of, and because of the large sums mutual funds pool, they can offer instant and very broad diversification to anyone with $25 a month. It's a wonderful thing.

By now you know ETFs are a cheaper way to accomplish diversification and quality asset allocation. So if you want to take a bite out of your investment costs and have more flexibility with your investments, here are some easy-to-emulate portfolio construction models and investment strategies using ETFs to help you build a solidly diversified portfolio with easily amendable asset allocation and excellent tax efficiency. There's enough information here to start you on the road to do-it-yourself freedom. For those who prefer to work with an advisor, this chapter will give you a good understanding of the strategies your advisor will have at his or her disposal so that your investment portfolio will not be held back just in the interests of keeping it simple. Advisors can add value, especially when they're free to use every tool in the arsenal to build your wealth. You'll notice, too, that there's still a role in these strategies for actively managed mutual funds for those asset classes not yet covered by ETFs and for those sectors where you might believe active management can still exploit some inefficiencies.

Keep in mind that ETFs can be bought or sold only inside a brokerage account. If you don't already have a brokerage account, it may seem like an unwelcome complication, but once set up, the flexibility and convenience the account provides makes it hard to ever want to do without it. A brokerage account is useful because you can hold just about everything but the junk in your basement in it. This means you can consolidate all your investments in one account if you'd like (with the exception of bank GICs which can't be transferred to another institution). You can easily open up an account with a full-service broker or an online discount broker and there is no charge to open an account.

Time to put meditation aside and examine how to put ETFs to a practical use.

Core and Satellite

Core and Satellite is a popular portfolio construction method especially for the equity side. It starts by allocating the largest chunk of money to the least risky equity holding; namely, a broad-based equity ETF. Surrounding that core like electrons are smaller investments in industry sectors, management styles, market capitalization and individual stocks. This method is also known by the trademarked name "Core and Explore" propounded by Charles Schwab in the U.S. and Canada. The core of the portfolio is passively managed, but the exploratory parts can be either passively or actively managed. An important consideration for the electrons is their maneuverability. They're the ones you may wish to use to dart in and out in anticipation of changing market conditions or hold longer term as a secular play. They're the ones the money manager is counting on to boost returns above the index benchmark.

Core/Satellite Equity Allocation Strategy (fig. 12)

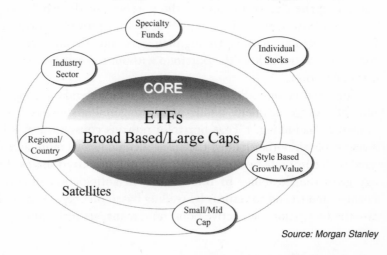

Source: Morgan Stanley

Schwab Canada worked extensively with Eric Kirzner, University of Toronto Professor of Finance, to hone their Core and Explore™ model to the Canadian environment. They adjusted for Canadian tax considerations, the depreciating Canadian currency and the changing nature of Canada's economy from resource-based to technology-and-services oriented. Out of Kirzner's work arose fourteen model portfolios, (seven for registered, seven for non-registered accounts), in increasing aggressiveness and all virtually on the efficient frontier. These are asset allocation models that optimize returns for a predetermined level of risk.

As the savvy client knows, the asset allocation sets the return expectations. A good allocation finds a balance between what the client needs to earn on his portfolio and his risk tolerance. Schwab is far from unique in stressing the critical importance of a good, client-specific asset allocation as the foundation for portfolio management. Even mutual fund companies have had fairly sophisticated, proprietary asset allocation programs for years. Mackenzie Financial Corp.'s STAR program is one example. Schwab, however, is notable for the way it implements these allocations.

Craig Ellis is a portfolio manager for Schwab Canada in Toronto. He deals with managed accounts of $250,000 or more, and gives portfolio construction guidance to the firm's investment advisors. He says after a client's initial asset allocation is determined, Schwab's approach is often to recommend that client's put half of each asset class in a passive vehicle—most usually an ETF—"because that forms the base of stability." Then the other half of each asset class is more actively managed by selecting individual stocks or by overweighting sectors with sector ETFs. Ellis says this approach works especially well with technology, where individual stocks can be very risky; whereas a diversified portfolio of a broad selection of technology companies mitigates the business risk of individual stocks while still giving the chance to capture the potential of the whole sector. Ellis also praises this Core and Explore™ design for providing lots of room for tactical portfolio changes, letting managers and advisors overweight sectors on the active side of the portfolio without throwing off the structural asset allocation.

For fixed income, Schwab frequently recommends putting 50% in a portfolio of government bonds with staggered maturities (this is also known as "laddering.") That portfolio remains constant and is held passively while the other half of the fixed income side is more actively managed with corporate bonds, income trusts and preferred shares. This strategy gives the flexibility to trade bonds in anticipation of interest rate changes and to add to returns by trading based on changes in credit quality—the two major ways active bond fund managers make money.

Although Ellis and other Schwab money mangers don't do this, it is also possible to "core" the fixed income portion of your portfolio with ETFs. A proper combination of Barclays Global Investors (BGI) Canada's iG5 and iG10 funds achieves an ongoing exposure to a set portion of the yield curve with Government of Canada bonds. This leaves room to "explore" with actively managed corporate or high yield bond mutual funds. Later this year, additional fixed income ETF offerings are expected on both sides of the border, and with them, added flexibility for the fixed income side of your holdings.

You may not realize it, but there are more benefits to bond ETFs than may immediately appear. Individual investors like you and me have to buy bonds through brokerages that hold them in inventory. Although there is no commission charge on a bond purchase, there is an invisible charge taken by the house on the sale of a bond that is factored into the yield your bond delivers. A bond that might cost $900 per $1,000 face value will be sold to you for the purposes of example at $910 per $1,000. That extra $10 over wholesale cost is the brokerages' built-in (and most often undisclosed) commission. Until recently, you and I were not privy to the wholesale cost of bonds. Until E-BOND Ltd., a Toronto-based on-line bond trading service, came along last year, investors had no accurate way of telling how much of a cut the bond desk was taking on a bond transaction because the bond market prices were veiled from us. That's still the case for most of us not yet familiar with the three on-line bond providers now operating in Canada. Without using their pricing service, the best you can get is a feel for current interest rate levels from looking at the yields of other bonds of a similar nature—if you can get current quotes of those bonds—and using this to judge the fairness of the yield on your own bond purchase.

With bond ETFs all you have to worry about is the brokerage commission to buy the fund and the annual MER. You can bet the ETF is getting a better yield on their Government of Canada bonds than you would be able to get, simply because of the size of the purchase. You can also bet that a $29 commission is a lot less than the money you lose in yield on an individual bond purchase. The real question is if the .25% MER is also less than the yield hit you'd take on an individual bond buy. It is definitely way less than the MER on a conventional bond fund which can easily run you .86% for an index bond fund to 1.88% for AGF Canadian Bond Fund and more.

Building Blocks

Very similar to the Core and Satellite approach is the Building Blocks method of portfolio construction. In this model, decreasing amounts of money are allocated to increasingly risky equity groups, sort of like those wooden building blocks kids love to play with, though it is more conventionally represented by the pyramidal design in our illustration. The base starts with a very broad-based passive investment such as TD Asset Management's TSE 300 ETF or iShares Russell 3000. Then, in decreasing weight, might come a growth and/or a value mutual fund, then perhaps a mid cap ETF, followed by a sector ETF in an area like technology, and then finally, the smallest building block of all—individual stocks.

Equity Building Blocks (fig. 13)

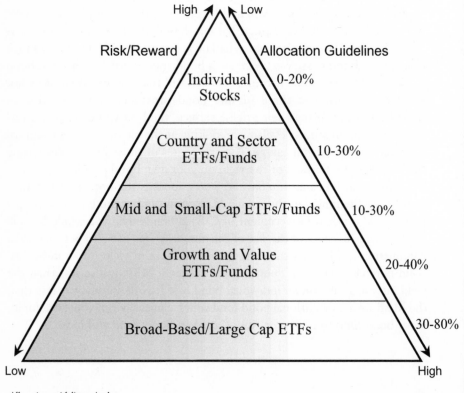

Allocation guidelines: Author

Source: Morgan Stanley

One of the many beauties of this approach is that your portfolio's return will probably stay fairly close to the return of its main holding; in this case, the TSE 300 ETF. It also gives a disciplined framework so you shrink your exposure as the riskiness of the investment increases. It's a big temptation to make sizable bets on hot industries. The Core and Satellite and the Building Block strategies let you have some exposure to a favoured sector, style or stock, but in moderation and with due consideration for the inherent risk.

Naturally, not every possibility needs to be included in portfolios following this general core approach. Likely you'll find it enough to tilt your passive core with a favoured sector or a promising stock, but if you're game to try all the flavours, the good news is that Canadians can use domestic ETFs for just about every area represented in the pyramid except for the growth-and-value tier. There are iShares in the U.S. based on the Russell Growth and Value indices, and for a combination of style and capitalization there are iShares on the S&P/Barra indices. StreetTRACKS' U.S.-based ETFs use Dow Jones indices also combining style and capitalization. So far Canada doesn't have any style-based ETFs. For RRSP portfolios, then, the best implementation is a style-based actively managed mutual fund.

As for the foreign content element of a Building Block portfolio, you're free to take 30% of your blocks and invest in U.S. ETFs that are counterparts to your Canadian position, though this may be impractical if your portfolio is not large and the 30% means buying less than a board lot of an ETF. You could also invest the growth and value portion of the pyramid in international mutual funds with those style biases, and to top up to 30%, swing in a U.S. sector ETF or a mutual fund specific to a U.S. or global sector. (See the sample portfolios below.) There are a limitless number of ways to utilize this strategy.

Core and Satellite and Building Block: Portfolio Construction Guidelines

• This portfolio construction style is very versatile.
• There are an "infinite" number of portfolios using combinations of ETFs, mutual funds, stocks, bonds and alternative investments.
• In general, smaller portfolios should restrict holdings to a few broad based ETFs to provide sufficient diversification at a reasonable cost.
• If distribution reinvestment and dollar cost averaging are desired, make sure the portfolio contains some mutual funds that allow this activity. (As investor demand grows, it is likely that more brokerages will offer this service on the larger, more popular ETFs.)

Core Components :
Broad Market/Large Cap Base

Exposure	ETFs		
	Type	Non-Registered	Registered
CANADA	Broad	TTF, TCF	
	Large Cap	XIU, XIC, DJF	
UNITED STATES	Broad	IYY, IWV, VTI	XSP
	Large Cap	IVV, SPY, IWB	
INTERNATIONAL	Broad	EFA	XIN

Step 1: Select one ETF from each desired **exposure** (one from broad OR one from large cap) and weight appropriately.

The Building Block method and the Core and Satellite approach anchor your portfolio in a passive index while giving you quite a bit of room to do some tactical maneuvering with a portion of your portfolio. You can adjust from value to growth when the economy starts heating up, or back to value as a more defensive play. You can tilt from sector to sector as you anticipate action and of course you can still enjoy your individual stock picks. Hard to imagine an easier to maintain portfolio that'll let you have so much fun.

So how much should you allocate to core and how much to satellite? As a rule of thumb, the more risk averse you are, the greater the percentage of your portfolio should be put in the passive core—even up to 100%. Your portfolio, then, will perform in-line with the asset classes you've chosen. No better, no worse. It's a trade off. You've given up the possibility of out-performing the market for the promise of not underperforming it (except by the amount of the small MER).

At the other extreme would be the 100% satellite portfolio—the swing for the fences approach. But as in baseball, when you focus on the home runs, you will often strike out. Most investors will find comfort in a core position ranging from 50% to 70% of their portfolio, with the conservative crowd approaching 100%. As always your investment decisions have to be in-line with your financial goals and risk tolerance.

Satellite / Tilt Components

Strategy	Exposure		ETFs
STYLE/CAP	Small Cap Value		IJS, IWN, DSV
	Mid Cap		IJH, MDY, XMD*
INDUSTRY SECTOR	Energy		XLE, IYE, OIH, XEG*
	Financials		XLF, IYF, IYG, RKH, XFN*
	Healthcare	Broad:	IYH, PPH
		Biotech:	BBH, IBB
	Technology	Broad:	IYW, IGM, MTK, XLK, XIT*
		Telecom:	IYZ, TTA, WMA
COUNTRY/REGIONAL	Europe	Broad:	IEV, EZU, EKH
	Asia Pacific *(Japan, Hong Kong, Singapore, Australia)*		EWJ, EWH, EWS, EWA
	Emerging Markets *(Mexico, Brazil, South Korea, Taiwan)*		EWW, EWZ, EWY, EWT

* 100% RSP Eligible

- **Step 2:**   Layer on to the core, one or more ETFs for each desired **exposure** to strategically "tilt" the portfolio

Rebalancing

The success of these investment strategies depends on disciplined rebalancing. Over time your carefully allotted percentages are going to come unstuck. Not all the assets will grow in proportion to one another. What started off as a 10% position may have grown to 20%, and your core may look a little gnawed in comparison. Rebalancing is the process of bringing your portfolio's asset classes back in-line with an optimal allocation.

As any one knows who has sold a winner to buy losers, this takes intestinal fortitude. The big temptation is to continue to let winners run. That's when greed overtakes reason. It is always best to leave something for the next guy. By rebalancing you capture your gains and plow them into asset classes that have yet to make their move. You lose out a little on the high end but chances are you capture the full movement from off the bottom.

Rebalancing at least once a year has a smoothing effect on returns, which increases the benefits of compounding.

Unfortunately, rebalancing an ETF portfolio comes with commission costs and probably a tax bill (outside a registered account). This means you have to decide how religiously you want to keep to your ideal asset allocation. Rebalancing to adjust for a 5% deviation isn't worth it in a small portfolio, but it could be in a large portfolio. These are judgements you have to make, perhaps in consultation with a financial advisor or accountant. Don't let the tax tail wag the investment dog. Rebalancing has to be done to get the full benefit of these strategies, an important part of which is their defensiveness.

Sector Rotation

Sector rotation is a fairly aggressive investment strategy that ETFs make very easy to execute, but unfortunately, not any easier to get right. Sector rotation managers invest in industry sectors they believe are poised for significant advances. Strategies vary greatly but generally fall into two camps based upon the expected holding period. Intermediate sector rotation is usually measured in months and attempts to capture cyclical moves. Secular strategies are based on multi-year trends.

The aim is to buy into a sector when it is still out of favour and to sell when it has peaked. Trouble is, nobody has a reliable crystal ball. Analysts have spent lots of time tracking historical sector performance in hopes of discovering some pattern or predictability to the ascendant sectors. Let's just say it's still an art, but one that plenty of managers think they can exploit. Plenty of ordinary investors unknowingly do sector rotation when they buy and sell industry-specialized mutual funds such as internet and technology, health sciences funds, precious metals and funds with a preponderance of financial stocks like AIC Advantage Fund. Sectors go in and out of favour, but with a little cunning and some luck, most everyone thinks they can pick the next hot sector. As the technology stock crash has shown, though, a big part of sector betting is knowing when to leave something for the next guy, or how to sit through some gut wrenching downturns. Exiting a sector before its decline can be as important as jumping onto it before its rise.

To give you some idea of how volatile sector investing can be, the following is a chart courtesy of Morgan Stanley Equity Research on the historical performance of major sectors.

Historical S&P/MSCI Sector Performance

Best ← Performance → Worst

1990	1991	1992	1993	1994	1995	1996	1997	1998	1999	2000
Consumer Discretionary 13.8%	Healthcare 53.2%	Financials 24.1%	Information Technology 19.3%	Information Technology 20.3%	Healthcare 58.2%	Information Technology 44.8%	Financials 49.0%	Information Technology 78.5%	Information Technology 79.7%	Utilities 57.1%
Consumer Staples 13.5%	Financials 48.9%	Consumer Discretionary 18.4%	Industrials 17.7%	Healthcare 13.5%	Financials 53.7%	Financials 35.5%	Healthcare 42.3%	Telecom Services 53.1%	Materials 25.6%	Healthcare 25.6%
Energy 13.4%	Consumer Staples 42.7%	Telecom Services 16.7%	Telecom Services 15.8%	Consumer Staples 8.7%	Telecom Services 41.8%	Consumer Staples 26.6%	Telecom Services 41.1%	Healthcare 43.5%	Consumer Discretionary 24.8%	Financials 24.8%
Industrials 12.7%	Consumer Discretionary 36.6%	Materials 11.1%	Energy 15.7%	Materials 6.6%	Consumer Staples 40.2%	Energy 25.9%	Consumer Staples 34.4%	Consumer Discretionary 41.2%	Industrials 19.8%	Consumer Staples 19.8%
Healthcare 11.1%	Industrials 32.4%	Industrials 10.1%	Materials 15.6%	Energy 3.6%	Information Technology 39.1%	Industrials 24.9%	Consumer Discretionary 33.3%	Consumer Staples 15.5%	Telecom Services 18.9%	Energy 15.5%
Telecom Services 8.8%	Materials 26.4%	Utilities 6.8%	Consumer Discretionary 14.7%	Industrials -2.6%	Industrials 38.8%	Healthcare 21.6%	Information Technology 27.8%	Utilities 14.9%	Energy 18.2%	Industrials 4.9%
Financials 7.4%	Utilities 23.9%	Consumer Staples 6.1%	Utilities 13.5%	Financials -2.9%	Utilities 32.7%	Materials 15.4%	Industrials 27.0%	Industrials 11.5%	Financials 3.8%	Materials 14.4%
Information Technology 6.6%	Telecom Services 13.5%	Information Technology 2.4%	Financials 11.3%	Telecom Services -4.7%	Energy 31.0%	Consumer Discretionary 13.6%	Energy 25.2%	Financials 11.4%	Utilities -9.3%	Consumer Discretionary -20.0%
Materials 6.4%	Information Technology 11.9%	Energy 1.9%	Consumer Staples -4.4%	Consumer Discretionary -7.6%	Materials 20.8%	Utilities 5.7%	Utilities 24.8%	Energy 0.8%	Healthcare -10.3%	Telecom Services -38.8%
Utilities 6.2%	Energy 6.9%	Healthcare -15.2%	Healthcare -6.7%	Utilities -11.6%	Consumer Discretionary 20.3%	Telecom Services 0.2%	Materials 8.1%	Materials 6.6%	Consumer Staples -15.5%	Information Technology -40.6%

Source: Morgan Stanley

Performance for all cited indexes is calculated on a total return basis with dividends reinvested. Categories are based upon S&P/MSCI sectors.

Historical Performance by Style

Performance	1990	1991	1992	1993	1994	1995	1996	1997	1998	1999	2000
Best	Growth	Small Cap	Small Cap	International	International	Value	Growth	Value	Growth	Growth	Mid Cap
	Large Cap	Mid Cap	Mid Cap	Small Cap	Growth	Large Cap	Large Cap	Large Cap	Large Cap	Small Cap	Value
	Value	Growth	Value	Value	Large Cap	Growth	Value	Growth	International	Mid Cap	Small Cap
	Mid Cap	Large Cap	Large Cap	Mid Cap	Small Cap	Mid Cap	Mid Cap	Mid Cap	Value	International	Large Cap
	Small Cap	Value	Growth	Large Cap	Value	Small Cap	Small Cap	Small Cap	Mid Cap	Large Cap	International
Worst	International	International	International	Growth	Mid Cap	International	International	International	Small Cap	Value	Growth

Source: Russell, MSCI, S&P, Morgan Stanley
Performance for all cited indexes is calculated on a total return basis with dividends reinvested. Indexes used for categories include: MSCI EAFE for International, Russell 1000 Growth for Growth, S&P 500 for Large Cap, Russell 1000 Value for Value, Russell Midcap for Mid Cap, and Russell 2000 for Small Cap.

The current crop of ETFs make sector investing easy. Not only that, but ETFs bring an efficiency to sector investing that is hard to emulate because of the broad index approach they take. Instead of relying on a manager to make good representative picks in the sector at hand, an ETF simply snaps up the sector index and is done with it. There's no active manager risk, and you can be assured that you're going to be along for the ride, though perhaps not always the entire ride because of concentration restrictions.

At the time of this book's printing, there were four sector ETF offerings in Canada, all by BGI Canada. These iUnits were in energy, information technology, gold, and financials. More sector ETFs were expected in the future. In the U.S., there's an astonishing 46 sector ETFs (including 15 sector HOLDRS out of 17 HOLDRS in total). What follows are the sectors currently represented by ETFs and HOLDRS in the U.S.

iShares Dow Jones Sectors
Basic Materials
Chemicals
Consumer Cyclicals
Consumer Non-cyclicals
Energy
Financials
Financial Services
Healthcare
Industrial
Internet
Real Estate
Technology
Telecommunications
Utilities

Select Sector Spiders
Basic Industries
Consumer Services
Consumer Staples
Cyclical/transportation
Energy
Financial
Industrial
Technology
Utilities

HOLDRS
B2B Internet
Biotech
Broadband
Internet
Internet architecture
Internet infrastructure
Oil Service
Pharmaceutical
Regional banks
Retail
Semiconductor
Software
Telecommunications
Utilities
Wireless

iShares Goldman Sachs Sectors
Networking
Semiconductor
Software
Technology

streetTRACKS Sectors
Wilshire REIT Index
Morgan Stanley High-tech 35 Index
Morgan Stanley Internet Index
Fortune e-50 Index

HOLDRS are fixed baskets of securities that trade on a stock exchange (see Chapter 7). HOLDRS have no concentration limitations, but U.S.-based ETFs, including sector ETFs, must abide by some concentration rules: no more than 25% of a fund's assets can be invested in a single security, and the sum of all securities in the fund making up more than 5% of the fund cannot collectively exceed 50% of the fund's assets. This requirement to be diversified is most likely to impinge on sector ETFs because of their relatively narrow focus. There is no similar concentration restriction on ETFs in Canada, but BGI Canada's iUnits sector ETFs has a 25% cap on the weighting of any one company in its Canadian sector funds. The BGI restriction is in keeping with the 25% cap the S&P folks have imposed on their own index. Such restrictions ensure a diversified portfolio, but they can affect the tracking, and will affect it when highly weighted companies become market favourites as Nortel Networks did in early 2000 when it took over more than a third of the TSE 300's weighting.

Jumping in and out of sectors is for the self-confident, active investor or an investor with an investment advisor of similar qualities, but if you get it right, it can give you spectacular returns. One very capital intensive way to play the sectors involves buying up all the Select Sector Spiders in weights that you judge to be most opportune. Since all nine Select Sector

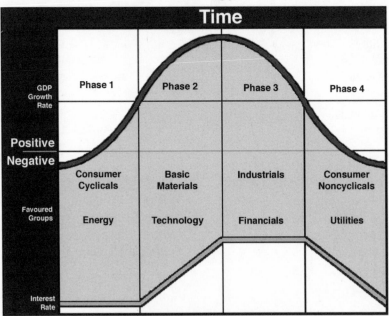

Sector Rotation Strategy Model (fig. 14)

Reprinted with permission from *Technical Analysis of STOCKS & COMMODITIES*™ magazine.
©1997 Technical analysis, Inc., (800) 832-4642, *www.Traders.com*

Spiders equals the entire S&P 500 Index, you would have broad market exposure with your own customized sector weightings. Not only that, but you are then free to trade the sectors individually. Ideally you'd be selling the falling sectors and riding the winning sectors and using the tax loss on the non-performing sectors to off-set the capital gains on the ascendant sectors. You can do this, too, with the iShares Dow Jones Sector ETFs, which together make up all of the Dow Jones U.S. Total Market Index.

For those whose investment stakes are not so large, there are more modest ways of sector investing. Analysts have found some basic sector rotation patterns to be fairly consistent across market cycles based on the reaction of sectors to interest rate movements.

Morgan Stanley have honed sector interest rate sensitivity to a fine point. They studied the last six business cycles and found that equity returns averaged 15.7% for the first six months following a second U.S. Federal Reserve interest rate cut, and 18.4% for the twelve months following the second rate cut. In an Equity Research Report called "Using ETFs to Capitalize on Sectors Favored for Recovery," the Morgan Stanley equity team says

As soon as investors became convinced that the Fed was committed to promoting recovery, as evidenced by its second interest rate cut, aggressive sectors started to outperform defensive ones. After the second rate cut, investors began to focus on sectors that were positioned to benefit from economic and earnings recovery.[3]

Average S&P Sector Returns During Fed Easing Cycles Since 1981

6-month period following the second Fed Easing

	Average Return (%)
Financials	19.0
Consumer Discretionary	18.5
Health Care	16.7
Information Technology	13.9
Consumer Staples	13.7
Industrials	13.0
Telecom Services	11.6
Materials	10.9
Energy	10.3
Utilities	8.5

12-month period following the second Fed easing

	Average Return (%)
Information Technology	20.9
Consumer discretionary	19.9
Health Care	19.0
Financials	16.7
Industrials	16.5
Consumer Staples	15.7
Materials	13.8
Telecom Services	10.9
Energy	9.6
Utilities	6.7

Source: Morgan Stanley Equity Research, January 20, 2001

Most sector rotation strategies are correlated to interest rate movements but there are any number of economic factors that might serve a similar purpose with enough cleverness and research. Technical tools can be applied just as easily to sector ETFs as to individual stocks. One technical analyst whose company refused to let his name be used, writes regular reports summarizing three technical parameters for each ETF in North America. The report is useful for seeing how investment opportunities are changing by region and by sector. The report tracks price momentum, the ETFs 40 week moving average, and the trend in its daily highs and lows. If the daily highs and lows are both getting higher, if the ETF is above its 40 week moving average, and if it is showing positive momentum, the ETF is a buy as long as conventional fundamentals don't contradict the positive outlook. A deterioration in the technicals with some fundamental correlation for this triggers a sell recommendation or a defensive option strategy. Using technical tools with ETFs makes them all the more interesting to brokers and investors who want to use ETFs in active trading strategies using sector and/or regional tilts. The fact that the target investments are diversified portfolios rather than individual stocks does mitigate risk, too.

Seasonality

There are numerous seasonal patterns in the Canadian equity market, its sectors, and some individual stocks. Seasonality is a popular topic for quantitative analysts. Hidden among the barrage of market data, they look for and sometimes find odd regularities or associations. Perhaps the most well-known of these is the correlation between the U.S. markets and the U.S. presidential cycle. Usually the fourth year of an administration finds the market booming. Markets will continue going higher after the election of a new president and during his legislative honeymoon. Markets start coughing with the worst of it around October of second year (midterm). After that the cycle starts again and markets begin moving up.

Some commonly observed seasonal patterns with the TSE have lead to the saying "Buy when it snows. Sell when it goes." Buying the broad Canadian market at the end of November and selling it at the end of March for the past 17 years would have been more profitable than just holding the index in 13 of the past 17 years.

Industries and individual stocks show seasonality, too. There appears to be seasonal patterns in Canadian oil and gas stocks: "Buy when it's coldest. Sell when it's hottest." That advice means buying at the end of December and selling at the end of July. Had you done that for the past 13 years, you would have returned an average of 10.8%, 10 out of 13 years. If you'd done the opposite and bought at the end of July and sold at the end of December, you would have averaged -4.9% during the past 12 years 9 times out of 12.

While recognizing that equity markets, sectors and stocks do often have seasonal characteristics, investors should use a mix of technical, quantitative and fundamental analysis before buying any investment. When you're ready to pounce on a perceived upswing, ETFs make a lot of sense for equity markets and sectors. During periods of seasonal weakness consider selling covered calls on your ETFs.

Regional Tilts

ETFs are also well situated for regional rotation or tilts. When you think Japan is about to emerge from its ten-year-plus slumber, socking some money into iShares MSCI Japan might be for you. Foresee political unrest in Hong Kong? Short iShares MSCI Hong Kong. There are 21 country-specific ETFs (all iShares). If a single country is too narrow a bet for you, a clutch of geographically related country ETFs will serve in its place. There's even a European Monetary Union (EMU) iShare. Regional coverage, however, still has some gaps. For one thing, the entire Far East as a region is unrepresented, so is Latin America. No doubt new products are being developed and will rectify this lacuna in time (and with the cooperation of foreign governments).

For the more conservative, you might just want to get more global exposure in general. Right now there are two ETFs and a HOLDRS that can give you that. SSgA's Global Titan has about 50 blue-chip stocks from around the world. BGI's iShares S&P Global 100 holds 100 large global companies, and Merrill Lynch's Market 2000+ HOLDRS has 54 large stocks from an assortment of countries. But these products are all considered foreign content for RRSP purposes. Which brings up an important point. In your drive to get international exposure with ETFs, be careful to take note of RRSP eligibility. Don't hold BGI's new RRSP global ETFs outside of an RRSP account. They're designed to be 100% RRSP eligible, and as a result, all the income from the i500R and the soon to be launched EAFE ETF is taxed as interest income at your highest marginal rate. Non-registered accounts, as a result, should avoid them. (See Appendix C for new products under development.)

Global Sector Investing

Now that ETFs have made tactical sector and country investing devilishly easy, globalization may very well have diminished its usefulness. Take a deep breath. There's evidence that sector investing is most effectively done across global markets, at least in developed countries. Salomon Smith Barney (SSB) published an equity research report in May entitled "The Global ETF Investor." It argues that globalization has meant that many developed markets move in close synchronization with each other, especially those countries in the European Union. This has spawned a trend away from country-based investing to global sector-based investing in developed markets. (In emerging markets the country effect still seems strong.)

But take heart. There's nothing you can do about this right now—no product to buy, no strategy to study. Soon though, you can expect a spate of global sector ETFs to hit the market. Not surprisingly, a series of ETFs based on S&P's ten new global sector indices are awaiting Securities and Exchange Commission (SEC) approval. "...[T]he introduction of global sector funds will give investors a way to diversify that does not currently exist," says the SSB report. The report also notes that the number of sector ETFs listed in Europe "has grown dramatically," a trend worth paying attention to. The only constant in the investment world is change.

Style Weighting

The investment management world is divided into two halves: value managers and growth managers. You might say they're arch rivals and they seldom thrive together. During the technology frenzy in the late 1990s, growth investing completely eclipsed value. There were even headlines about famous value investors like Warren Buffett and John Templeton being icons of times long gone. Technology was to so profoundly change our productivity that price to earnings ratios no longer had any significance, and these old guys just couldn't accept the world had changed around them. Companies without earnings were exploding with promise and their stock prices rode along with the optimism. Then, suddenly these companies exploded right in their investors' faces. And the bargain hunting value style of investment management reasserted its dominion in 2001.

In a pure textbook sense, growth and value are opposing money management styles. In the realities of the marketplace, only a minority of money managers are extremists. Most subscribe to an approach that includes both camps to some extent, so let's lay out the camps. Staunch growth managers look for companies with faster than average gains in earnings over a specified period, usually a few years. They don't take much notice of price-to-earnings ratio, or price-to-book ratios. During the tech bubble, some growth managers didn't even hold out for actual earnings growth. A company with the likely prospect of above-average earnings growth was enough to light up their buy buttons. Sometimes growth managers are really momentum investors in disguise, jumping on stocks with prices that show a lot of upward movement.

This would make pure value investors cringe in horror. These are the old-fashioned, bargain-minded folks who look for companies with good fundamentals but in an industry that's fallen out of favour. Value managers have to hold their noses to buy a stock with a price to earnings ratio over 20. Contrast that with all the growth managers who bought Nortel Networks when its P/E was over 100.

In some years, typically when the economy is contracting, value managers look very smart. In other years, growth managers get the glory. For the entire period between 1994 and 1999 large cap growth stocks delivered much higher returns than value stocks, but from 1994 to 1997 value stocks led the pack.[4] The prudent mutual fund investor should have a mix of both investment styles. With ETFs you can go one better and actually trade on anticipation of broad investment style changes, or tactically weight your portfolio with a growth or value bias. You might, for instance, want to go heavy on growth at the beginning of an economic expansion, and then tilt your portfolio in favour of value as the expansion slows. Below is a list of the 16 style-based ETFs.

Broad Market Growth
iShares Russell 3000 Growth

Broad Market Value
iShares Russell 3000 Value

Large Cap Growth
iShares S&P 500/Barra Growth
iShares Russell 1000 Growth
streetTRACKS Dow Jones U.S. Large Cap Growth

Large Cap Value
iShares S&P 500/Barra Value
iShares Russell 1000 Value
streetTRACKS Dow Jones U.S. Large Cap Value

Mid Cap Growth
iShares S&P MidCap/Barra Growth

Mid Cap Value
iShares S&P MidCap/Barra Value

Small Cap Growth
iShares S&P SmallCap/Barra Growth
iShares Russell 2000 Growth
streetTRACKS Dow Jones Small Cap Growth

Small Cap Value
iShares S&P SmallCap/Barra Value
iShares Russell 2000 Value
streetTRACKS Dow Jones Small Cap Value

These style ETFs are based on three different indices each of which defines "value" and "growth" in different ways (see Appendix B for more details). Before you buy one, make sure you know just what kind of value or growth you're getting into. As of February 2001, there were 19 companies in the Dow Jones U.S. Large Cap Growth Index that were also in the

S&P 500/Barra Value Index, and 30 companies in both the Dow Jones U.S. Large Cap Value Index and the S&P 500/Barra Growth Index.[5]

Options

Options may conjure complicated, obscure trading strategies that only Nobel Prize winners can really understand and only their mothers can love. But in truth, there are some simple and conservative option strategies that can and should be used by more investors to minimize risk and increase returns. One of the great advantages of ETFs is that they can use all the same option strategies commonly used for single stock holdings just so long as there are option contracts available on the ETF. So far, there are options on all the HOLDRS, all the Select Sector Spiders, and some of the larger, more popular ETFs.

What follows below is a list of the ETFs with options and where the options trade. Currently the sole Canadian-based ETF option trades on the Montréal Exchange, but more are expected in the not-too-distant future.

ETFs and HOLDRS with Options

Ticker Symbol	ETF	Option Exchange
Size- and Style-based		
QQQ	Nasdaq-100	A,C,P,PS*
MDY	S&P MidCap 400 SPDR	AMEX
IWB	iShares Russell 1000	AMEX
IWM	iShares Russell 2000	AMEX
IWO	iShares Russell 2000 Growth	AMEX
IWN	iShares Russell 2000 Value	AMEX
VTI	Total Stock Market VIPERs	AMEX
OEF	iShares S&P 100	CBOE
FFF	Fortune 500 streetTRACKS	AMEX
XIU	iUnits S&P/TSE 60	ME*
Sectors		
XLB	Basic Industries SPDR	AMEX
XLV	Consumer Services SPDR	AMEX
XLP	Consumer Staples SPDR	AMEX

XLY	Cyclical/Transportation SPDR	AMEX
XLE	Energy SPDR	AMEX
XLF	Financial SPDR	AMEX
XLI	Industrial SPDR	AMEX
XLK	Technology SPDR	AMEX
XLU	Utilities SPDR	AMEX
FEF	Fortune e-50 streetTRACKS	AMEX

HOLDRS

BHH	B2B Internet	AMEX/CBOE
BBH	Biotech	A,C, PS
BDH	Broadband	AMEX/CBOE
EKH	Europe 2001	AMEX
HHH	Internet	A, C, PS
IAH	Internet Architecture	AMEX/CBOE
IIH	Internet Infrastructure	AMEX/CBOE
MKH	Market 2000+	AMEX
OIH	Oil Service	AMEX/PS
PPH	Pharmaceutical	AMEX/CBOE
RKH	Regional Bank	AMEX/CBOE
RTH	Retail	AMEX/CBOE
SMH	Semiconductor	AMEX/CBOE
SWH	Software	AMEX/CBOE
TTH	Telecom	AMEX/CBOE
UTH	Utilities	AMEX/CBOE
WMH	Wireless	AMEX/CBOE

*A= AMEX, C = CBOE (Chicago Board Options Exchange)
PS= Pacific Stock Exchange, P= Philadelphia Stock Exchange ME= Montréal Exchange

Covered Call Writing

One of the most common and conservative option strategies is "covered call writing." Writing a call on a stock or ETF is simply selling a contract that gives the contract buyer the right, but not the obligation, to buy the asset at a specific price at some point before the expiration of the contract. A covered call just means you own the asset you are writing the option on. If you didn't own it already, that would be, in the street's vivid language, a "naked call."

Suppose you own 200 i60 units at a current market price of $45 and you believe the market is going to stay fairly flat for the next three months. You could write a call option on your 200 units to sell them at $47.50 any time during the next three months. You'll receive a premium for the sale of the option, for example $.50 per share, to equal $100 (200 x $.50). As long as the market does not go above $47.50 (what's known as the "strike price") you'll keep your units. If you end up having to sell your units, you've lost out on any appreciation of the units above $47.50, but you've pocketed the $100 premium. Options come in a wide variety of expiration dates. Conventional options can go as far out as nine months. Beyond that there are Long-term Equity Anticipation Securities (LEAPS) that go out as far as three years. In July 2001, the longest maturity for an option on an i60 was a March 2003 call LEAP. (It was for an exercise price of $45 where the bid was $5.20 at close of market on July 27, 2001.)

Put Options

If you want to protect the value of your ETF position, you can buy a put option at a strike price of, say, $40. Buying a put gives you the right, but again, not the obligation, to sell the ETF at a certain price before the expiration of the contract. You have to pay the premium, but in return, you get a guaranteed price for your current holding. The option premium in this case is just like paying an insurance premium, because you are essentially insuring your ETF's value for the period of the contract. If the market value goes below $40 near the expiration of the contract, you could exercise the put and sell your ETF position for $40 per unit or sell the put and lower the effective cost of your ETF position.

Call Options

A call option gives you the right to buy a security at a specified price before the expiry of the contract. In exchange for paying a premium, you get the opportunity to capture future gains on an index without having to buy the index. You risk the option premium and that's all; whereas if you bought the ETF and it dropped in price, you could be exposed to a much greater loss and you'd have a whole lot more money tied up.

As you can imagine, ETFs are suitable for all kinds of option strategies, limited only by imagination and the availability of options. If you're just starting with options, it's a good idea to enlist the help of an options licensed full-service broker who can help you direct your strategy, remind you of expirations and generally lead you through the process. Chapter 5 will show you how one investment advisor uses covered calls to enhance his clients' returns.

Short Selling

ETFs can be sold short like any other stock. Short selling involves selling something you don't own in the anticipation that its price will go down. In order to do this your brokerage house must borrow the stock which you must eventually return by buying on the open market. The short seller pays interest to the stock lender until the lender requires the shares returned or until the short seller voluntarily closes the position. To close the position, the short seller has to purchase the stock at the then-current market price and return it to the lender. If the price has gone down, the short seller has made a profit by selling high and buying low. If, on the other hand, the stock has gone up in price, he's lost money by selling high and buying back even higher. Perhaps it sounds like Russian roulette, but short selling ETFs might be thought of as less risky than short selling individual stocks.

First of all, there's a huge bank of ETF shares available, so you're unlikely to get something known as a "short squeeze," in which so many shares are loaned out that there are too few in circulation to comfortably buy back and close all the short positions. This causes the price of the shorted shares to go up and ruin the strategy.

Second, it is arguably easier to forecast general index trends than it is to predict the future value of an individual stock. Suppose you think the U.S. market is going to decline because it is approaching the second year of the a presidential administration's term. You can short sell a Spider or a Diamond. If you've made the right prediction, you get to buy back at a lower price the ETF you previously borrowed and sold.

Most importantly, because of their diversified nature, ETFs are exempt from the uptick rule in the U.S. market. In the U.S., a short sale is allowed only in a rising market. A short sale can occur only if the last sale was at a higher price than the sale before it (an uptick) or if the last sale was flat, the previous sale to that must have been higher. ETFs can be shorted on the same price or on a downtick, which is a tremendous advantage in a falling market.

In Canada, while no stock can be sold short into a declining market, there is no uptick rule. A short sale must be done at a price no less than the price of the last board lot trade in that stock. Even Canadian-based ETFs have to behave themselves and observe this rule. It prevents short sellers from driving a stock down mercilessly.

You would want to short sell an ETF either when you are confident the index is going to go down or in order to hedge a long position in the same index, though buying a put option is a far less dangerous strategy to accomplish the same end.

ETFs propel Barclays name to forefront

PP Aug 4 05

82% OF U.S. ETF SALES

BY MATTHEW KEENAN

Barclays Global Investors NA surveyed brokers who cater to wealthy individual investors five years ago and found its name awareness was about 50%. In a follow-up study last year, 98% were familiar with the company.

The difference for San Francisco-based Barclays Global was its aggressive push of exchange-traded funds, which are pools of equity investments that can be traded any time the stock market is open.

The unit of London-based Barclays PLC became the fastest- growing U.S. ETF firm last year, taking in about 82% of U.S. ETF sales. Fuelling its rise were individual investors, who accounted for 60% of the firm's US$45-billion in fund sales and represented the majority of Barclays ETF buyers for the first time.

"We've been out evangelizing and selling for a long period of time, so the message was starting to get through," said J. Parsons, a managing director at Barclays.

Typically, ETFs enable investors to buy or sell a basket of stocks or bonds that comprise an index, such as the Standard & Poor's 500 Index or the Nasdaq Composite Index. While mutual funds are priced once daily, ETFs have prices that fluctuate throughout the trading day, and investors do not have to wait until the close of the markets to trade them.

Twelve years after the introduction of ETFs, investors bought US$55-billion in U.S.-based ETFs in 2004, more than tripling the US$15.8-billion sold a year earlier, says the Investment Company Institute, a mutual fund trade association based in Washington.

Conventional stock and bond mutual funds, which finished the year with 36 times the assets of ETFs, had US$209.8-billion in sales. "ETFs have just gotten to be mainstream," Parsons said.

Bloomberg News

cution

this particular case, we saw two
ationships with Masonite and KKR

and we also helped execute the deal
KKR's bid. The original idea and its
Canadian corporate history.

liver creative ideas and solutions have
ch insight and commitment are integral

Many of these ETF strategies involve some sort of market timing. Tilts, rotations, style weightings, all of these require a bet on the shape of things to come in the market. That's why John Bogle, the founder of Vanguard Group and arch advocate for index mutual funds, says that ETFs are like giving investors a loaded shotgun. ETFs are easy to trade; therein lies both their beauty and their power to harm. Frequent trading most often results in poorer returns because the investment decisions are made in the heat of the moment and are often disconnected from a long-term strategy. Market timing is a tool to be used in moderation, and is not recommended for novice investors who are best advised to hold a core broad index and per-haps, a small assortment of style/cap indices.

The Easiest of All

After you've waded through complicated portfolio strategies, you might be ready to settle into the couch, put your feet up and become par-alyzed by indecision. That's when you either call an investment advisor (if only you knew a good one) or manfully resolve do the easiest thing possi-ble without abdicating your responsibility altogether: employ the Couch Potato Strategy. This is a strategy formulated by Scott Burns, a U.S. per-sonal finance journalist in 1991. It has the virtue of being dog simple, drop-dead easy and really cheap. Simply put half your money in an S&P 500 Index and the other half into a U.S. Government bond fund and put on your slippers. Rebalance to 50–50 once a year and guess what? From 1973 to 1990, the strategy would have returned an average of 10.3%, outscoring 70% of managers in the 17 years. It continued to do well through the 1990s, according to Glenn Flanagan and Tim Whitehead, who adapted this approach for Canadians in an article for the June 1999 issue of *MoneySense* magazine. Their Canadianized version for RRSPs has a third in a Canadian bond index fund, a third in a TSE 300 Index Fund and the last third in a fully RRSP eligible S&P 500 Index Fund. Backtesting the portfolio (because there were no RRSP eligible index funds around a few years back) the pair determined that the Canadian Couch Potato Portfolio returned an average 13.7% over the past 25 years: "Its performance easily outdistanced both the TSE 300's performance over that period (10.9%) as well as Canadian long-term bonds (11.8%)." You can check on the Canadian Couch Potato Portfolio's current returns at *www.moneysense.ca*. It continues to outpace the TSE 300 (with MER).

Of course, the costs of the portfolio would become positively miserly if instead of index funds you employed ETFs to do the heavy idling. There's an ETF for all three asset classes now, so you can afford a glass of wine while you're lounging on the couch.

Canadian Couch Potato ETF Portfolio

Weighting	ETF	MER
17%	iG5 (XGV)	0.25%
17%	iG10 (XGX)	0.25%
33%	TD300 or TD300C (TTF/TCF)	0.25%
33%	i500R (XSP)	0.30%
100%	Portfolio Totals	0.26%

At a .26% MER for an ETF Couch Potato Portfolio, this strategy is as cheap as it is easy. It has only one shortcoming: it doesn't include stocks outside of North America. A different core equity strategy might include international markets using an iUnit on the MSCI EAFE Index.

An Interview with Paul Mazzilli

Paul Mazzilli is an executive director at Morgan Stanley in New York, and Director of Exchange Traded Fund Research. He generously agreed to an interview on July 13, 2001.

Donna Green: You've written a lot about using investment strategies using ETFs, especially the Core and Satellite approach.

Paul Mazzilli: Yes, Core and Satellite sounds so simple but it took a long time to get there. Now its even in the Chartered Financial Analysts (CFA) manual for training. I had worked in a prior job with a group that worked with some of the big, smart pension plans in the U.S. We found that currently as much of 40% of major pension plans are indexed. That's the core. It's hard to beat the markets in general, so why not have all your portfolio in something that looks just like the market at a very low cost, well diversified way? That's the whole core strategy.

DG: What should be the core?

PM: I'm writing a research report this week on the different cores, S&P 500, Dow Jones, Russell 3000, Wilshire 5000. Interestingly, they all pretty much represent the broad market and move together. I'm not comfortable giving asset allocation ranges because everybody's situation is different. People should work with their financial advisor to figure that out.

DG: And outside the core?

PM: On top of the core you can have sector allocations, growth versus value allocations, large cap versus small cap, real estate, international. Traditionally these smart pension plans would do it through outside managers. Now you can do it with ETFs.
    Finally, on top of the pyramid there's individual stock selection. We're not saying you should index everything. As a matter of fact, some of these very large pension plans, like

an IBM or a General Electric, with as much as a $100 billion in assets, have their own research analysts who probably focus on less than 150 stocks. And these are the most sophisticated plans in the world. They're saying, "We're going to minimize risk by having a core; we're going to add value by asset allocation decisions to different sectors or styles, international markets, and then we're going to really focus in on stock picking where we can add value, but we've reduced our risk because it's a small part of our portfolio." In that section if you can beat the market, your overall portfolio is going to beat the market, too. Individual investors can emulate this.

DG: Is there anything ETFs are especially good for?

PM: Diversified asset allocation. People tend to forget about overall asset allocation, growth versus value, different sectors, bonds, foreign markets which all the academic studies show make for the efficient frontier. If you want to get into sectors you have no exposure, to you can do it through ETFs.

If you wake up and have the idea you want to go long financial stocks because you think the Fed cutting rates is good for financials, how do you do it? You can get an idea but it takes days to figure out which stocks in that sector to buy. You may buy two stocks and it turns out that one of them has an earnings disappointment. You may have made a great call on the sector but been exposed too much to one stock. With an ETF, if you decide you want to go long financials, the minute the market opens you can be long that sector; and more importantly, you are long that sector in a very diversified way so if one stock blows up, but the sector does well, you are protected.

Fees are much lower on ETFs, too. The average U.S. ETF [MER] is about 30 basis points. The average conventional mutual funds is about 140 basis points and the average [MER] for a U.S. index fund tracking the S&P 500 is 68 basis points. The iShares S&P 500 is 9 basis points. They're much more tax efficient, too. Index funds in their own right are very tax efficient, but what people don't realize is that other shareholder activity creates capital gains. We did a *study that showed for the last nine years since Spider existed, it paid two very small capital gains distributions. The average open-end index fund has paid 2% per year in capital gains because of redemptions.*

Last year was an extremely difficult market in the U.S., and yet there was a record $345 billion paid out in capital gains distributions and that came from portfolio turnover driven in part by redemptions. Some people had the misfortune of buying an Internet fund in March and finding it worth 75% less at year end but still got whacked with a capital gains distribution, because throughout the year, the fund was shrinking and selling assets it bought at lower prices in previous years and realizing gains. A big part of gains went to fewer investors at the end. In some extreme cases you could have got $.90 of gains on your $1 investment at year end. The only way [U.S.] ETFs create capital gains is through index reconstitution which would not happen to nearly this extent.

DG: Any advice to investors now?

PM: You have to be careful with some sector ETFs, what's in them versus what you think you are getting. Some of them can be more concentrated in a few stocks than you might think, and may be less pure than you think, also. The Technology Spider, for instance, includes some telecom names.

Right now many people have losses on their mutual funds. It may be a good time to capture those and go into an ETF.

And watch out for fees.

Notes

1) Brinson, Gary P., L. Randolph Hood and Gilbert L. Beebower, "Determinants of Portfolio Performance," *Financial Analysts Journal*, July/August 1986, pp. 39–44. (See *http://publish.uwo.ca/~jnuttall/asset.html* for an outstanding discussion of how the Brinson study has been widely misconstrued.)

2) Roger G. Ibbotson and Paul Kaplan, "Does Asset Allocation Policy Explain 40, 90 or 100 Percent of Performance?" Available on-line at *www.ibbotson.com/research/papers/Asset_Allocation_Performance/Does_Asset_Allocation_Expl*. Thanks to Dan Hallett for this reference.

3) "Using ETFs to Capitalize on Sectors Favored for Recovery," by Paul J. Mazzilli, Dodd F. Kittsley, James P. McGowan, January 29, 2001, Morgan Stanley Equity Research North America, p. 4.

4) "Style Investing with ETFs: Growth and Value Plays," by Paul J. Mazzilli, Dodd F. Kittsley, James P. McGowan, February 14, 2001, Morgan Stanley Equity Research North America, p.7.

5) Ibid., p.5.

Chapter 5
Using ETFs with an Advisor

In the crowded financial services industry, you are a valuable asset. Brokerages, financial planning firms, mutual fund companies, banks and insurance companies are struggling among the throngs to distinguish themselves in your eyes. They are all keenly aware that satisfying your needs efficiently is the key to their prosperity and ultimate survival. Part of the urgency motivating so much change in financial services is the growing commoditization of basic financial services. Just as you're likely to buy gasoline based solely on price, so increasingly sophisticated investors are likely to shop for financial services with a sharp eye to fees and costs. The Internet has empowered investors, not just through the wealth of low cost choices available for stock trading, but mostly through the explosion in the breadth and depth of investment information available at the click of a mouse. Brokerage firms used to have something of a monopoly on respected analysts and technical specialists. Today, these same analysts are fighting for credibility, undermined in fact or in perception by their firms' corporate underwriting activity.

If you're like most, you'd like to use a trusted and competent financial advisor to help you coordinate all your financial needs—investing, insurance, tax planning, estate planning. Trouble is, most of us feel we've got too little money to be of interest to any advisor with those kinds of skills, or we're afraid of paying too much for more promise than delivery in an industry notorious for its inherent conflicts of interest. We end up continuing to buy the mutual funds du jour through our familiar mutual fund salesperson, and promising ourselves at some point to get thoroughly organized. In many cases that probably means deciding to completely revamp your portfolio yourself and sign up with an on-line discount broker. (You may even have bought this book in anticipation of doing just that.)

There's nothing wrong with such a do-it-yourself ambition except that every year it's put off may be taking you another year further away from your goals. It's also unnecessarily complicating your life, because the industry has grown sensitive to the worry about corrosive costs and the conflicts of interest between advice and commissions. The industry's response has been the development of a variety of fee-based programs, sometimes also known as "fee-for-service" programs.

Fee-based Programs Can Save You Money Over a Portfolio of Mutual Funds

All the major brokerage firms have at least one fee-based account type because fee-based programs have become the fastest growing programs in the industry and for good reason. For one flat fee (based on a percentage of assets) you get asset allocation planning, investment advice, ongoing contact with an advisor whose interests are perfectly aligned with your own, and a consolidated statement, usually with on-line access. Minimum account size is $100,000 to $150,000, and commonly, a fixed number of free trades are included. Fees vary from firm to firm but the range at press time was .85% to 2.5% with most around 1.5%.

Happily, ETFs and fee-based advisors go together like a soup and sandwich. A fee-based advisor wants to justify his fee by saving you money over a mutual fund portfolio with an average MER of 2.3%, so she's motivated to get you the best products with the lowest costs. No conflict there.

This type of fee-based account is not a program so much as a different business model—a new way of structuring your relationship with a financial specialist. It's a relationship in which the costs are spelled out explicitly, unbundled from the investment products and left open to scrutiny, and for larger accounts, negotiation.

"People don't have any idea how much they're paying in fees," observes John Hood, a fee-based investment counsellor running his own firm in Toronto. "I was looking at a portfolio referred to me that was full of mutual funds. The client was paying $50,000 a year in management fees, which was ridiculous." That's not so extraordinary either. A $2 million portfolio at an average MER of 2.3% will cost $46,000 a year in management fees, $10,000 to $20,000 of which goes to the advisor as a trailer fee. A million-dollar portfolio, something most of us aspire to upon retirement, costs $23,000[1] a year if fully invested in mutual funds with average MERs. Hood charges a flat 1% of assets for his services on $400,000 minimum accounts. On a million-dollar account, that's $10,000 in fees—a far cry from $23,000. Often you'll find fee-based advisors who vary their fee with increasing account size.

It's not a clear-cut savings of $13,000, however. Sometimes the investments themselves have costs. Bonds have commissions built into their prices and stocks have trading commissions. ETFs and low cost, no-load mutual funds have MERs, too. And as is the case with all mutual funds, the MER does not include the trading commissions on trades done within the fund. Always ask your advisor the total costs of your investments, including MERs and expenses over and above the MER. In a fee-based environment, you want to be sure you're in an arrangement that is genuinely better (and cheaper).

Fee-based Programs Go Hand in Hand with ETFs

Because of this drive to keep fees competitive and total costs low, Hood uses ETFs extensively in his client portfolios. But not just because of their razor-thin costs. "ETFs allow me to compete [with the big firms] simply because of their performance. I know, particularly in the U.S., that I'm going to outperform 90% of the portfolio managers simply because I use an indexed based product on a long term basis," he says.

"Another advantage of ETFs is that it clarifies things," Hood notes. "Clients know roughly where they are just by knowing how the indexes are doing."

The simplicity has other strengths. "A lot of planners," continues Hood, "have a client meeting every year, get the $13,500 RRSP contribution and dribble it in bits and pieces into the latest hot funds. In ten years the client's going to have 40 funds. It's nuts. It's diversification cubed." These fund du jour folks can very well end up with an inefficient, high cost portfolio that dramatically underperforms.

But Hood has also seen advisors convert a mutual fund portfolio with 30 funds into a portfolio with 40 ETFs. "That doesn't make any sense either," he says.

To his mind, a $700,000 portfolio can comfortably employ about 15 ETFs. More than that and he thinks the portfolio is either over diversified or has lost its focus.

Hood uses ETFs extensively on the equity side of his portfolios. For fixed income he uses bonds and a covered call writing strategy. "I buy stocks that pay a dividend and sell long-term options against them. That lets me significantly boost the yield on the income portfolio," he says. So between ETFs and his blue-chip covered call writing strategy on the fixed income side, he says he's able to effectively compete with big brokerage houses and their research facilities.

How Two Advisors Use ETFs With Their Clients

Hood is far from alone in understanding the advantages of ETFs in fee-based programs. Keith Matthews is another fee-based investment advisor with a passion for ETFs. Matthews is Vice President, Sales and Marketing, and a fee-based advisor with PWL Capital Inc. in Montréal. PWL Capital uses ETFs widely in the equity components of their client portfolios.

"For .75% to 1.5% we will build you the best portfolio possible. I am now going to go out into the universe of all possible products for the best after-fee portfolio. When we look at the thousands of different mutual funds out there—dealing with management drift, management change I get surprises. They're not tax efficient. I can't control the inflows or the outflows of cash into the portfolios that impact my client. When you look at all these different aspects, you can't ignore the power of exchange traded funds.

"Studies show clients are better off working with investment advisors. The no-load mutual funds have given better rates of return than load mutual funds on paper, but the actual returns captured by clients has been much higher in load portfolios. Having an advisor pays dividends in the long-term world. Staying the course, fee for discipline, for long-term asset rebalancing, these have been proven to be of tremendous value to clients," Matthews says.

"A fee-based manager is trying to maximize your after-tax return. It's all about after-tax. Over a ten-year period, managing in a buy and hold environment, making slight modifications, using ETFs and a variety of other securities, you will get a better after-tax return relative to the other alternatives available out there. Period," Matthews says unequivocally.

PWL Capital uses individual government and corporate bonds, real estate investment trusts (REITs), a mix of large, mid, small cap ETFs and some sector exposure through ETFs. They use ETFs extensively for Canadian, U.S., and European exposure. For European equities they use iShares 350 Europe Fund and Dow Jones Global Titans, an ETF that holds 50 of the biggest and bluest of the world's global companies. As for other regions and asset classes, the firm considers them too volatile for their high-end clients. PWL's minimum account size is $500,000.

"ETFs empower investment advisors to do very exact asset allocation," states Matthews. "There's nothing passive in that. Handing the investments decision off to a fund manager is really being passive. Where's the accountability in that?"

Passion for the fee-based approach runs deep in many advisors who have set themselves apart in this way. Matthews is a case in point. "Fee-based is about how can I best grow your portfolio over ten years—after costs, after taxes—not how can I generate the most amount of commissions from you."

A Cost Survey of Different Fee-based Arrangements

As a consumer, though, you have to be cautious about the kind of program you chose with a fee-based advisor because fee-based doesn't always mean rock-bottom pricing. There's an assortment of programs and arrangements a fee-based advisor can recommend, and some programs are even more expensive than a portfolio of conventional mutual funds.

Generally, the most expensive fee-based accounts are a kind of wrap program that pools investors' assets in some way—either with mutual funds or with proprietary pooled funds. Wraps are accounts that provide ongoing monitoring and asset allocation rebalancing for a fee based on a percentage of invested assets. Typically they are sold by one party but managed by another, which distinguished them from fee-based investment counsellors who actually execute the investment decisions themselves. These pooled wrap programs are offered by mutual fund companies, brokerages, banks and trust companies.

Mutual fund wrap programs use an assortment of retail mutual funds as a sort of fund-of-funds approach. You pay a fee for a consolidated allocation service as well as the standard MER on the underlying funds. Examples of these programs include Mackenzie's STAR program and CIBC's Choice Funds among others. These programs have low minimum investments from $2,500 to $5,000.

Pooled wraps use proprietary in-house mutual funds known as "pools." These pools usually have lower MERs than conventional load funds, but the programs themselves also impose a service fee. Minimum account sizes range from $10,000 to $100,000. AGF Harmony, CI Insight and Frank Russell Canada's Sovereign programs (distributed by RBC Investments and TD Evergreen) are examples of pooled wraps. A balanced portfolio in these three programs could run from 1.92% to 3.15%. Other programs of the same ilk can run from 1.77% to an astonishing 3.60%.[2]

A third kind of wrap program that might be offered by a brokerage would be a segregated wrap. These programs use an investment manager or a number of different managers who invest your money directly in individual securities. They can often be customized to take into account your current holdings, but they have high minimum investments from $250,000 to $1,000,000. Fees are quite variable from company to company and often negotiable to some extent. Typically a company might give the advisor a 25 basis point bargaining window, half of which comes from the advisor's remuneration, but anything greater than a .25% discount on fees usually comes out of the advisor's cut. Program fees range from as much as 2% to as low as .40% for a $2,000,000 portfolio mostly in fixed income. Most, but not all, of these accounts come with a fixed number of free trades per year.

In mutual fund and pooled programs, transaction charges are typically over and above the program fee and the MER of the funds. Despite their costs, pooled programs in particular are often touted by investment advisors as being tax efficient for a few reasons. The investment service fee on non-registered accounts only is tax deductible, and some pooled funds calculate and assign the capital gains tax liability of each investor as they exit the pool so that the remaining investors don't get stuck paying the tax for the clever investor who bailed out before a distribution. These features, however, don't come anywhere near compensating for the cost of the programs themselves. Except for accounts with very large minimums, in almost all cases you'd get off a lot cheaper on the whole by simply holding load mutual funds and getting your advisor do to an annual rebalancing to an asset allocation you had determined together.

"...[A] hybrid approach that uses regular mutual funds and other low-cost products (i.e., exchange traded funds, bonds, et cetera) can provide investors with a very well-diversified, tax-efficient, and low-cost portfolio and provide ample compensation for your advisor," says Dan Hallett, Senior Investment Analyst with Windsor, Ontario-based Sterling Mutuals Inc. in his study of pooled wrap programs in an article in *Canadian MoneySaver* magazine last year.[3] His conclusion? Stay away from these wrap programs and find a better way.

The better way is to work with an advisor to find the best and lowest cost investments around. That mandate becomes less complicated when it is in the context of a transparent fee-based relationship.

Just as you have to be careful of institutional fee-based programs, you also have to exercise some discrimination with the portfolios of fee-based advisors. Not all portfolios are equal, especially when it comes to costs. Two advisors may both charge 1% in fees, but their portfolios could end up being significantly different in total costs after the embedded costs on the recommended investments are taken into account.

A fee-based advisor has the same tools at his disposal as other advisors, but has the freedom of choosing investments that don't pay a commission. The most cost-effective portfolio would be composed of individual bonds and stocks and ETFs in an account with an unlimited number of free trades. The least cost-efficient portfolio would be one entirely of load funds with a fee on top of that, which believe it or not, is still available in the marketplace.

Somewhere in the middle is a fee-based account holding 0% front-end load funds, but watch out for this. Front-end equity funds pay 1% a year in trailers to the advisor which is discretely charged to you through a plump MER. Fee-based advisors should be making their money on your fee, not on your embedded costs. Sometimes, though, advisors can't find the right type of fund in a no-load fund or with an ETF and must resort to a front-end fund at zero commission. Your advisor may want, for instance, an actively managed fund for emerging markets or Latin America. There's nothing wrong with this so long as you understand the advisor is, in effect, double-dipping—getting a fee and if not a commission, then also a trailer fee funded through the higher MER you are paying on that fund. Scrutinize the asset allocation in these cases in particular. Plenty of advisors believe exotic asset classes don't add much but volatility.

To better accommodate fee-based advisors, fund companies have come out with different classes of funds that are essentially no-load. They have no redemption charges because they don't pay the advisor a commission on the sale of the fund, and they sport reduced MERs. The "F" class units have stripped the commission and trailer costs out of the MER leaving only the fund company's cost of running the fund. "F" here stands for "fee-based." Another reduced MER class is called "I" class, standing for "institutional." I class units have MERs slightly higher than F units because they still pay an advisor a small trailer fee. They are designed for clients with high minimum investments. Mackenzie Financial Corp.'s I class, for instance, is exclusively for those with $500,000 invested in Mackenzie funds, and possibly in the context of a fee-based arrangement with an advisor.

"The vast majority of clients don't know that I class units pay the advisor more than is disclosed up front in the fee-based arrangement," observes John De Goey, a financial advisor with Assante Capital Management Ltd.'s office in Toronto. "Clients don't ask about trailers or read the fine print. The net effect is that the client thinks 1% is fair, and the advisor thinks a 1.25% is fair so they both feel they've struck a good bargain but it's likely the client won't understand just what the advisor is being paid," says De Goey. "How much is fair compensation is open for debate, but the disclosure of this compensation is not debatable. It should be absolutely transparent."

The moral of the story is to be sure you know exactly what and how your advisor is being compensated. Fee-based accounts can hold more within them for your advisor than you might think. De Goey uses an assortment of relationship models with his own clients, but he prefers the fee-based one he has designed. It has broad-based ETFs at its core, and no-load and zero front-end load funds added to that for some active management in sectors he believes are less efficient.

Below are the investments De Goey commonly draws upon for his clients' portfolios. They are listed below by asset class.

Fixed Income passive	iUnits iG5 Bond Fund
Fixed Income active	Phillips, Hager & North High Yield Bond Fund (no-load)
Canadian Equity passive	iUnits S&P/TSE 60 Capped Index Fund
Canadian Small Cap	Ivy Enterprise Fund (0% front end)
International Equity passive	iUnits EAFE Index RSP Fund (forthcoming)
U.S. Equity passive	iUnits S&P 500 Index RSP Fund (i500R)
Emerging Markets	C.I. Emerging Markets Fund (0% front end)
Global Small Cap	C.I. Signature Global Smaller Cos. Fund (0% front-end)
Tangibles	Sentry Canadian Energy Growth Fund (0% front-end)

De Goey charges 1.20% on accounts under $250,000. Between $250,000 and $499,999 it's 1.08%, and after half a million it's .96%. This is his fee only, which includes GST. It does not include transaction costs (which at Assante is $95 per stock or bond trade) nor does it include MERs on the ETFs or the mutual funds. You may not think taking the MERs into account adds much but watch what it does to the all-in costs. De Goey calculates the total costs for an 80% passive portfolio of his design is 2% annually. At 60% passive it is 2.35%, the average MER for a Canadian equity fund; but as he sees it, he is offering his clients better tax efficiency, tax deductibility of fees on non-registered accounts and a personalized investment policy statement.

These costs could be brought down by using F class mutual funds (or more ETFs for that matter) instead of 0% front-end load funds. De Goey has crunched the numbers and figures the same portfolios would come in at 1.94% for the 60% passive portfolio and at 1.74% for the 80% passive portfolio, including the advisory fee but excluding GST in all cases. For administrative reasons that are beyond his control, De Goey cannot yet offer his clients a robust selection of F class funds. At this point many non-bank- owned firms have been slow to adopt a complete platform that can accommodate the use of F class units. But with competitive pressure mounting, this situation will change sooner than later.

This highlights another issue you should be on the look out for. Firms, by their organization and licensing and by their back office systems, limit the product universe available to their representatives. Furthermore, plenty of financial planners can't sell bonds, individual stocks or ETFs because they're not licensed to do so. These financial products require a securities license. Mutual fund salespeople are required to have a mutual funds license only, which does not equip them to sell or even administer individual securities. These advisors are restricted to mutual funds because they have not undertaken to obtain a securities license or because their firm has not structured itself so as to be permitted by regulators to hold securities licenses on behalf of employees, which is a necessary condition of having securities licensed personnel.

If you hire a fee-based advisor, first make sure the firm is able to transact securities like stocks and bonds and ETFs, and that the advisor herself is securities licensed. Paying a fee for someone to simply select mutual funds is a little like golfing with one arm tied behind your back: it's better than being in the office but it's not terribly effective. Then make sure your advisor has no other restrictions in acting on your mandate of "Build me the best portfolio possible." Too many times the actual portfolio falls short of the ideal because of avoidable obstacles. Don't tolerate the obstacles. Find a firm and an advisor who can give you the universe—of investment products anyway. Why limit your range of investment possibilities and your chance at better returns?

Since a fee-based investor pays a flat fee, based on assets under administration, he can be assured his advisor is choosing the best investments for his account, not the investments which generate the most revenue for the advisor.

Why Advisors Have an Interest in Going Fee-based

This may surprise you, but advisors have powerful motivation to be transitioning to fee-based arrangements, too. "A fee-based investment book of business is worth more than a traditional transactional business," says Matthews. "The book of business has more stable cash flows and is easier to transfer to another advisor." Add to that the fact that fee-based arrangements tend to attract higher net worth clients and position the advisor as more of a money coach or consultant than a salesman, and your advisor has got lots of incentive to give you the most efficient portfolio possible for a fee.

Just how much that fee should be is up to you to decide. Under $100,000 the best strategy is almost certainly to do it yourself with a simple Core and Satellite strategy or the Couch Potato Portfolio. From $100,000 to $250,000, a 1% fee is getting off easy as most fee-based advisors reserve the magical 1% charge for larger portfolios. After $250,000 you're in a good position to negotiate the fee, especially with the fixed income portion of your portfolio.

Remember, your advisor has as much interest in adopting a fee-based arrangement as you have. You can't get what you don't ask for, so bargain hard for the best deal you can get. Your advisor, if she's enlightened, will appreciate that bargaining because in the end, if you're both satisfied with the arrangement, you'll be a loyal client and he'll have a steadier cash flow. Then again, you must realize that you'll be writing a cheque every quarter or authorizing a monthly automatic debit to your investment or chequing account to pay these investment advisory fees. But don't kid yourself. Lower transparent investment costs are certainly in your best interest. Higher hidden charges, while being out of sight and out of mind, are detrimental to your portfolio's long-term returns and to your ultimate security.

John Bogle, founder of the Vanguard Group, has spent most of his life urging the investment industry to "give investors a fair shake" with reasonable fees. Below he share his insights about fee-based advisors. Although his is a no-load company, he believes in the value of advisors for most people, with a caveat to the costs.

> People have to think very carefully about how much that fee ought to be. I don't think 1% is unreasonable for $50,000. But when you get up to very large amounts, 1% is a huge amount. Get out a compound interest table. Take a look at the difference between 10% and 9% over an investment lifetime of 50 years. Just that little 1%: the difference is staggering. A dollar at 10% is going to be worth $117 in 50 years. A dollar at 9% is going to be worth $74. If you want to put $10,000 around that, it's $1,117,000 versus $740,000 to the investor at a 1% difference. That's $430,000 to the croupier. Think of that. A third of the return is taken by the croupiers. The investor puts up 100% of the capital and takes 100% of the risk to get two-thirds of the returns. People have to focus on the long term and the impact of costs.

> Advisors should do their fishing in a low cost pond. Of all the strategies, that absolutely works—that's it. You can take any comparison of any mutual fund you've ever seen in your life and cut it any way you want. If you compare the high cost quartile with the low cost quartile over any reasonable period of time, the low cost quartile wins. That's as close to a certainty as you get in this world.

> To my mind, anything that gives investors lower costs and greater flexibility is a good thing, and there's nothing preventing ETF investors from holding on to them indefinitely. If anything, it's cheaper to hold an ETF long-term than it is to hold an index mutual fund long-term.

Why Your Financial Advsior Might Not Recommend ETFs:
An Interview with Duff Young

Duff Young is CEO of FundMonitor.com, a Toronto-based provider of research and portfolio analytics for financial advisors. He graciously agreed to an interview for this book, dated July 11, 2001.

Donna Green: Not all financial advisors can deal with ETFs, isn't that right?

Duff Young: There are challenges to working with a financial advisor if you are an ETF fan sometimes. Specifically, I'm talking about financial advisors who are licensed only to sell mutual funds. I believe in financial advice and do not sell my research to do-it-yourselfers or discount brokers. My clients are financial advisors. That said, I think that many advisors have to change precisely because of ETFs and the very compelling nature of what they offer. I'm telling advisors every day to either upgrade their license or move to a firm that can offer a full range of securities. They don't want to become stock jockeys, and I don't want to push them away from their strength in financial planning. I'll tell you candidly that I do notice that the fully licensed guys aren't necessarily the cat's meow either. To often you see financial advisors now becoming a stock jockey. Let's be serious: brokers are not investment managers. Very often clients are jumping out of the pot of mutual fund MERs into the fire of a heavily traded individual stock portfolio.

DG: Should an investor wanting ETFs simply seek out a broker?

DY: A broker doesn't spend 100% of his time picking stocks, so he is fundamentally less well-equipped than is a mutual fund manager. A broker has to deal with clients all day long, to sell and soothe, and coax and report to clients. I would venture to say that whereas an investment manager spends

80% of his time picking stocks, a stockbroker couldn't spend 20%.

The middle ground, the Promised Land, is somebody who does financial planning and can get you ETFs. That is the perfect place to be, and it is still a small but increasingly common minority. You can find this type of person who is an expert at financial planning but capable of selling securities at the fee-based shops, of course, and people like this are at all the brokerage firms. Probably a good 15% to 20% of their population fit this description beautifully and a similar proportion of mutual-fund-only dealers are inclined to use the services of jitney brokerage arrangements to facilitate individual securities trades on behalf of their clients. This is a wonderful trend that I vigorously encourage even though it is not without its administrative headaches. I suspect we will not get the regulatory okay to allow financial planners the privilege of recommending ETFs, but it is deserved.

It is illegal for a mutual-funds-only licensed advisor to actually do anything that is in furtherance of a trade in securities. A financial planner has to be very careful. Sadly, you can't ask your planner whether an ETF is right for you because, technically, he can't answer. That's a big issue dealing with a financial advisor.

In reality, today a good financial planner who is not fully licensed does a tongue-in-cheek kind of recommendation: "Well, yes, I certainly like the U.S. market today. I certainly like passive investing for a certain part of your portfolio, Mr. Johnson. And CIBC and a few other firms do have some decent index funds but they are expensive. Now there are cheaper alternatives available. Hmm, what do you think of that?" Playing the "nudge, nudge, wink, wink" game is an important reality for most investors in dealing with a financial planner today.

Your guy isn't a bad guy, but you can't ask him about ETFs and expect an honest answer. Number one, he can't really answer; it's illegal. Number two, he's got some biases, although that may be changing because he might be biased towards fee-based soon, and technology is probably going to encourage that.

DG: How does an investor play the "nudge, nudge, wink,

wink" game?

DY:

[Client] *"Do you think it's important to be really cheap in passive investing?"*

[Advisor] *"Yes."*

"Do you know of any lower cost index funds than the one you are recommending?"

"Yes."

"Is the Spider a cheaper index fund?"

"Yes."

"Would you be angry with me if I were to put 30% of my portfolio's core holding in Spiders?"

"No."

"Are you making a formal recommendation?"

"No."

I'm saddened by these regulatory limitations. A lot of advisors are very good people who would be happy to play the "nudge, nudge, wink, wink" game.

DG: Will financial advisors embrace ETFs?

DY: *I think financial advisors should use ETFs because they make so little of the 2.3% MER* [on mutual funds] *anyway. There's no new net growth in money coming in* [in mutual fund sales], *so there's no deferred sales charges coming to these guys. They are living only on trailer fees. Trailers are only 50 basis points on 2.3%. A financial planner would be far better off to charge you 60 basis points and get you a bunch of iUnits. You'd only pay 80 basis points, he's making 20% more money, and your costs would fall by 65%. Those are the mathematics of unbundling.*

Soon there will be a better backbone in place that will allow fee-based planners to monitor and charge on assets at various institutions, and that will fuel demand for ETFs because planners will be able to recommend, monitor and access fees based on ETFs that reside elsewhere. (If we mean financial planners who aren't fully licensed, then we have to change "recommend" to the "nudge, nudge, wink, wink"game.)

DG: Will ETFs change the marketplace?

DY: *Paradoxically, the arrival of this new cheap competitor instead of making the rest of the marketplace more cost competitive is going to make the rest of the marketplace more wild. In order to justify its fees, which will not change, active managers are going to have to start swinging for the fences a little bit more. Far too many of them have been closet indexers all along. Ironically, I expect average MERs are going to skyrocket because the market is going to polarize. ETFs will grab the cheapskates' business and in a search for balancing a portfolio with really active stuff, I think hedge funds are going to take off. They are expensive, but worth it, and appropriate in a balanced portfolio when complemented with ETFs.*

Notes

1) A $23,000 management fee cost on a million dollar portfolio assumes an 80% equity, 20% fixed income asset allocation with some above average MER equity funds like international or specialty funds offsetting lower MER fixed income funds to average 2.3%.

2) Much of the current market information on wrap programs came from Dan Hallett, Senior Investment Analyst with Sterling Mutuals, Inc. in Windsor, Ontario.

Dan wrote an insightful and well-researched two-part article about pooled wrap programs in *Canadian MoneySaver* magazine, "Pooled Wrap Programs: The Asset Management Maze," February 2001, March 2001. Hallett updated the survey in July, 2001 for Sterling Mutuals. For further market recognizance, see *www.cifunds.com/insight/competitive.htm#top* for a very broad, though dated survey of pooled and segregated programs (as of May 1999). The fees are out of date.

3) Ibid.

Chapter 6
Taxes: Implications and Strategies

An RRSP is a Canadian tax haven. Your retirement investments are as good as sunning themselves on a beach in the Cayman Islands while they're nestled in an RRSP account, but your investments outside an RRSP are battling the harshest Canadian element of all: taxes. Outside of a tax sheltered account, taxes are the biggest expense most investors confront, bigger than commissions and management fees. This chapter will take you through the tax considerations of ETFs, both domestic and U.S.-based, and explore some tax strategies using ETFs. For the purposes of this discussion, we'll assume your investments are taking the full brunt of Canada Customs and Revenue Agency (CCRA), formerly Revenue Canada, outside a tax sheltered account and held on capital account.[1]

From a personal tax point of view, made-in-Canada ETFs are just like Canadian mutual funds. At the end of the tax year you get a T-3 detailing the nature and amount of income from your ETF. There will generally be some dividend income, some capital gains, a small amount of interest income and possibly some foreign income, just like a mutual fund (though mutual funds that are structured as corporations instead of trusts generate T-5s rather than T-3s).

Just as with mutual funds, the income an ETF receives may come from capital gains on security trades, dividends from holdings and interest. This income flows out of the fund to unitholders in the form of distributions and that's what you pay tax on. Mutual funds and ETFs make distributions in order to save tax at the fund level and to minimize the total tax paid overall. Income kept in the fund will always be taxed at the highest tax rate, whereas unitholders may have a lower personal marginal tax rate and thereby get to keep more of the distribution in their own pockets. That's why less total tax is paid when the fund's income is distributed to unitholders rather than being retained within the fund.

And again, like mutual funds, the tax character of a Canadian ETF's distributed income is retained when it is passed to unitholders. A dividend stays a dividend and a capital gain stays a capital gain, giving unitholders the advantage of the dividend tax credit and the 50% break on capital gains.

In absolute terms, ETFs generally distribute far less income than most actively managed mutual funds. As we discussed in Chapter 1, because ETFs do so little buying and selling within the fund, ETFs are remarkably good about keeping their gains to themselves and not troubling investors with large distributions. Even the i60's noteworthy distribution in 2000, by ETF standards a relatively large 3.1% of NAV, compares very favourably to many actively managed funds.

Taxation of Distributions

Distributions from US-based ETFs also retain their tax character under U.S. tax law. The only trouble is that American character isn't given the same accord by Canadian taxation officials. U.S.-based ETFs are classified under U.S. tax rules as regulated investment companies (RIC). Distribution of dividends to Canadian residents from a RIC are subject to a 15% withholding tax. Distributions of capital gains from a RIC, however, don't incur withholding tax. But the bad news is that this dividend income is not eligible for the dividend tax credit which is reserved for the dividends of Canadian corporations. Nor does the capital gain portion of the distribution retain its character. You may not, however, be required to include all of the distribution from a U.S. ETF in your income under a new Canadian tax rule.

An investor who receives a distribution from a U.S. trust will be taxed on the amount of the distribution that represents income of the trust as calculated under Canadian tax rules. Since most U.S. ETFs are trusts (though some are corporations), this might have you thinking you can ignore 50% of the capital gains income from a U.S.-based ETF trust. The problem is that as an investor you can't know how the ETF's capital gain was calculated in the first place, and so you can't know positively how much of that distribution to include in your income. The two countries have different ways of calculating capital gains. The practical upshot of this is that Canadian ETF investors are not safe in assuming they can discount the U.S. capital gain by 50%. If you do and subsequently get questioned by CCRA, the burden of proof is on you; and since there's no way to determine how the U.S. gain was arrived at, CCRA wins by default. Furthermore, this new rule doesn't apply to ETFs that are corporations, in which case, all the distributions are included fully in income anyway.

Janice Russell, Tax Partner and the leader of the Canadian Investment Management Tax Practice of PricewaterhouseCoopers LLP, notes, "Canadian holders of iShares may be fully taxable on iShare distributions but will be eligible for a foreign tax credit in respect of withholding tax paid." The same applies to any U.S.-based ETF, not just iShares. In other words, you won't be taxed twice on your U.S. ETF income. The foreign tax credit will apply to the money withheld by the U.S. government, yet that Canadian tax bill may very likely be calculated on every penny of U.S.-based ETF income without dividend tax credits or an advantageous 50% inclusion rate for capital gains because of the practical difficulties in applying the Canadian tax rule.

Adjusted Cost Base

Distributions always bring to the wary investor's mind the menacing adjusted cost base (ACB). The ACB of an investment is its average cost including acquisition costs (trading commissions) and reinvested distributions. You need the ACB to figure out the capital gains on an investment because it's the sale price minus the ACB that determines the capital gain (or loss). Fortunately, there is no special consideration in calculating the adjusted cost base of ETFs. It's pretty straightforward.

ACB = (total purchases + acquisition costs + reinvested distributions) ÷ units purchased

Remember that quarterly ETF distributions are paid out in cash (unless your brokerage has a rare arrangement to reinvest them) but the end-of-year capital gains distribution gets reinvested. That capital gain distribution does become part of your ACB. Your trading commissions to buy the ETF units are also included in the ACB.

Triggering Your Own Gains

Apart from the capital gains embedded in a distribution, you can trigger a capital gain yourself by selling an ETF you own. Be it Canadian or U.S., you do get to avail yourself of the 50% capital gains inclusion rate when you make a profit on the sale of your ETF. That means that you are subject to tax at your marginal tax rate on only 50% of the realized gains. The other 50% are tax free. So if you are looking to maximize your after tax returns with U.S. investments, you would favour U.S. investments with few distributions and a good potential for capital gains upon the sale of the investment. That describes a number of U.S.-based ETFs.

Spiders, for instance, are famously tax efficient even for a Canadian investor. Since their inception in 1993, Spiders kicked out only $.09 in fund-generated capital gains, and last year distributed only $1.50 in income, all the while rising from US$45 a share to US$120. Last year the MidCap Spiders distributed a parsimonious $.78 in income and no capital gains while trading around US$100. You can learn the distribution history of all the AMEX-listed ETFs at *www.amextrader.com* under the ETF section by clicking on "portfolio composition" and then "distribution history." Be careful, though. A long history of minimal distributions doesn't always mean history will repeat itself. Last year some European iShares paid out hefty distributions after years of very minimal income. The iShares MSCI Germany, for instance, paid out $2.53 on a share trading in the teens.

The best defense against surprise distributions is knowing what's in the underlying portfolio. Concentration reductions and index reconstitutions are the most common reasons for large distributions in an ETF that normally runs without so much smoke.

If you're concerned that the Canadian taxation of a U.S.-based ETF will offset the ETF's fundamental tax efficiency, stick to the large and mid cap U.S. funds. They have low turnover within their portfolios and correspondingly lower distributions. Taxable accounts should be cautious with style-based ETFs and the small caps as these regularly move companies in and out in keeping with the changes within the indices themselves, and thus throw out more distributions. For reasons explained below, U.S.-based ETFs are structurally more tax efficient than Canadian ETFs because they generate fewer capital gains; thus even if you have the potential to pay more tax on the distributions from a U.S.-based ETF, in most cases you're getting far fewer distributions than you would get with a Canadian mutual fund holding the same assets.

In-kind Redemptions at the Fund Level

At the personal tax level there's a considerable difference between the tax treatment of U.S. and Canadian-based ETFs. There's a big difference at the fund level, too. In the U.S., in-kind redemptions are non-taxable. An in-kind redemption happens when those giant creation/redemption units of around 50,000 ETF shares are exchanged for the underlying securities in the fund, what's known as an "in-kind redemption." This is not treated as a deemed disposition under U.S. tax law, which means that U.S.-based ETFs don't incur a capital gains tax liability from in-kind redemptions. It doesn't work the same way in Canada. Here, an in-kind redemption is viewed as a deemed disposition by the fund and the fund is thereby liable to pay the capital gains tax or distribute the capital gains to unitholders for them to subsequently pay the tax. This difference in tax treatment makes U.S.-based ETFs more tax efficient than Canadian ETFs and less likely to distribute capital gains than Canadian ETFs.

Superficial Loss Rules

Canadian investors do have one small tax break over their American counterparts. It's not much but it's something.

Both countries want to prevent what's known in Canada as superficial losses—trades that trigger a loss simply to offset some previously incurred capital gains. The hallmark of a superficial loss, to CCRA's mind anyway, is repurchasing the disposed investment within 30 days of having sold it. This move shows the purpose of the sale was to cash in on some tax losses, sometimes known as "crystallizing" the loss, and not to get rid of a dog. Suppose you sold a Spider for a loss but immediately bought an iShares S&P 500. Your underlying positions would be virtually identical. You simply sold one S&P 500 ETF and replaced it with another. In Canada your tax loss would be safe because you own different properties even though their constituents are the same (keeping in mind the provisions of the general anti-avoidance rule). In the U.S. most tax experts believe your capital loss would be disallowed.

U.S. Estate Tax Considerations

U.S.-based ETFs are attractive investments for Canadians looking for U.S. index exposure, so it's important to understand the consequences to your estate if you should die with a significant position in U.S. investments.

Canadian residents who are not U.S. citizens are subject to U.S. estate tax on the value of their U.S. assets owned at death. U.S.-based ETFs are U.S. assets so they get included in the tally. Whereas Canada taxes only the increase in value of assets owned at death, the U.S. system taxes the entire value at death. If you're a Canadian resident who is not a U.S. citizen and your worldwide estate is less than US$1.2 million, there is nothing to worry about with respect to your U.S.-based ETFs. They won't be subject to U.S. estate tax. If, however, your worldwide estate is greater than US$1.2 million, your U.S.-based ETFs will be taxed. The good news is that your ETFs are eligible for an estate tax exemption equal to the greater of US$60,000 or the enhanced exemption provided under the Canada/U.S. treaty. Under this treaty, U.S. assets are eligible for an exemption equal to a standard exemption of US$675,000 multiplied by a formula that divides the U.S. assets by the value of the estate's worldwide assets. The standard exemption of $675,000 is going up to US$3.5 million by 2009.

The U.S. has repealed the U.S. estate tax for 2010. It is fully expected this repeal will last for 2010 only and that thereafter some standard exemption amount will be reinstated. Keep in mind that Canada gives foreign tax credits for U.S. estate tax to minimize the chance of double taxation. In the best case, the investor pays the higher of the two taxes, but quite likely the payment is split between the U.S. and Canadian tax collector. As Russell prudently warns, "Canadian residents with large U.S. holdings, including ETFs, should consider obtaining estate planning advice to deal with the issue of U.S. estate taxes."

Foreign Reporting Requirements

CCRA, ever vigilant, doesn't want Canadians investing abroad without the knowledge of the government lest someone avoid paying their fair share of tax. Canadian residents who own specified foreign property that at any time of the year exceeds $100,000 in total value, must file a Foreign Income Verification Statement (T1135) with their personal income return. The "specified foreign property" includes shares of foreign corporations and interests in trusts so you know what that means. Foreign-based ETFs would have to be reported if your total specified foreign property is greater than $100,000 Canadian, unless they meet certain exemptions and some ETFs do.

Tax Saving Strategies

Avoiding Mutual Fund Distributions

At the end of a mutual fund's fiscal year, the fund distributes its income if it has any. Sometimes these distributions can be large and as a result trigger a proportionately large tax liability. This is especially painful when your distributions are automatically reinvested in new units of the fund. You don't see any cash from the distribution but nevertheless have to send money away to cover the tax liability. In a money-losing year, that adds insult to injury. There is a way to avoid this: sell the fund before the record date for the distribution and avoid the distribution altogether. Doing this may, however, trigger capital gains and unbalance your asset allocation. There's not much you can do about the capital gains, but you can keep your assets covered by buying an ETF that is comparable to your fund's holdings. This judicious mutual fund sale might save you some taxes if the tax on the fund distribution is greater than the tax on half your capital gain. Replacing the fund with a similar ETF will mitigate the asset allocation damage that selling a strategic mutual fund could have on your portfolio's overall balance. Just be careful not to walk into a distribution on the ETF side. A call to the ETF sponsor for a distribution estimate would be a good idea.

Tax Swaps

The technique we described above is called a "tax swap," which is the sale of one security for tax purposes and the immediate purchase of a similar investment. It is done not only to escape mutual fund distributions, but often with the intention of crystallizing a capital loss in order to offset a capital gain now or in the future. (Capital losses can be carried forward indefinitely.) Swaps allow investors to maintain or alter their market exposure and asset allocation when they take a loss. You could, for instance, dump a gold sector mutual fund and buy an iUnits Gold Index ETF. You'd gain the tax loss on the mutual fund but still have similar gold exposure and no worries about the superficial loss rules. Swaps work well between mutual funds and ETFs, be they sector plays or broad indices. And with the growing number of ETFs it's now possible to swap between different ETFs in the same sector or asset class.

This is an especially appropriate strategy if you feel your targeted market sector is bottoming. You gain some tax management flexibility, and as your ETF is fully invested, you get to ride the sector's full upswing when it happens.

Tax Loss Harvesting

This is an evocative name for biting the bullet. Suppose you find yourself with some capital gains tax liability, and you also have a stock with a loss but in an industry you think will revive. You can sell your loser, declare a capital loss to offset your capital gain liability and then buy a sector ETF in the industry you still want to cover. After 30 days you can sell the sector ETF and repurchase your original languishing stock. In this way, you will have avoided the superficial loss rule but still have kept your industry exposure. With any luck, you might have also picked up your original stock at no more than you sold it for.

Equitizing Cash

Pension funds and other big institutional investors use ETFs widely for something called "equitizing cash." The name doesn't sound appealing, but the technique is popular. Equitizing cash simply involves taking cash and turning it into a low risk equity, usually an extremely liquid, broad-based equity ETF. Equitizing enables managers to be in the market just in case one of those big up days hits, the kind of days pundits say make up only 1% of the time but account for half your returns. (Of course, you also have the risk of hitting a day everyone would rather forget.) For taxable accounts, it has the happy result of avoiding interest income, which is taxed heavily, in return for potential capital gains and dividend income.

Individual investors can equitize just like the big institutions. Is your interest income becoming a tax burden? ETFs provide a way to turn that interest income into less punitively taxed income with little loss of liquidity and the benefit of market exposure, although with some added risk. Of course, this has to be done in the context of your entire portfolio because taxation shouldn't be the only investment consideration, though it's one that is too often neglected: it's only the after-tax return that pays for those trips to Hawaii.

Micromanaging Tax Liability in an Index

Broad indices like the S&P 500 and the Dow Jones Total Market are made up of a number of industry sectors. In the U.S., all these sectors are represented by ETFs so it's possible to own a whole index by buying all of its component sectors in the right proportions via ETFs. The nine Select Sector Spiders, for instance, fully replicate the S&P 500. Naturally, your total costs will be higher using this strategy, as you'll have higher MERs and incur many more commission charges, but the advantage is in being able to micromanage each sector's losses and gains. As one sector slumps, you can sell it to use that loss to off-set the surge of another sector. You can even try to enhance your returns by custom weighting the various sectors rather than keeping them in sync with the broader index. If you already own a lot of technology or financial stocks, you might want to underweight those sectors, for instance. Got a hankering for consumer staples? Here's the chance to easily overweight that sector. It's not a strategy for a couch potato, that's for sure.[2]

Taxation of Option Strategies

Option strategies can be taxed in two different ways depending on whether the options are on capital account or on income account. The general rule of thumb is that an option strategy is speculative and thereby on an income account and fully taxed. If, however, an option is used to hedge an investment you already own, it is not considered speculative and the option will be treated as on capital account.[3] The following discussion will assume you are using options on capital account. (Refer back to Chapter 4 for an explanation of the option strategies discussed below.)

Call Options

The purchaser of a call option has paid a premium for the opportunity to buy a security—an ETF for instance—at a certain price by a certain date in the future. Should the option expire without being exercised, the premium paid becomes a capital loss in the taxation year in which the option expires. If, instead, the option is exercised, the option premium is added to the cost base of the ETF. A call option holder has one other course of action open to her. She can sell the option on the secondary market before its expiry. The net gain or loss that results from that sale is a capital gain or loss in the year the option is sold.

The premium paid to the writer of a call option is considered a capital gain. If, however, the option is exercised, the option premium is instead added to the proceeds of the security sale. That way it becomes part of either a capital gain or a capital loss.

Put Options

Similarly, the premium paid to the writer of a put option is treated as a capital gain. If, however, the option is exercised, the premium is subtracted from the cost of buying the ETF units. This means the adjusted cost base of the ETF will be lower than it would be otherwise, leading to higher capital gains when those ETF units are sold. (Remember someone who writes a put promises to buy at a certain price up to some specified time in the future. Someone who buys a put is buying the right to sell at a certain price some time in the future.)

If a put option expires unexercised, the buyer of that put can claim the premium he paid for it as a capital loss in the year the put expired. If, instead, he sells the put on the secondary market, the net gain or loss is taxed as a capital gain or loss in the year it is sold. Should the put be exercised, the premium paid to buy the put is deducted from the proceeds of the ETFs sold. The result is a reduction in the resulting capital gain, if there is one, or alternatively, an increase in the capital loss.

When the writer of either a put or a call buys an off-setting option to protect his position, the cost of acquiring that off-setting position is treated as a capital loss.

Knowing how your option strategy will be taxed will be a factor in determining its viability as a strategy.

Short Selling

Short selling, the practice of selling shares you don't own, is speculative so the proceeds are generally taxed as on income account, which means the profits are fully taxed; however, taxpayers can make a 39(4) election which respect to their Canadian securities that will have the effect of treating all their Canadian stock transactions as on capital account. (There is no similar election for options or foreign securities unfortunately.) This is a once-in-a-lifetime declaration and there's no going back once you've made it. (Traders and dealers aren't eligible.)[4]

One Future Tax Hiccup for ETFs

ETFs are remarkably tax-efficient inventions, but a Canadian tax law threatens the ETF's smooth-running internal mechanism. The new tax law will impact ETFs in 2003 unless the Department of Finance comes to its senses and amends the provisions before then. There will be a lot of lobbying by Canadian ETF sponsors and some mutual fund companies to have this law changed. Nevertheless, you should be aware of what's at stake so you can add your voice to the many should it become necessary.

To get a handle on this problematic tax issue, it's necessary to understand how mutual fund trusts, of which ETFs are a kind, are currently taxed at the fund level—especially with respect to redemptions.

Suppose you redeem 100 units of XYZ Equity Funds for a capital gain of $200. The fund may have to sell some securities in order to get the money to pay you for those 100 units you redeemed. When it does this it may also incur a capital gain of, say, $200. Potentially there are two parties paying tax on the same $200 capital gain: the fund and you. To prevent this double taxation, the fund is given a credit against its capital gains liability in proportion to the capital gains tax you will pay. This arrangement is something known as the "capital gains refund mechanism."

A change to the tax laws intended to help trusts has inadvertently thrown a wrench into the workings of the refund mechanism—changes that would have serious implications for ETFs held in non-registered accounts—unless it is changed. The change has to do with the tax treatment of in-kind redemptions in trusts. Normally, redeeming a trust unit like an ETF for its underlying securities is a taxable event to the trust. Suppose for a moment you have 50,000 units of i60s hanging around and you decide to redeem them in-kind for the underlying 60 stocks. The i60 fund takes the i60 units and gives you the 60 stocks those units represent. The fund has now disposed of those underlying stocks and has to calculate its capital gain on the difference between the purchase price of those securities delivered to you and the market value on the day of the transaction. (Mutual fund trusts actually use the average purchase price, but disregard this for the purposes of this example.) Normally, at the same time you would have to calculate your own capital gain based on the original cost of the ETF units and the value of the stocks you are delivered. There are now two parties paying tax on only one capital gain. The capital gains refund mechanism allows the trust to off set its capital gains liability to the extent of the taxable proceeds to the former unitholder, which is you. This is where the problem arises. The tax law change would allow you to declare as proceeds the original cost of the securities to the fund—not the value of the redeemed securities.

That's a pretty good deal for you, but the trust is stuck paying the capital gains on in-kind redemptions rather than the redeeming unitholder. The capital gains refund mechanism won't work properly because it refunds only to the extent of the tax you pay. If you are getting a break, the fund is picking up the tab; and because trusts flow out their tax liabilities, all ETF unitholders will end up footing the tax bill for this and all other in-kind redemptions. Redeeming unitholders are, essentially, escaping their rightful share of capital gains tax. Janice Russell from Pricewaterhouse-Coopers says this arrangement will give unitholders an incentive to redeem their units rather than sell them on the market as ETFs are intended to work. "It's an oversight by the Finance Department," Russell says. "They thought they were helping trusts, but [the changes] leave a gain in the trust that gets distributed to the wrong person." She says some pooled funds will also be affected by this change, though most conventional mutual funds won't be affected because they don't accept redemptions in kind. Currently funds can and have elected out of this rule until 2003. "It's incumbent on the ETF industry to get this rule changed," says Russell. She's very hopeful it will be changed because it has an unfair consequence. The Ministry of

Finance is not renowned for being kind, but it does try to be just.

Sometimes it takes a hew and cry to get the Ministry of Finance to take notice. The following discussion a good example of a bad tax policy being reversed through the determined efforts of fund companies and investors alike.

The Tax on ETFs that Almost Squished the Spider and Its Peers

An e-mail from an accountant to a financial journalist started a last minute campaign that very probably saved U.S.-based ETFs from a draconian tax that would have made them wildly impractical for Canadian investors.

A public-spirited accountant sent financial journalist Jonathan Chevreau an e-mail in response to a general article Chevreau had written on ETFs for the *Financial Post*. The e-mail warned of an impending tax law no one outside of tax circles seemed to be aware of. The earnest journalist heeded the heads-up and alerted the financial community to the danger with less than two months to the government's September 1, 2000 deadline for comment.

The draft tax legislation in question was an attempt to plug an enforcement problem relating to offshore trusts (the kind the Bronfmans had). The legislation proposed that Canadians pay tax every year on 100% of their gains on foreign investment entities, whether the gains are realized or not. So, if you owned a Spider and it went up $1,000 in one year, you would be required to declare that $1,000 and pay tax on the full $1,000 (not the 50% capital gains inclusion rate) even if you didn't sell it. The same would apply to U.S.-based mutual funds and a lot of other investments apart from foreign trusts. As it stands now, you are required to pay tax on these capital gains only when you actually realize those gains by selling the investment for a profit, at which time you pay tax on only 50% of that profit.

"It had fairly widespread implications," says Dan Hallett, Senior Investment Analyst with Windsor-based Sterling Mutuals Inc. and one of the vocal opponents of the legislation.

The definition the legislation had for a foreign investment entity was basically any business structure of any kind—be it a trust, a corporation or otherwise—not governed in Canada and with at least 50% of its assets in investment properties. And the definition of investment properties was so broad it included cash, real estate, derivatives and common stocks."

Since U.S. ETFs hold U.S. common stocks, the legislation would have taken in ETFs, U.S.-based mutual funds and U.S.

company stocks that have a large investment component; for example, Microsoft with its substantial dealings in put options. Canadian investors holding U.S.-based ETFs, mutual funds and a number of U.S. stocks would then be required by the law to recognize their capital gains every year and pay tax on the full amount. This requirement would, in effect, put such investments off limits to Canadian investors who have nothing in common with the Bronfmans, except maybe a bottle of whiskey. But it gets worse. As Hallett perceptively pointed out, the legislation would also ding ordinary Canadians invested in conventional Canadian mutual funds.

He cited Fidelity Far East as an example of a Canadian mutual fund that would be hard hit by the legislation. At the time, the Fidelity fund had more than half its assets in four Far East holding companies. The fund's accrued gains on those four securities totalled nearly 40% of the fund's net asset value. If unitholders had to suddenly pay tax on all those unrealized gains, it would cause a run on the fund.

Sources hired by CI Funds to research the effects of the legislation estimated 20% to 30% of U.S. stocks would get caught in this law aside from any other foreign stocks, which would have a big effect on all Canadian mutual funds holding U.S. equities.

"To some extent, this legislation was construed as something that would hurt investors who bought index products from the States and was construed as a benefit to the fund industry," recalls Hallett. "Once you looked at the depth of the implications, though, it definitely would have hurt the fund industry as a whole."

Realizing that, the Investment Funds Institute of Canada (IFIC) made a presentation to the finance ministry on behalf of the Canadian mutual fund industry outlining these problems. John Mountain, Vice President of Regulation for IFIC says simply that the proposed legislation "was way too broad."

Given the profound implications of the proposed tax law and the short time before the comment deadline expired, there was an urgency to get the law pointed in the right direction. As a result of this last minute flurry of anxiety, the finance ministry proposed to exclude U.S.-regulated investment companies. This exclusion would let U.S.-based ETFs and mutual funds slip out of the net, but Hallett's concern with respect to domestic mutual fund holdings still isn't addressed. "The Fidelity Far East example illustrates why excluding regulated investment companies [RICs] is not a complete solution. There are other legal structures [apart from RICs] that would still be adversely affected."

"I think the intention of the proposed law is well meaning," says Hallett. "There certainly should be a law that prevents the very wealthy from taking such huge amounts of money out of the country without any tax implications. I don't have a solution, but I'd like to think there is a way to plug the loopholes that existed previously without hurting the people in the country who aren't involved in those activities."

A revised draft of the legislation was expected in the summer of 2001.[5]

Notes

1) Being held on capital account is opposed to being on income account. It means that only 50% of capital gains would be taxed and 50% of losses would be deductible. When investments are held on income account, there is no break for capital gains.

2) Thanks to Paul Mazzilli, Executive Director and Director of Exchange Traded Funds Research at Morgan Stanley in New York, who wrote about this strategy most recently in "ETF Strategy Guide," July 2001 put out by MS Equity Research Department.

3) For a full discussion of income versus capital accounts, see Canadian Customs and Revenue Agency's (CCRA) Interpretation Bulletin IT479R. You can find this at *www.gov.ca*. Go to CCRA and search on "Transactions in Securities."

4) Taxes are a can of worms. When the tax rules with respect to short selling were devised, ETFs weren't even a twinkle in the TSE's eye. As a result, the short selling tax rules don't apply to trust units. This is unfortunate because the party lending the ETF units to a short seller is thereby deemed to have disposed of them and should declare the capital gain or loss resulting from that deemed disposition. It is to be hoped that the Ministry of Finance will see the unfairness of this and amend the rule.

5) For more information on this see Dan Hallett's article "Tax Proposal in Canada Raises Questions," on *www.indexfunds.com*. Search by author's name. Also *www.bylo.org*, a private Canadian investor site, was involved in spearheading investor opposition to the proposed tax law. See the discussion at *www.bylo.org/usmfetftax.html*.

Part Three

Where ETFs Came from and
Where They Are Going

Chapter 7
Lifting the Hood

Remember when Japanese cars suddenly made North American cars look like gas-sucking tanks? ETFs are revving up to do the same thing to the mutual fund industry. It won't lead to a rollicking demolition derby because the funds industry will respond with innovations of its own, and you've got the best chance of understanding future new products by knowing the inner workings of today's innovations. Here we'll lift the hood to look at some detailed issues affecting ETFs. These issues are not inherently complicated, but you do have to get close to the oil to understand the finer points. We'll show you how you can know you are getting a fair price for an ETF, how dividend payments and other sources of cash work inside an ETF, and the differences between American and Canadian ETFs. We'll also discuss the interesting but little-known hazards of index construction as they affect ETFs. For those not mechanically inclined, feel free to skip to the next chapter.

Record-keeping

First a word about the physical management of ETFs. They don't come in certificate form and no ETF will issue a stock certificate. Ownership is tracked on an electronic book-based system coordinated through the transfer agent. So don't look to tuck a stock certificate into a safety deposit box or surrender a stock certificate as collateral for a loan. However, you may be heartened to know that ETFs don't flood you with the shareholder information for all the underlying securities. You receive shareholder information for the ETF itself and have voting rights only with respect to the business of the ETF, not its underlying securities, similar to any conventional mutual fund.

Are You Getting a Fair Price?

The value of an ETF unit is initially set at a fixed percentage of the underlying index. For i60 units it's one-tenth the S&P/TSE 60 Index. (For iUnits sector funds it's one-quarter the index value; Dow Jones Canada 40 the divisor is one-twenty-fifth; TD's 300 and Capped 300 ETFs are one-three-hundredth.) When the S&P/TSE 60 Index is at 465 an i60 should be around $46.50. Of course, that would be way too easy. Dividends and other sources of cash (which do not get reinvested) also have to be factored into the unit price.

BGI Canada's Web site says, "The trading price of an ETF is approximately equal to the trading value of the underlying securities held in the fund, plus any undistributed net income." This information is correct as far as it goes, but unless you know what that "undistributed net income" is, you can't calculate the net asset value (NAV) for yourself. And it's important that you know this otherwise you can't determine if you are buying an ETF at a fair price which means one that is close to NAV. (The price of most ETFs track their respective NAVs very well most of the time, but it's always prudent to check.)

The undistributed net income is made up of the estimated cash amount per unit, and something known as a "distribution price adjustment." The estimated cash amount is a tally of dividends received by the fund but not yet declared as distributions. The distribution price adjustment reflects an amount per unit declared as distributions (and therefore deducted from the NAV) but not yet paid to unitholders. Normally, the distribution price adjustment will be zero since there is merely a seven-day gap every quarter between the declaration of distributions with ETFs and their payout to unitholders.

To figure out how much you should be paying for an ETF use the following formula.

$$\frac{\text{Current index value} + \text{estimated cash amount per unit} + \text{distribution price adjustment}}{\text{(divisor)}} = \text{NAV}$$

The divisor is the ETF's fraction of the index. In the i60's case, the divisor would be one-tenth. The numbers for the estimated cash amount and the distribution price adjustment per unit are not as easy to come by.

Only the fund administrators know that information, and even at that, the daily cash amount is an estimate done one day in advance. For iUnits, you can find these numbers on BGI Canada's Web site, *www.iunits.com* under "Fund Values" and then under "Holdings." BGI Canada, the sponsor of the iUnits, updates the NAV for all its Canadian ETFs daily on the site so you don't have to do the calculation yourself. TD Asset Management's site, *www.tdassetmanagement.com*, also gives a NAV value per unit as of the close of the previous day's market and how that changed from the last daily close. They also report an estimated cash amount and a distribution price adjustment. State Street Global Advisors, the sponsor for the Dow Jones Canada 40 ETF, is expected to launch a stand-alone Web site for their Dow Jones funds but until then the estimated cash amount, distribution price adjustment and other time sensitive facts are available from an e-mail the company disseminates daily to subscribers.

Things are a lot easier in the U.S. for savvy ETF investors. The American Stock Exchange (AMEX), where almost all ETFs trade, broadcasts every scintilla of information you would ever want to know about an ETF through eight ticker symbols per ETF. Take the famous S&P Depositary Receipts (Spiders) for illustration. The chart below shows the eight ticker symbols for Spiders.

Ticker Symbols for SPDRs

SPY	Trading Symbol	SXV.SO	Shares Outstanding
SXV	Intraday Value	SPX	Benchmark Index Symbol
SXV.NV	Net Asset Value	SXV.EU	Estimated Cash Amount
SXV.DV	Net Accrued Dividend	SXV.TC	Total Cash Amount Per Creation Unit

Source: www.amex.com

The market value for Spiders (SPY) is quoted in real time; it is the trading price for the Spiders shares. The "intraday value" is the estimated value of the underlying portfolio calculated every 15 seconds. With this and the estimated cash amount, it's easy to see how much of a premium or discount the market price represents. The "net asset value" (SXV.NV) is computed per share at the close of the market each day and includes the value of the underlying securities plus portfolio cash (accrued dividends) and minus accumulated expenses. The "net accrued dividend" (SXV.DV) is a tally of dividend income calculated per share as of the end of the previous day. The same is true for "shares outstanding" (SXV.SO) calculation. The "estimated cash amount" (SXV.EU) is, as its name implies, an estimate for the current day based on the actual cash holdings in the fund at the close of the previous day.

Ticker Symbols for DIAMONDS

DIA	Trading Symbol	DXV.SO	Shares Outstanding
DXV	Intraday Value	INDU	Benchmark Index Symbol
DXV.NV	Net Asset Value	DXV.EU	Estimated Cash Amount
DXV.DV	Net Accrued Dividend	DXV.TC	Total Cash Amount Per Creation Unit

Ticker Symbols for Qubes

QQQ	Trading Symbol	QXV.SO	Shares Outstanding
QXV	Intraday Value	NDX	Benchmark Index Symbol
QXV.NV	Net Asset Value	QXV.EU	Estimated Cash Amount
QXV.DV	Net Accrued Dividend	QXV.TC	Total Cash Amount Per Creation Unit

Source: www.amex.com

Having this information available by ticker symbol makes it easy and straightforward to get timely information about the financial underpinnings of an ETF. (You can find all eight ticker symbols associated with every ETF that trades on AMEX on the AMEX Web site, *www.amex.com*.)

Shockingly, many Canadian brokers don't have access to these ancillary ETF ticker quotes because it is an election on their data service that costs money. Don't be surprised if even your full-service fellow charging you $95 a trade doesn't get these tickers.

Nevertheless, the values for these ticker symbols are cranked out around 4:00 p.m. in New York. As it happens, a number of ETFs trade until 4:15 p.m. New York time, but rather than getting a sharper price at the end of the trading day, the spread between bid and ask widens at the end of the day. If you're going to buy an ETF, it's often best to avoid this period.

Below is a list of the ETFs that trade from 9:30 a.m. to 4:15 p.m. in New York. (All others stop trading at 4:00 p.m. Eastern Standard Time.)

- All broad-market ETFs
- iShares Sector Index Funds
- iShares International Index Funds
- streetTracks Dow Jones series

The AMEX Web site is like the Wall Street Journal of ETFs with a huge wealth of information about all their listed ETFs. The American Stock Exchange is clearly committed to ETFs because ETFs are its revenue lifeline. The beleaguered Toronto Stock Exchange (TSE) hasn't quite awakened to the importance of ETFs, even though i60s are one of the most actively traded shares on the exchange. The TSE's site (*www.tse.com*) has scanty ETF coverage but has pledged to beef it up in the future. When you think of it, the TSE should be an exceptional reference on Canadian ETFs since they were the sponsor for Canada's first exchange traded fund, TIPs. (After ten years TIPS merged with BGI Canada's the 160 Fund in 2000.) With the Canadian ETF universe now numbering more than a dozen funds and counting, it's likely the TSE will rouse itself soon.

Liquidity

Liquidity is the ease with which an investment can be bought and sold without substantially affecting the market price of the investment. Trading volume is a good indication of liquidity. The more a stock trades, the more liquid it is. Typically, the more liquid an investment, the narrower the spread between the bid and ask price. ETFs with big assets are highly liquid: the Qubes, Diamonds, Spiders, the iShares S&P 500; most of the style and capitalization ETFs, like the iShares Russell series; and the S&P Mid Cap and Small Cap series. In general broad market ETFs trade swiftly and frequently and are widely held.

Liquidity seems to be a concern with the lightly traded country iShares such as MSCI Australia ETF with an average daily trading volume of 15,000 shares and the MSCI Belgium ETF with $10 million in assets and only 5,000 shares traded on average a day (as of July 2001). Normally such thin trading volumes would pose a problem for an institution that would want to move 10,000 or more shares, for example. Spreads do widen in these circumstances, but remember, ETF prices are ultimately tied to the value of the underlying securities. As long as these securities are liquid and the arbitrage mechanism is not impeded, the price of even a thinly traded ETF should stay fairly resonant with the NAV. Even if the ETF itself is not a model of liquidity, the liquidity of the underlying portfolio should prevent excessive price discrepancies. According to an ETF report put out by Goldman Sachs Derivative & Trading Research (June 29, 2001), "...the dollar volume of the trading activity in the underlying stocks is more significant in assessing liquidity than the dollar volume of the ETF."

How Is Cash Handled?

You might wonder how cash can get so plentiful in an ETF portfolio that you must take it into account in order to make sense of an ETF's price. After all, isn't one of the reasons ETFs are superior to mutual funds because they have so little cash? Well, yes, ETFs proportionally have a lot less cash than most mutual funds because they don't have to deal with redemptions in cash or cash influxes waiting to be invested. ETFs strive to be investment rich and cash poor, but try as they may, they still have some pesky cash hanging around.

ETFs get cash from a few sources. First, their underlying stocks generate dividends. Most ETFs pay out their dividends quarterly and their capital gains annually, but between payouts, the dividend income must be mopped up. Canadian equity ETFs don't reinvest the dividend income they receive into the underlying securities. Instead, they put that money into a separate account. That account generates interest income, out of which is paid the fund's expenses. As a result, Canadian equity ETFs don't distribute interest income but only dividend income, and capital gains.

Cash can sometimes arise from the creation of new ETF units between dividend quarters. The creation of new ETF units requires three things: the basket of securities to make up the ETF; cash for dividends already received on those securities; and cash equal to the value of any accrued dividends. The cash for the accrued dividends gives rise to a return of capital at a future distribution.

Cash within bond ETFs, like the iG5s and iG10s, is distributed semi-annually as interest income when it is received. Interest income received by the fully RRSP eligible i500Rs, on the other hand, is reinvested in the fund.

And because these are pretty streetwise critters, ETFs also scarf a few dollars from lending their securities to short sellers. This was a source of income for TIPS when it was around and TIPS' exemption from the general prohibition for funds against lending securities was passed on to the i60's. In early 2001, regulators changed the rules to permit all mutual fund trusts to lend their securities. Now all Canadian ETFs and mutual funds that are structured as trusts can lend out their own securities and charge a fee for doing so.

Canadian vs. U.S. ETF Structure

The legal structure of investments may seem like a pretty arcane thing, but these legal discrepanciees can make a difference to your costs and ultimate returns. All ETFs in Canada now are structured as mutual fund trusts so they all must conform to the same rules and labour under the same restrictions. Their U.S. counterparts, however, come in a few legal varieties and this structure makes a difference in how they treat their dividend income, whether or not they can lend securities, and how they are permitted to track the index.

Structure Comparison of ETFs

Characteristics	Mutual Fund (U.S.)	Unit Investment Trust (U.S.)	Grantor Trust (U.S.)	Mutual Fund Trust (Cdn.)
Dividends	reinvested until quarterly distribution	not reinvested	paid directly when received	not reinvested
Index strategy	may optimize	replication only	cap-weighted basket	may optimize
Loan securities	yes	no	no	yes
Derivatives	may use	may not use	may not use	may use
Funds	iShares, streetTRACKS, Sector SPDRS	SPDRS, 400 SPDRS, Diamonds, Qubes	HOLDRS	iUnits, DJ40, TD ETFs

Source: Morgan Stanley Equity Research for U.S. ETFs, author for Canadian ETFs

Exchange Traded Investment Trusts

The oldest ETFs, Spiders, Diamonds, Qubes and the S&P 400 Mid Cap Spiders, are exchange traded unit investment trusts (UITs). With the UIT structure, dividends and income are not reinvested, the underlying securities cannot be lent and the index must be replicated. Optimization is not permitted. (See Chapters 2 and 3.)

Exchange Traded Open-end Index Mutual Fund

Sector Select Spiders, and all iShares and streetTRACKS ETFs are exchange traded open-end index mutual funds. This more contemporary structure permits the funds to reinvest dividend income the moment it is received, and it gives the funds the flexibility to optimize their index strategies if they so desire. Lending securities is also permitted, so this is by far a more flexible structure for ETFs.

Both ETF structures distribute dividends and capital gains, so there is no tax treatment difference for a U.S. resident between the different legal structures. (There's no difference in tax treatment between these structures for Canadian residents either; unfortunately, all U.S. ETF distributions are treated as ordinary income by Canadian tax collectors.)

Exchange Traded GrantorTrust

This type of trust is a legal structure used by HOLDRS. HOLDRS are very different from index-linked ETFs. Some might say that, strictly speaking, they're not ETFs at all, but because they are generally included in ETF discussions we have included them here. Most HOLDRS initially contain 20 stocks that are never changed or rebalanced in any way. Investors receive the dividends directly and have voting rights. It is almost like owning the 20 stocks individually, except that they can be traded easily as a group. HOLDRS do not lend securities, reinvest dividends or use derivatives. (See the end of this chapter for a more extensive discussion of HOLDRS).

The Canadian ETF Structure

ETFs in Canada are structured as mutual fund trusts. A trust preserves the tax characteristics of its income and passes it on to the unitholders. So when a Canadian ETF issues a distribution, it lands in investors' hands as dividend, interest or capital gains with their respective tax treatments. This structure permits the manager to optimize an index if desired, and as of 2001, mutual fund trusts have been permitted to loan securities.

Look before you hedge

CHANCES ARE THAT YOUR FINANCIAL adviser is trying to sell you on the merits of hedge funds. These funds, which use alternative investing strategies, are all the rage because they performed relatively well during the last three years, when most mutual funds sucked wind. But before you make your adviser's day and say yes to whatever fund he's touting, consider a few facts he may not mention.

The most important of these facts is risk. While most mutual funds restrict themselves to buying some combination of stocks or bonds, hedge funds use more exotic tactics to boost results. For example, they can go "short" by selling stocks they don't own in an attempt to benefit from falling stock prices. They can also "lever" your investment by borrowing additional money in order to magnify the size of the bets that they place.

These strategies can be very successful and result in double-digit returns. Problem is, they can also backfire and if they do, your hedge fund will plummet faster than a falling brick. Until a few years ago, hedge funds were restricted to rich investors—people who could afford to take a big loss. Today thresholds have been lowered so that you can buy some hedge funds for as little as $500. But the fact that hedge funds are more accessible doesn't make them appropriate for all portfolios. You must ask yourself if you can stomach losing money.

This is a real danger. Your adviser might tell you that a good hedge fund will make your portfolio *less* volatile because a hedge fund can go up even when stocks go down. But while this is true in theory, it's difficult to know if it's true of any single hedge fund. Yes, hedge funds as a group tend to have low volatility when you look at measures like standard deviation. But other critical measures of volatility—such as "skewness," which measures the probability of winning big or losing all your money—show that hedge funds are still dangerous. A big loss in a single year can cripple them.

Proponents of hedge funds like to quote figures that show that such funds, as a group, have done very well. Keep in mind that those returns are partly due to what's known as survivorship bias. That is, only funds that have survived the dismal markets of the past few years are included in the statistics. Those that blew up are no longer included in the averages because they no longer exist. As a result, many hedge fund indexes overstate the group's returns and understate its volatility.

To make matters even more complicated, we don't have enough of a track record to assess the host of new players that have popped up since 2000. Of the 82 hedge funds listed in Morningstar Canada's database, only 22 have three-year track records and only four—four!—have five-year track records. In most cases, you are buying an unknown quantity. Three years is simply not long enough to determine whether good returns are due to skill or luck.

A hedge fund can be a good addition to your portfolio only if you're aware of the risks and you understand exactly what you're investing in. The following tips can help steer your choice:

• Avoid funds that charge a management expense ratio (MER) of more than 3.25%, including performance fees. Big fees eat up profits and leave little for you.

• Don't fall in love with any single manager. Hedge funds that follow similar strategies tend to have similar returns. So no matter how good a manager's track record, you shouldn't be paying more in fees than similar funds are charging.

• Start with a "fund-of-funds." These funds invest in a number of different funds, giving you diversification across different managers and investment styles. The result? Less risk. TD Private Wealth operates a good fund-of-funds that is well worth looking at.

• Ensure the fund isn't overly leveraged, since too much leverage means risk. Leverage of three times (which means the fund borrows up to $3 for each dollar you invest) should be the max. This should be spelled out in the prospectus.

• Invest no more than 5% of your portfolio in hedge funds. Your adviser might recommend taking this allocation from the bond side of your portfolio. Don't do it. Treat hedge funds like equities because their ride could be bumpy. **M**

If your adviser recommends adding a hedge fund to your portfolio, ask some tough questions

Kelly Rodgers, CFA, provides investment consulting to high-net-worth individuals and nonprofit organizations. Her Web site is www.rodgersinvestmentconsulting.com. For previous columns by Kelly go to our Web site at www.moneysense.ca.

Dividends

The current crop of Canadian-based equity ETFs distribute their dividends quarterly and their capital gains annually in December. The iUnits bond funds distribute interest income semi-annually and capital gains income annually in December.

ETF quarterly distributions are made in cash to unitholders. If you find those quarterly cheques a nuisance, ask your brokerage about a dividend reinvestment plan. So far, only one brokerage in Canada (RBC Investments) offers this, but with more demand others will follow. That will save you a commission and allow you to keep your money tracking the total return index.

Capital gains generated from the ETF's own internal buying and selling are distributed in the form of additional units of the ETF at the end of each year, but only for an instant. In December an ETF with a capital gain distribution will issue more units of itself in an amount equal to the value of the capital gain distribution. When this distribution "in-kind" happens, more units are created but the underlying value of the assets remains unchanged. This means that the price of all the ETF units must go down so that when all the units are added up, the total value of all the units still equals the original asset value. For an instant you own more units at a fractionally lower price. You'll note that this is exactly what happens with conventional mutual funds when they make a distribution: the units are increased by the amount of the distribution, but the value of all the units is decreased by the amount of the distribution. There is no change in the value of your total holdings.

The difference with an ETF, though, is that it immediately "consolidates" all its outstanding shares, knocks the number of units back down to the pre-distribution number and boosts the unit price back to its pre-distribution level. After this, you are left with an unchanged number of shares at the pre-dividend price but with a higher adjusted cost base. The value and number of your units hasn't changed, but the fund has passed on to you a capital gains tax liability in proportion to the distribution. The good news is that your adjusted cost base increases by the amount of the capital gains distribution, so when you subsequently sell your ETF, your ultimate capital gain will be less than it would have been without receiving the dividends.

Remember, you are still required to pay tax on this capital gains distribution even though you received it in-kind temporarily, in the form of increased units. The unit consolidation is done so investors aren't left with fractions and odd numbers of shares from distributions. (It's easy to sell 100 units but not so easy to sell 103 units and quite impossible to sell 103.33 shares on a stock exchange.) But more important than that, the divisor would be thrown off if the number of ETF units increased while the share value dropped.

Distributions from U.S.-based ETFs to Canadian residents are treated uniformly as income and are therefore taxed at your highest marginal tax rate. Distributions from Canadian-based ETFs are more tax-advantaged because they retain their tax character as dividends, interest or capital gains.

Index Construction Free-floats

Putting together an index may not seem like a tough job. Take the stocks of 100 companies with the largest market capitalization on a stock exchange, and you've got an index. The bigger a company's capitalization, the greater that company's influence on the index. What could be more straightforward? But take a look below at all the listed securities excluded from the Dow Jones Canada Index.

- Preferred shares
- Convertible notes
- Warrants
- Rights
- Mutual funds
- Units
- Limited partnerships
- Closed-end funds (for the most part)
- The bottom 1% of stocks by market capitalization
- Stocks where 75% or more of shares are controlled by
  another corporation or state entity.
- Stocks with more than ten non-trading days over the past quarter
- Stocks with low average daily turnover

Source: www.dowjones.com/corp/index_directory.htm

That's a lot of dance partners ruled out before the music even starts, but this is a big ballroom where every move counts and every discrimination is for a reason.

Indices are constructed with two goals. First, an index should be an accurate representation of a market or market segment, otherwise the fluctuations don't mean very much. Second, an index should be investable. In other words, index investors should be able to reproduce the index easily by buying its components. This is where some foreign indices fall short. A company may have a very large market capitalization, but when few of the shares are available for trading, it becomes difficult to reproduce the index. This can happen when a company holds many of its own shares or the shares of another company also on the index. Foreign ownership restrictions on stock purchases, imposed by some countries, further reduces the investability of an index, as does major stock holdings by controlling shareholders, company management or governments.

Most index sponsors have addressed this issue by designing indices and their weightings based on the "free-float" of a company's stock available to foreign investors in the market instead of being based on total market capitalization. Morgan Stanley Capital International, the world's top provider of global stock indices, is in the process of converting from market cap to free-float adjusted market cap indices. The change is anticipated to dislodge so many stocks currently included in major indices that MSCI is doing it in stages to be completed by June 2002. At the same time, they're trying to increase their market coverage from 60% to 85% to get a more accurate representation of the markets by their indices. The changes will make MSCI indices more meaningful benchmarks for investors, but global fund managers aren't delighted: these changes will fix some notoriously easy-to-beat indices.

The free-float issue isn't as straightforward as it may seem, however. According to Glenn Doody, Director of Canadian Index Operations at Standard and Poor's in Toronto, the TSE was one of the first index sponsors to adjust their index to free-float in 1977 when they introduced the TSE 300. S&P, by the way, has converted almost all its indices to free-float with the exception of the S&P 500 which doesn't need it because of the healthy liquidity of the stocks within that index.

There are, however, degrees of compliance with free-float ideals. Surprisingly, Canada's market is one of the few in which S&P has disregarded ownership restrictions in its index construction. Doody says Canadian restrictions on foreign ownership of media and communication companies, airlines and financial institutions would leave a Canadian index with too few companies to be representative of the market. "Market representation and liquidity are always a trade-off," observes Doody. Optimal Canadian market representation requires the inclusion of many companies on which the government has imposed foreign ownership restrictions. S&P's domestic Canadian indices have opted for the best representation rather than for perfect foreign liquidity. The Dow Jones people, at least for the purposes of their global index, do their market cap calculations based on free-float, but their free-float calculations take into account only block holdings of 5% or more. If a country, Japan for instance, has many small block holdings, the Dow Jones free-float will not be sensitive enough to adjust for that.

Doody also noted a few other issues in index construction.

Exchangeable shares (shares that can be exchanged for another security either in the same company or in another company), were removed from all S&P Canadian indices last year. Multi-class shares were another sore spot recently rectified. Some companies, Bombardier for instance, have different classes of shares independently listed on different indices. Bombardier B was in the S&P/TSE 60 Index and Bombardier A was in the S&P/TSE Small Cap ndex, but Bombardier itself is a large cap company. With Bombardier and other dual class companies like it, S&P amalgamated the classes into the largest, most liquid class and determined which index that class should be put. "Securities shouldn't be in the index," says Doody. "Companies should be in the index."

No doubt there will be other refinements to indices as time goes on and their uses become more diverse. "Fifteen or twenty years ago, indices were mainly used to measure markets. Today, more and more you are seeing indexes with products associated with themderivatives and ETFs," says Doody.

For investors, knowing something about the problems involved in constructing an index puts their performance and those of a fund manger in perspective. All the financial sophistication in the world has yet to make it a science.

Smelling the oil yet? Understanding some of the issues in index construction and maintenance will help you choose the right index to track with an ETF. (For a complete list of the indices that have ETFs associated with them, please see Appendix B. There you'll also find mention of how the indices are constructed and run.)

Take a few minutes to review the history of ETFs, where they came from and why. It's been said that history repeats itself. Who knows, but maybe some of the failed products that came before ETFs might find the time is finally ripe to reassert themselves. Also, in Chapter 8 you'll find some predictions about what's next on the scene in exchange traded funds.

What Most Confuses Investors About ETFs: An Interview with Stephen Rive

Steve Rive is General Manager of iUnits for Barclays Global Investors (BGI) Canada Limited. He oversees the development and ongoing management of iUnits. Before joining BGI Canada Steve worked at stock exchanges in Canada and the Far East helping develop and market new products. The interview below took place in July 2001.

Steve Rive: All this heavy, under-the-hood stuff is invisible, to the investor but the result of it is a much more cost-effective way to distribute a fund. The brokers take care of handling the orders. They provide the monthly statements for investors and the tax reporting. That's a big efficient system already set up. There's no magic as to why the MERs are so low on ETFs. It's because it's inherently a more cost effective way to distribute a fund, and you get the benefit of being able to buy and sell during the day and being able to use limit orders where you actually choose the price at which you want to buy and sell. You can have it sitting there and it will only trade when it reaches the price you want.

There is one technical point, though, that does seem to cause some confusion among investors and advisors, and that is how ETFs treat their capital gains. All mutual fund trusts, which includes ETFs, distribute their income to the trust once a year and that includes any realized capital gains. We have realized gains because of redemptions and index adjustments. The fund is no richer or better off when it has realized a gain. All that's happened is that a tax liability has been   generated. Think of a situation where you've invested $50,000 in a stock. It goes up to $100,000 and you sell it. You now have $100,000 in cash. The day after you make your sale you are no richer than before you made the sale but suddenly you owe tax on that $50,000 of capital gain when it went from $50,000 to $100,000. When these realized gains are distributed by an ETF, there isn't any new wealth in the fund to be passed on to unit holders. All the ETF is doing is passing on this realized gain.

All mutual fund trusts distribute this gain in the form of additional units. A traditional fund gives you more units and lets the net asset value of all the units drop by the amount of the distribution. If you had $10,000 before, you'd still have $10,000 after a distribution but in more units at a lower price per unit. In our case, though, after we issue more units we immediately reconsolidate the number of shares so that the number of units outstanding and the price are the same as before the distribution. In both cases, ETFs and mutual funds, the value of your holdings is unchanged by a distribution. If you had $10,000 before the distribution, you've still got $10,000 after, but you then have this pro rata share of the tax liability of the gains realized inside the ETF.

The key point, and what a lot of people don't realize, is that with a traditional fund, when you get those additional units your price is dropping as well, so you're not really any better off than you were before. There's no material difference between what we do and what a traditional fund does. In both cases, when the dust settles the only thing that's happened is that the value of your holdings are unchanged, but the fund's liability for capital gains tax has been flowed through to unit holders on a pro rata basis.

For some reason people haven't really thought that through. They see more units and they feel comforted: "Okay, I've got a capital gains liability, but I've got some more units." In fact, of course, they're no better off than they were before. ETFs reconsolidate the new units, thereby keeping the price of each unit as it was before the consolidation. If we didn't do that people would have fractional shares and the divisor [tracking factor] would be thrown off. This reconsolidation has caused a lot of confusion for brokers, investors and even back office people at the brokerage firms.

It is an important point because the reconsolidation mechanism is ultimately how the unit price on the exchange is able to track the net asset value of the underlying fund during the day.

Another thing investors find confusing is the tax reporting. A lot of people call us asking after their T-3 slip. Unlike a conventional mutual fund company, we don't produce any tax slips at all for investors. Because ETFs are exchange traded, it's the broker who prepares the T-3.

Except for those two points, ETFs seem to be pretty well understood by our investors.

A Note About HOLDRS

Somewhere between a whole index and a hand-picked portfolio of your own making lie HOLDRS. HOLDRS are exchange traded baskets of securities, each typically containing 20 different stocks related by industry sector. These elect stocks remain in the portfolio unchanged for the life of the trust unless corporate events cause changes to the stock itself like reconstitution, delisting, et cetera.

HOLDRS stands for "holding company depositary receipts" and despite that intimidating handle, they're really the proletarian version of ETFs. For the cost of a stock trade and few other expenses, you can buy an instant portfolio with a very focused sector concentration. HOLDRS cover specialized sectors like business-to-business Internet companies, Internet architecture firms and more diversified, established sectors like Telecommunications, Utilities and Pharmaceuticals. Unlike mutual funds and ETFs, HOLDRS have no MER or any other ongoing fees or costs apart from a small annual trustee fee ($2 to $8 per 100 shares of HOLDRS) that is paid out of dividends and other distributions. If the portfolio doesn't generate enough income to pay the trustee fee—not a farfetched scenario when dealing with Internet companies the trustee fee is waived to the extent it can't be paid from distributions.

Because they do not have to comply with the concentration limits that apply to mutual funds and ETFs (in the U.S.), your HOLDRS portfolio will never be forced to sell a winning stock. This will spare you the sting of unwanted capital gains and the disadvantage of a smaller holding in a good investment. With HOLDRS, as with an individual stock holding, you can ride a winner as long as it runs and you decide when to sell it and trigger your gains.

HOLDRS also bring that wonderful creation/redemption process pioneered by ETFs into the clutches of ordinary retail investors. You can easily redeem HOLDRS for all its underlying securities, which gives you the freedom to sell the shares you don't want on the open market and keep the rest. The trustee charges a $10 fee per round lot of 100 HOLDRS shares for this service. Less likely but also possible, you can create 100 HOLDRS by surrendering the requisite number of shares of the underlying portfolio to the trustee who, for $10, will issue you HOLDRS in exchange. ETFs, like Spiders and i6o's, permit this creation/redemption only with huge share volumes of 50,000 or more which means in practice that only institutional investors and arbitrageurs can take advantage of that feature.

HOLDRS, on the other hand, are bought, sold, created and redeemed in multiples of 100 shares and only in lots of 100. (ETFs, you'll remember, do come in odd lots.) Of course, because you can't buy anything less than a round lot of 100 HOLDRS, the proletariat buying these keepers had better have enough money for 100 shares. In spring 2001, that would have meant forking over as much as US$13,400 for Biotech HOLDRS, or as little as $700 for the beat up B2B Internet HOLDRS.

Apart from their accessible redemption feature, HOLDRS are retail friendly in another way, too. You get the voting rights associated with all the underlying shares. This is in marked contrast to all other baskets of securities, including mutual funds and ETFs. In these structures, the beneficial owners do not get voting rights to the underlying securities. Social investors, eager to influence corporate behaviour through their voting rights, will appreciate this feature of HOLDRS and the flexibility to divest themselves of companies within the portfolio that don't cut the mustard ethically.

Along with these voting rights you'd better get yourself a bigger mailbox because you receive all the investor relations mailings from the 20 or so underlying companies, too. The two non-sector HOLDRS (Market 2000 and Europe 2001), have around 50 companies in each of their baskets. If you take pity on your mail carrier's back and your recycling box, you can elect to receive much of these corporate mailings electronically.

Cheaper to hold and more flexible than ETFs, HOLDRS, as a structure, have a lot going for them. The actual execution, however, could use some work. Merrill Lynch's portfolios, with two exceptions, are highly sector-specific, and as such, expose you to a lot more risk than a broad market index or even a sector mutual fund with a greater number of holdings. The risk hasn't been academic either.

In spring 2001, not one HOLDRS year-to-date return was in positive territory. One-year returns ranged from +9.18% for Pharmaceutical HOLDRS to -92.39% for B2B HOLDRS. Internet and Internet Architecture were not much better at -89.51 and -81.07% respectively.

The prospectus for HOLDRS lists an interesting risk factor that has proved more problematic than most would have expected. Under "Temporary price increases in the underlying securities," the prospectus says, " [and] purchasing activity in the secondary market associated with acquiring the underlying securities for deposit into the trust may affect the market price of the deposited shares." In other words, gathering up the shares to build a HOLDRS could inflate the price of the individual securities. Merrill Lynch was the subject of a class action suit by investors in the B2B Internet HOLDR who claimed securities were put into the HOLDRS at inflated prices, possibly due to some sort of manipulation at their Initial Public Offering (IPO) stage. (For more information on the suit see *www.holdrs.com/holdrs/main/index.asp?Action=QuoteH&symb=BHH* to view press releases about the class action. Allegations have not been proven in court.)

On March 14, 2000, the B2B Internet HOLDRS traded at US$108. By April 3, 2001 they were at $4.26.

There's another, more fundamental problem with HOLDRS. The portfolio is a snapshot in time. What goes in at the beginning stays in unchanged unless there's a spin-off, merger, consolidation or other corporate event that would cause any of the underlying securities to be withdrawn from AMEX. Until late 2000, all such events would be treated as though you owned the securities individually. You would receive directly the new share reissues, the buyouts, et cetera. and they would not be reflected in the fund. This means the number of holdings in the fund could shrink and the corresponding concentration of the remaining stocks would increase. Gradually your investment would become less diversified. An amendment to the rules governing HOLDRS now permits them to retain stocks resulting from those stock rending corporate events, but this doesn't entirely ameliorate the structural problem.

Suppose a private biotech company discovers a cure for cancer. They go public and their stock immediately rockets skyward. A Biotech HOLDRS put together before that company went public would miss out entirely on the biggest Biotech shooting star in history. An index continually refreshes its holdings to keep up with market activity, so any index-based product like an ETF will not miss out on the next Viagra. The static portfolio construction will haunt any HOLDRS and especially those in rapid growth sectors; the very sectors these products have chosen to exploit.

Even leaving aside this problem, market appreciation and losses will, over time, change the balance of the HOLDRS underlying securities relative to each other. The longer you keep a HOLDRS, the more risky and less representative the portfolio may become.

Internet HOLDRS is a good example of the danger. Internet HOLDRS was launched with AOL at 19.6% of the original portfolio. Time-Warner swallowed AOL and now AOL Time-Warner Inc. stock takes up 47% of the portfolio yet only 20% of Time-Warner's revenue comes from Internet-related businesses.

HOLDRS is a signature product designed and offered by Merrill Lynch & Co., Inc. in the U.S. and they've been popular. First introduced in 1999, there are now 17 HOLDRS trading on AMEX with over US$4 billion in assets. That, in spite of Merrill Lynch's unfortunate habit of launching these highly specialized Internet and Technology plays at very close to the market top. Many early HOLDRS investors saw their high tech portfolios plummet, some by as much as 93%. But dismal timing aside, these products have a number of attractive features and few worrisome drawbacks, too. So far, no other financial firm has come out with a competing product to Merrill Lynch's HOLDRS, but there's industry speculation that other brokerages might take a run at them with their own keepers.

Lest you worry that the absence of an ongoing management fee will make HOLDRS a fleeting product, take heart. Merrill Lynch has not turned altruistic. HOLDRS finance themselves by charging a 2% underwriting fee at the initial offering (for 10,000 HOLDRS or more the underwriting fee is 1%), a charge that is paid only once and does not spill over into the secondary market.

Before grasping a HOLDRS for your own take a good look at the costs. Although a 2% underwriting fee may not seem unreasonable, keep in mind that the upside potential of a HOLDRS initial public offering (IPO) is not like the promise of a new stock IPO. HOLDRS are baskets of securities that have each already had their own public debut. Just repackaging them into a HOLDRS and launching that as an IPO doesn't automatically create any new upside potential. You may find an underwriting fee palatable for a stock IPO with great expectations, but where's a similar excitement with a HOLDRS IPO? Also, scrutinize that annual trustee fee. Should the price of 100 HOLDRS fall dramatically, you could be paying more money in trustee fees than the MER on an ETF. All HOLDRS trade on AMEX and all have options associated with them

For More Information on HOLDRS go to *www.holdrs.com*, an extensive site with prospecti.

Chapter 8
The Past and Future of ETFs

Modern Portfolio Theory and the Efficient Markets Hypothesis together were the intellectual underpinnings of indexing, but indexing as an investment strategy wouldn't have been a practical in real life without the technology to make trading a list of stocks possible all at once. In the late 1970s institutions started taking advantage of new electronic order delivery systems on the New York Stock Exchange (NYSE) and the American Stock Exchange (AMEX) that allowed them to trade groups of shares effectively as a single basket. "Program trading" got its name from the computer programs that were designed to generate lists of stocks to be transacted through the electronic order delivery system. The new electronic system made it possible for a large number of different stocks to be bought or sold more or less simultaneously for a fixed commission, and so virtual basket trades began.

Then in 1982, the Chicago Mercantile Exchange (CME) introduced an index future on the S&P 500 that proved hugely popular because it was a more efficient way to effectively trade a whole index.[1] An index future is a contract that pays you the cash equivalent of the value of the market at a set time in the future. By buying a contract that promises to pay you the cash value of an index in the future, it is as though you have bought all the stocks in the index, when all you've actually purchased is a contract.

Index futures revolutionized portfolio management. Trading index futures was a pretty good proxy for buying and selling all the stocks in an index and an improvement over doing just that. Futures contracts were dirt cheap to trade and quickly became highly liquid.

Program trading and a heavy use of index futures were the main working parts in something known as "portfolio insurance" that prospered from 1982 until the market crash in October 1987 and something that some have blamed for the crash itself. Two finance professors at Berkeley, Hayne Leland and Mark Rubenstein, developed software in the late 1970s that was designed to control the risk of an entire portfolio. Their program calculated how much the equity component of a portfolio could go down relative to its cash position before the whole portfolio fell below a specified bottom. When stocks were going down the software dictated how much money had to be stripped from stocks and plowed into cash. When stocks were going up more money was taken from cash in favour of equities. Applying this program trading with S&P 500 Index Futures gave them a dynamic strategy to control the risk of an entire portfolio. By 1986, the professors' company, Leland, O'Brien, Rubinstein Associates, Inc. (LOR) was managing US$60 billion through software licensing agreements.

"Our computer models worked right on target. It was a really reliable product," said Rubinstein in an interview for this book. "Our simulations showed that even through the great depression that would have disturbed us a little bit... [B]ut the results might have been acceptable, and in almost all the rest of the time, it works like a charm."

The charm lasted until October 19, 1987. That day the market fell so fast and furiously that portfolio insurers couldn't liquidate their positions swiftly enough to protect against loses. The market dropped 20% in one day, and according to Rubinstein, 20% of the sales of stocks and index futures that day were from portfolio insurers who would have sold more if they could have, making it all that much harder for the market to stagger back to its feet.

After that experience the Securities and Exchange Commission (SEC) wanted to encourage the development of low cost equity basket-type products not associated with the futures market which had not impressed regulators with its resilience under stress.

Index Participation Shares

That's when a number of equity basket products started being developed in parallel. The first of these was Index Participation Shares (IPS) which came in a few varieties. The most popular was AMEX's "Equity Index Participations," based on the S&P 500 Index.

IPS were simply stocks that paid returns linked directly to the underlying index. They could be sold on the secondary market or redeemed for cash—but not for the underlying securities because there weren't any secu-

rities behind them. The IPS were a claim on the return of a futures contract on the S&P Index. The first IPS started trading in May of 1989. Not
long after a Chicago court ruled that IPS were actually futures and should
trade on a futures exchange and be under the jurisdiction of the
Commodity Futures Trading Commission. No futures exchange picked up
the innovative product, possibly because they didn't want it competing
with their own index futures, and IPS died.

SuperTrust

Meanwhile Leland, O'Brien and Rubinstein were hatching a different
portfolio product. In 1988 they made an application to the SEC for something they called a SuperTrust that was to hold a basket of securities identical to the S&P 500 Index. It was a complicated product containing
SuperShares and SuperUnits. It took LOR five years to painfully wend
their product through the SEC. By the time it emerged, AMEX was just a
few months short of launching its own portfolio product which turned out
to be kryptonite for SuperTrust.[2] Despite having the biggest launch in the
history of any fund product to that point, (US$2 billion), SuperTrust failed,
partly because it was too complicated. AMEX's elegantly simple product,
the famous Spiders, made it to the market three months after SuperUnits,
in January 1993, and completely eclipsed LOR's regulatory groundbreaking
product—the very first exchange traded fund proper.

TIPS

The demise of IPS in the U.S. was something of a stroke of good fortune for Canada because the Toronto Stock Exchange had an IPS of its
own sort in the making. In March of 1990 the TSE launched TIPS,
Toronto 35 Index Participation Units, based on the Toronto 35 Index, a collection of Canada's biggest and most liquid companies with wide industry
representation. Unlike the American IPs, however, TIPS was a trust containing a basket of securities matching the Toronto 35 Index. The trust
issued units as a claim on the trust. These units could be bought or sold on
the TSE, or in sufficiently large numbers, redeemed for the underlying
securities in the trust. TIPS was immediately embraced by institutional
investors and went on to popularity even among retail investors. So, by
some odd reversal of our usual national fortune, the TSE launched a world
first: the first successful ETF.

According to Gord Walker, Director of Derivatives, Markets and Marketing at the TSE from 1991 to 1996, TIPS was the model for Spiders. He believes a copy of a TIPS prospectus was attached to the SEC application for Spiders. Walker was responsible for launching and overseeing Canada's second ETF in 1995, called HIPs, based on the Toronto Stock Exchange 100 Index. (TIPS and HIPs were rebranded into TIPS 35 and TIPS 100 in 1999.)

Although TIPS and HIPs were an attempt to bring Bay Street to Main Street, the products were far less popular with retail investors than the TSE expected. They were, however, hugely popular with institutional investors because of their convenience and their penchant to run on very little. TIPS and HIPs did not have a management fee. These ETFs repaid the TSE for the operating expenses of the fund only through interest made from lending the securities of the fund to short sellers, and the interest the fund earned on stock dividends, which were banked before their quarterly distribution to unit holders. That worked out to .04% annually, and as it turned out, less than the fund needed to pay its own way.

Walker is convinced that more individual Canadian investors would have bought TIPS had the retail investment community had more of a motivation to sell the product. TIPS, like all ETFs, are up against mutual funds, many of which pay a sales commission and regular trailer fees for as long as the client holds the fund. An ETF sale nets a broker a small stock trading commission, which is nothing like the 5% or so of a mutual fund sale, and usually nothing more thereafter.

Nevertheless, institutional interest in TIPS was strong, and TIPS became among the most actively traded securities on the TSE. In a way, TIPS was a victim of its own success. Its very economical MER of .04% forced the TSE to subsidize the operating expenses of the fund and tied up resources that could be directed to its equity listing services, so the exchange decided to off load responsibility for the product onto an outside provider. Barclays Global Investors Canada Limited won the contract to manage TIPS by merging it with the already existing i60 Fund. In March of 2000, TIPS 35 and TIPS 100 were both merged with BGI Canada's i60 Fund and its comparably robust .17% MER. The combined entity made the i60 amongst the largest mutual funds in the Canadian equity category. At $5 billion that's enough money to keep even a big company interested in maintaining the product.

Spiders, of course, went on to great fame and glory, too, even if it did have to crawl over the bodies of a few dead products.

ETFs Today: Spiders, WEBS, Diamonds, Qubes, VIPERs

Spiders, appropriately enough, spawned WEBS (World Equity Benchmark Shares) in 1996. These ETFs were based on international equity indices and are now known as iShares MSCI Country Funds. There are now an astonishing 21 of these representing the indices of as many countries. Before there could be eentsy-weensy ETFs, the arachnid theme was abandoned in favour of more industrial sounding names like Diamonds (January 1998) based on the Dow Jones Industrial Average and Qubes (March 1999) for the Nasdaq 100 Index. Nearly 70 more ETFs have followed. Perhaps the biggest indication of the irreversible momentum of ETFs was Vanguard Group's launch on May 31, 2001 of its own ETF, the first in what is expected to be a series of VIPERs (Vanguard Index Participation Equity Receipts). Vanguard's first ETF is based on an optimized basket of Vanguard's Total Stock Market Index Fund which is itself based on an optimized basket of about 3,400 stocks in the Wilshire 5000 Index. The Total Stock Market VIPER is an ETF, and simultaneously, a new share class of Vanguard's existing index fund. The company has already filed with the SEC to launch another ETF tied to the Wilshire 4500. A pioneer in index mutual funds for the retail investor, Vanguard is one of the largest mutual fund companies in American with a staggering US$550 billion under administration. They clearly see the writing on the wall.

Canadian and International ETFs

BGI Canada's i60s entry into Canada in 1999 led the way for ten other ETFs from BGI and one slated for launch in August of 2001. TD Asset Management and State Street Global Advisors introduced their own ETF products this year, and these are almost certainly not the last from them or from others. New exchange traded products are bursting forth like daffodils in the spring and product sponsors are savvy enough to understand the future importance of these flowers. In Canada alone there's $416 billion tied up in mutual funds. Why shouldn't product manufacturers be trying to siphon some of that money for themselves?

Global markets are introducing ETFs rapidly, too. Domestic and regional ETFs are traded on exchanges around the world—on DeutscheBorse, Euronext in Amsterdam and Paris, in Sweden, Switzerland, the United Kingdom, Hong Kong, India, Israel, Singapore and South Africa. Thailand is even expected to be offering ETFs soon.

Different regulatory regimes spur innovative ETFs. Germany was the first country to introduce actively managed ETFs in November of 2000. Six months later, Germany had seven index-based ETFs (most run by HypoVereinsbank AG) and eleven actively managed ETFs sponsored by DWS Investments, a unit of Deutsche Bank. The Deutsche Borse of Frankfurt restricts the actively managed ETFs on its exchange from trading beyond a set bid/ask spread. It does this because the normal arbitraging that keeps index ETF prices in line with their NAVs isn't available for the active funds. Institutional shareholders of actively managed ETFs learn about their portfolio positions with a two-day delay. Retail investors, on the other hand, get one-month-old information. Trying to arbitrage on that stale information would be like trying to make a sandwich with bread that was eaten a day ago. North American regulators want to keep a level playing field between retail and institutional investors, so it's highly unlikely such a disclosure regime would float on this side of the pond.

German institutional investors seem to favour the index products while the actively managed ETFs are more popular with retail investors. In less than a year and a half, actively managed ETFs have attracted over US$16 billion. The popularity of ETFs in Germany owes something to costs of traditional mutual funds in at country that usually carry a sales charge, annual management fees and bank deposit fees.[3]

In Canada and the U.S., ETFs are required to provide continuous portfolio disclosure, which poses a problem for active fund managers who don't want to show their hand too flagrantly. There's good reason for that reluctance. If market participants get wind of a manager's intention to buy a security, others will buy it up first and push the price up before the manager has finished establishing his position. Similarly, once its known that a manager is selling a significant position in a stock, others will sell and grind down the price. That manager's cold sweat is known as "front running." Jurisdictions that permit actively managed ETFs have to come to some kind of compromise between continuous disclosure and portfolio confidentiality. Germany has one solution. It wouldn't fly in North America and it will be interesting to see what develops in other parts of the world.

BNP Paribas Asset Management Australia filed a prospectus in April for four actively managed ETFs under the Access brand. They were expected to have MERs of 1.85% to 2.1%, but would have an innovative savings plan option for a minimum $100 a month with a minimum $2,000 initial investment. At the time of this book's printing, they had been approved by Australian regulators and had just begun trading. Before BNP's announcement, Australia had one index ETF sponsored by Salomon Smith Barney but State Street Global Advisors was hot on their heels and expected to launch one of their own soon. BNP's Access ETFs are the first actively managed ETFs in the Asia/Pacific area.

The appetite for actively managed ETFs may be enormous. One mutual fund research company, FRC, expects actively managed ETFs to attract US$60 billion in their first year and as much as $500 billion within five years in the U.S. alone.[4] When it took nine years for index ETFs to garner $66 billion, FRC has serious expectations.

Whether or not actively managed ETFs take off, there's still plenty of room for the plain index variety to proliferate. ETFs are now listed on the major European bourses and in Singapore, Japan and Hong Kong. Proposed ETFs are in the works in Korea and India, and China may not be too far behind as China now has an equities index, the FTSE/Xinhau China 25 Index, which is seemingly designed for basket products like ETFs and index funds.

Cross-listings

There's also a flurry of cross-listing going on with ETFs globally. Cross-listing allows the securities from one exchange to be traded on another exchange. This gives retail investors the chance to buy and sell stocks that would otherwise never be available to them, and it increases the liquidity of the cross-listed security. (Institutional investors often have foreign intermediaries through which they can trade foreign securities.) The American Stock Exchange has arranged with Euronext (formed from the merger of the Amsterdam, Brussels and Paris exchanges) and the Singapore Exchange to offer some U.S. ETFs. Talk is underway with Australia and Japan for similar cross-listing opportunities.

Nasdaq has also announced plans to list Japanese ETFs on its electronic market in both the U.S. and Europe in the future. Nasdaq seems to have plans to provide a global trading platform for ETFs via its network in the U.S., Europe and Japan.

Cross-listing isn't good just for foreign investors. It also has benefits for North American investors when the cross-listing gives reciprocal access. Suppose you own an iShares MSCI Hong Kong and you sell it at 11 a.m. Toronto time. You get a price as of 11 a.m. Toronto time, but the underlying securities are 12 hours away tucked in their beds. Your 11 a.m. price actually reflects the market sentiment about what the Hong Kong market will do when it wakes up, so it is not a perfect tracking device. If, on the other hand, you owned a Hong Kong ETF that tracked the Hong Kong market, your 11 a.m. sell order would be executed the minute the Hong Kong market opened at that exact market price.

The flexibility to trade domestic ETFs in their own time zone will enhance tracking and increase liquidity. It's the financial markets equivalent of free trade.

ETFs may not just be the next generation of mutual funds: they may turn out to be the financial enterprise that boldly goes where no financial instrument has gone before.

The Evolution of ETFs

1978 Program trading, trading large blocks of different stocks simultaneously based on a computer program's instructions, starts.

1982 LOR's portfolio insurance takes off with the introduction of index futures in the U.S.

1987 October stock market crash puts the lie to portfolio insurance as it was designed. Regulators call for a different kind of stock basket product.

1988 LOR files a proposal to the SEC for a SuperTrust with SuperUnits and SuperShares, the first exchange traded funds.

1989 Index Participation Shares trade on AMEX and the Philadelphia Exchange. Shortly thereafter a Chicago court rules them futures and so eligible for trading on a futures exchange only. No futures exchange picks up the product and it is discontinued.

1990 Toronto 35 Index Participation Units launched by the TSE, becoming the first successful ETF in the world.

1992 SuperTrust units are traded on AMEX in November but are quickly eclipsed by a simpler product, Spiders.

1993 Spiders land on AMEX in January.

1996 WEBS (now iShares MSCI Funds) launched.

1998 Diamonds (Dow Jones Industrial Average ETF) launched

1999 Qubes (Nasdaq 100 ETF) launched in March and becomes one of the most heavily traded securities in the U.S.

2000 More than 75 new ETFs were launched worldwide.

2001	May 31 Vanguard Group launches its long awaited initial VIPERs ETF.

2001	July 31 New York Stock Exchange begins trading Spiders, Diamonds and Qubes.

ETFs in the Future: Global Sector Funds

The most immediate development in ETFs is probably going to be the introduction of global sector ETFs. These would be ETFs specializing in stocks in one particular industry sector but selected from countries around the world. Studies are beginning to show that good timing of sector plays can boost returns, and this applies in big letters to sectors across country boundaries.[5] Given the difficulty in individual stock picking—especially internationally—ETFs are the ideal product for sector plays. You can move in and out of them quickly and because no ETF so far hedges foreign currencies, you get full exposure to the currency effect on all the international stocks.

More Variety

ETFs in general are certain to become far more varied in kind. The world's first bond ETFs are in Canada with more of these to follow in the U.S. Even fully RRSP eligible ETFs are emerging to send clone mutual funds back to the test tube. In 2001 BGI Canada introduced the i500R Fund, a fully RRSP eligible fund pegged to the S&P 500 Index. Canada is also soon expected to get its first HOLDRS.

ETF innovations will not be limited to ordinary stocks and bonds. There's already at least three real estate investment trust (REIT) ETFs in the U.S. As long as it can be bought and sold with real time pricing, anything can be thrown into an ETF structure. A Lehman Brothers' report on ETFs written in September of 2000 predicted a hedge fund of ETFs would follow active and leveraged active fund ETFs.

Pools of ETFs

More immediately, it's not hard to imagine ETFs made up of pools of other ETFs. Spectrum Investments has already done this within a mutual fund. "Tactonics" is Spectrum's new global tactical asset allocation fund. It contains as many as 20 ETFs dynamically managed with a proprietary trend spotting computer model. Clearly, ETFs were the best tool the fund managers could find to implement their strategy. Unfortunately, Tactonics'

MER at more than 2% will still be as high as any other mutual fund. An ETF holding other ETFs in a dynamic asset allocation could do something very similar without the drawbacks of a mutual fund structure.

Actively Managed ETFs

So far the North American regulatory hurdle of continuous disclosure is holding back the introduction of actively managed ETFs, but industry sources do not think that will prove insurmountable. Even with current regulatory restrictions, though, exchange traded baskets of securities will continue to proliferate here and around the world because they're more efficient and flexible. Index mutual funds, step aside. Active funds, watch out.

Derivatives on ETFs

Mark Rubinstein who, along with his colleagues at LOR, was the U.S. ETF pioneer, feels the time is ripe for another generation of ETFs that have options associated with them as did his SuperUnits.

> Our product really [was] better than ETFs today because you could break it up and do more with it... I'm going to be quite surprised if some exchange traded funds don't effectively start doing this. In today's context it's going to be a lot easier to get regulatory approval for things like we were doing. There's a lot more awareness of derivatives and options.

Perhaps Rubinstein's design of options within units won't materialize but there are other ways to achieve the same end. The Montréal Exchange is expected to come out with options on a number of BGI's sector ETFs. A futures market in Canada on sector ETFs may not be far behind.

The Competition

All good products inspire competition and ETFs are no exception. Two Internet services in the U.S. allow American investors to buy and sell ready-made portfolios for a flat monthly fee. FOLIO*fn* at *www.foliofn.com* offers over 100 portfolios that cover markets, sectors, risk levels and famous investment strategies like the Dogs of the Dow. Each portfolio can hold up to 50 stocks. The Web site says, "It's as easy as selecting a mutual or index fund." What's more, FOLIO*fn* has the even more remarkable feature of allowing investors to customize the contents of their portfolios with up to two trades a day in as many as three portfolios—all for US$29.95 a month or US$295 a year. That's the equivalent of holding CDN$175,000 worth of i60s with an MER of .17% without trading commission. Quite a deal especially when you think of the added flexibility it gives you over a fixed ETF portfolio. Anything less than $175,000, though, and a straight ETF portfolio is considerably cheaper over two years or more, even with initial brokerage commissions. Hot on FOLIO*fn*'s heels is Netfolio (*www.netfolio.com*), a similar concept with a US$20 a month or US$200 a year subscription and immediate trading. Netfolio's chairman, CEO and founder is James O'Shaughnessy, the famous U.S. money manager and author of *What Works on Wall Street*. O'Shaughnessy was quoted in the *Wall Street Journal* as saying "I think the era of the communal bath is over and everybody's getting their own shower. We're seeing a move from the mutual to the personal."

Nancy Smith, Vice President of Investor Education for FOLIO*fn*, says there are plans to expand their service to Canada but no official date has been set. She points out that ETFs can be bought through their service and held in their accounts, or an investor can select one of the indices offered at *www.foliofn.com* and even customize it if desired. There's no MER or any other expenses beyond the monthly or annual fee. Of course, there isn't a big selection of famous-name indices to chose from at this point either.

Should these do-it-yourself ready-made but customizable portfolio services catch on, ETF sponsors might very well be forced to join them at their own game and radically revise the nature of their offering. Time will tell just how active investors ultimately want to become even when they're aiming for a predominantly passive investment approach. Don't give up your day job just yet.

Conventional mutual funds are not likely to lie down and play dead either. Mutual fund companies will almost certainly launch their own ETFs, as Vanguard has done. Sensing the change in the wind, some fund companies might even attempt to convert some of their existing funds to exchange traded funds.[6]

In a move that's got the American Stock Exchange worried, the New York Stock Exchange will begin trading the three most popular ETFs on its exchange on July 31, 2001. For the first three months of trading in Qubes, Diamonds and Spiders, the NYSE will not charge transaction fees. ETFs are the mainstay of AMEX, which has lost stock listings to NYSE and Nasdaq. This competitive move by NYSE underscores the market importance of these products less than ten years old in the U.S. and the promising future they harbour.

We've just entered the third inning of ETF development. Competition among the sponsors will continue to spawn more choice and innovative offerings. The game is only beginning to heat up. Tens of products are in the on-deck batting circle now. (See Appendix C for a list of products soon to be launched.) In two years there will be many more players and we can only guess what they'll look like. I hope I'll be back to report on them—with you.

Are ETFs the Death of Mutual Funds?: An Interview with FRC's Gavin Quill

Financial Research Corporation (FRC) provides competitive market research and analysis to the mutual fund industry from Boston, Massachusetts. Gavin Quill is a Senior Vice President with FRC and the Director of Research Studies. He oversees primary source research on many mutual fund industry topics and last year co-authored an FRC study entitled, *The Future of Exchange Traded Funds: An Emerging Alternative to Mutual Funds*. Below is an interview from July 10, 2001.

Gavin Quill: Last year you had constant repetition, "ETFs will inherit the earth." From conference to conference, everybody was trumpeting these things that were going to compound at stratospheric growth rates and just gouge the heart out of the mutual fund industry. I don't foresee that at all. One of the major findings of a study we did at Financial Research Corp. last year was that the majority of the cannibalization of assets into the new crop of ETFs was coming, not from mutual funds, but from individual stocks. Obviously ETFs are a hybrid between mutual funds and individual stocks and you'd expect them to draw business from aficionados of both products, but what we're finding is that the majority of the redistribution is coming from people who buy individual securities who are taking a more pooled approach. The press has really overplayed the death of the mutual fund.

I do have fairly optimistic views about the long-term prospects of exchange traded funds. But the optimism is built more around the successful introduction of actively managed ETFs than around the long-term substantial growth of the index-based versions.

On the index based side of ETFs we're forecasting we'll be around $200 to $250 billion four years out from now in the U.S. You can't deny that is substantial growth from the $70 billion we have now. But it's not going to eliminate index-based mutual funds and it's certainly not even going to scratch actively managed mutual funds, where you have $4 trillion in equity funds. You will not find an index-based ETF industry growing in the U.S. or Canada that would in any way parallel the mutual fund industry that already exists; at least while ETFs are index-based only.

There is a compelling superiority to ETFs versus index mutual funds in most cases. Nevertheless, you're not going to see the elimination of index mutual funds. In the real world, there is substantial inertia to investor behaviour. They stick with what's working well enough. They don't care that something has 10 basis points lower management fee or that it gives them some additional flexibility that they aren't sure they will ever use. Institutions behave more rationally than individual investors do and are far faster in aggregate to adopt the next superior product. Clearly, ETFs are superior in many fashions for the retail investor assuming he cared about those features and understood them fully.

But when [actively managed ETFs] are finally created, the dynamics of ETFs will change. People like actively managed funds—rationally or irrationally. In the mutual fund world only 10% of equity mutual fund assets are in index funds and that's after a gigantic run up in the last six or seven years. For whatever reason, individuals overwhelmingly prefer active management over passive management. This preference puts a ceiling on the potential long-term growth of ETFs as long as they are limited to indexed products. However, once you move to actively managed option, now you've got a viable competitor to the mutual fund industry.

I have no doubt that actively managed ETFs will eventually be approved by the Securities Exchange Commission. My expectation would be that we might see the first products brought to market in the forth quarter of 2002 or the first quarter of 2003. I see such a lucrative opportunity and so many benefits ultimately for the investing community. We have been forecasting in the first five years from the first actively managed ETF, that we would get to about $250 billion in the U.S. with an outside possibility of $500 billion. That's out of a pool of roughly $3.5 trillion of actively managed equity funds held by retail investors. Even under the very best case, 500 billion out of $3.5 trillion, that's only one-seventh the size, and it would clearly still not annihilate *the mutual fund industry. It would just be a respectable compliment to the mutual fund giant.*

Now along comes FOLIOfn. I am so impressed with what the folio people have created, the superiority and the innovation built into their products. It is very commendable and it will be superior for those who want to avail themselves of it. But I'm skeptical about how many people will want to avail themselves of it. You cannot extrapolate from what the very small minority of techno-savvy early adopters do and what the overwhelming majority of busy non-technologically focused, happy-with-good-enough investors are going to do. Most people want active management, and basically, the folio world is the the do-it-yourselfer world which is declining rapidly.

Folios are not primarily competition for mutual funds. They are, even more than ETFs, competition for individually held stocks. I think folios are going to draw their assets away from brokerage platforms. They are tremendous, exciting, superior on many dimensions, but I think it will be a long slow market penetration. But these could actually become very, very dominant helping financial professionals, who want to create their own portfolios for their clients.

The area of real growth for the next year or two while we're waiting for actively managed funds will be overseas. It's exploding in Europe, Australia and Asia. We're going to see the same kind of proliferation of products and assets that we've seen in the U.S. especially because of cross-listing. The AMEX is doing a tremendous job in being able to cross-list with Euronext and Singapore, and working with Japan and Australia for next year to get a whole lot more liquidity into these products.

I expect over the next decade we will see ETFs, mutual funds and folios all thrive together in the U.S., Canada and around the globe. Growing wealth, increasing pools of financial assets, retirement privatization and low interest rates, will create a prosperous environment with plenty of opportunity for each of these vehicles to grow at a healthy pace without having to kill off one of the others to succeed.

For more information on the history of equity baskets see *The Handbook of Equity Derivatives* (revised edition), Francis, Jack Clark, William W. Toy, J. Gregg Whittaker, editors; New York: John Wiley & Sons, Inc., 2000; "Index Participation Units," by Eric Kirzner, pp. 100–120; "Exchange-Traded Equity Funds—Genesis, Growth, and Outlook," by Gary L. Gastineau and Clifford J. Weber, pp. 121–141. Also, "Why Financial Instruments Fail or Succeed," by Jack Clark Francis, pp.631–650.

On SuperShares and SuperUnits, a fascinating product that was 15 years ahead of its time, see Mark Rubinstein's extraordinary Web site, *www.in-the-money.com*. Click on articles about SuperShares. Also interesting is his discussion of the development of portfolio insurance.

For an accessible and entertaining explanation of portfolio insurance see *Capital Ideas: The Improbable Origins of Modern Wall Street*, Bernstein, Peter L. New York: The Free Press, 1992; pp.269–294.

Notes

1) The history of index futures and other derivative products is instructively and entertainingly told in "The Whence, How and Why of OTC Equity Derivatives: An Introduction to OTC Derivatives for the Financial Investor," by Bruce Collins, Ph.D., Associate Professor of Finance, Western Connecticut State University. The paper is available at *www.wcsu.ct.stateu.edu/finance/newsletter/n/fall98.htm*.

2) Mark Rubinstein was one of three principals of Leland, O'Brien, Rubinstein Associates, Inc. (LOR), the California-based company that invented portfolio insurance, and subsequently, the first ETF in U.S., SuperTrust. The company is no longer active and Rubinstein remains a professor of finance at the University of California at Berkeley. He very generously gave an extensive interview for this book. Here is an excerpt from that May 2001 interview, demonstrating so poignantly the heartbreak of pioneers.

> *Rubinstein: We feel frustrated about the fact that now exchange traded funds are the big deal and even though we had the idea first, at least in terms of applying it, we didn't make it. We were a little company. We feel we've been cheated out of the intellectual credit for this. We were the first people to actually do it.*
>
> *We spent millions of dollars on attorneys trying to convince the SEC to allow us to do this. We were doing something that was obviously right and would be in the interest of investors. If ordinary options are in the interests of investors, these certainly would be. If index funds and mutual funds are in the interest of the investors, these are. So it made no sense to me. They asked us to go through all kinds of hoops and we couldn't just sit down at a table and talk to them.*
>
> *Prime and Scores* had already been approved and our product had an even better reason to exist because we were not trading calls on individual stocks. We were going to make it possible to buy calls on a widely diversified portfolio, and generally speaking, that's better for investors than individual stocks.*
>
> *But the SEC said they were ashamed that they had approved Primes and Scores. They didn't like them and they were going to make us go through a very long procedure instead of a short cut procedure for approval. It ended up taking five years. If the SEC had not done that, our business might be a lot different today.*
>
> *By the time they ended up approving [SuperShares], index securities in general and options were becoming more popular and there was a variety of*

them. AMEX ended up going ahead with their own product [Spiders], *but I'm sure if we'd gotten our product out a year or two before, they wouldn't have gone ahead and they probably would have helped us more in marketing. We were way ahead of the game in our thinking.*

John O'Brien...convinced large companies to buy huge quantities of SuperUnits and then break them up and sell them off to the market. I think we had the largest initial launch of any fund to that point, $2 billion.

Our product was really better than ETFs today because you could break it up and do more with it. Unfortunately, in the practical world there are other hurdles. The SEC won't let you do it, they'll put burdens on you.

The Achilles heel of our product was its complexity. [Because of this] *the SEC said every secondary transaction must come with a prospectus. We told the brokerages you can sell* [SuperUnits] *just like an ordinary stock, but then there was the prospectus problem. Brokerage companies didn't want to change their procedures until the product got popular.*

LOR exists as a shell. That's what happened to us. It shows you that when you try to innovate in financial markets, you're probably going to fail and you have to get the product just right; otherwise, someone else will come in who makes it just a little bit better and take the whole market, which is basically what Spiders did.

SuperUnits and SuperShares stopped trading in 1995.

*"Primes and Scores" were a popular but unusual product first introduced in 1983 by a company called Americus. Here's how Professor Rubinstein explains them in his unpublished paper "SuperTrust," available on his Web site, *www.in-the-money.com* by clicking on "Mark Rubinstein" and scrolling down the list of articles. The excerpt below is from page 8 of Rubinstein's paper.

The first trust was based on shares of AT&T. For each share of AT&T a shareholder turned over to Americus, he was issued a trust unit. In turn, the investor could split the unit into a SCORE and a PRIME. At the end of five years, the SCORE received AT&T shares with a market value equal to the capital gains above a preset "termination value" earned over the period (if any). The PRIME received all the cash dividends, AT&T shares equal to the remaining capital value of the trust, and shareholder voting rights.

A recombined PRIME and SCORE could be redeemed for a unit at any time and a unit could also be redeemed at any time. There were 28 different stocks being used in these Americus Trusts in 1988. An unfavourable taxing ruling in 1986 made the creation of any more of these trusts impractical. They have all since expired.

3) Coleen Moses, SEI Investments, April 24, 2001 e-mail broadcast.

4) Elba Vasquez, Vice President, Financial Research Corp. as referenced in "Actively Managed ETFs: Coming Soon to an Exchange Near You?", *www.TheStreet.com*, May 24, 2001.

5) See "The Global ETF Investor: Conference Highlights: Slicing the World—the Country versus Sector Allocation Debate," Salomon Smith Barney Equity Research publication, May 22, 2001.

6) An article written by Gary L. Gastineau, Senior Vice President at AMEX, and Clifford J, Weber, Vice President at AMEX, has suggested that even though it is too early to say for sure, it is possible that after a certain date in the future most or all new mutual funds will be exchange traded. "[T]he facts that exchange mtraded funds have some attractive characteristics not available in conventional funds and that these funds are frequently less costly for their sponsors to create and maintain, suggests that substantial gains in market share are likely." p.140, "Exchange-Traded Equity Funds—Genesis, Growth, and Outlook," *The Handbook of Equity Derivatives* (revised edition), Francis, Jack Clark, et al., editor. New York: John Wiley & Sons Inc, 2000.

Part Four

Appendix A
Fact Sheets on all Canadian ETFs

iUnits™S&P®/TSE™ 60 Index Participation Fund   Large Cap

Pricing and Fund Data

	June 29/01	52 Week Range
Price	$44.40	H $69.65
		L $40.45
Fund Ticker Symbol		XIU
Benchmark Ticker		SPTSE
MER		0.17%
Fund Manager		BGI Canada
Inception Date		Sept. 29/99
Net Assets		$4.53MM
Shares Outstanding (000)		93,632
Avg. Daily Trading Vol. (Jun/01)		$54.4MM
Underlying Securities		60
Original Index Divisor		1/10
Options Available		Yes
RSP Eligibility		100%

Distributions

	Income	Cap. Gains
Frequency	Qtrly	Yr-End

History (per unit)

	2000	2001YTD
Dividends	$0.42	$0.34
Return of Capital	$0.06	$0
Capital Gains	$1.67	$0
Total	$2.15	$0.34

Sector Exposure (%) June 29/01

Financials	30.7
Energy	12.1
Materials	12.0
Information Technology	11.8
Industrials	11.0
Telecommunications Srvcs.	7.6
Consumer Discretionary	6.3
Utilities	4.5
Health Care	2.0
Consumer Staples	1.4

Top Ten Holdings (%)

Nortel Networks	8.3
Royal Bank of Canada	6.2
BCE	6.1
Toronto Dominion Bank	4.5
Bombardier B	4.6
Bank of Nova Scotia	4.2
Alcan	3.8
Manulife Financial	3.8
Bank of Montréal	3.7
CIBC	3.6
Top Ten Total %	48.8

iUnits i60 fund vs. Total Return S&P/TSE 60 Index

Performance %   June 29/01

	1 Mo	3 Mo	YTD	1Yr	3 Yr	5 Yr	10 Yr
Market Price	-5.54	-0.03	-15.67	-27.92	-	-	-
Benchmark Index	-5.32	0.86	-15.15	-26.95	3.04	12.56	12.27

Fund Description

The iUnits S&P/TSE 60 Index Participation Fund (i60) is an open-ended mutual fund trust, listed and traded on the Toronto Stock Exchange (TSE), designed to replicate the performance of the S&P/TSE 60 Index. The Index consists of 60 large cap, liquid stocks balanced across 10 industry sectors and represents approximately 60% of the whole market. The Index is market capitalized weighted, float adjusted and is rebalanced quarterly.

Source: BGI Canada

iUnits™S&P®/TSE™ 60 Capped Index Fund   Large Cap

Pricing and Fund Data

	June 29/01	52 Week Range
Price	$49.15	H $52.80
		L $47.20
Fund Ticker Symbol		XIC
Benchmark Ticker		SPTSEC
MER		0.17%
Fund Manager		BGI Canada
Inception Date		Feb. 16/01
Net Assets		$262.55MM
Shares Outstanding (000)		5,323
Avg. Daily Trading Vol. (Jun/01))		$1.24MM
Underlying Securities		60
Original Index Divisor		1/10
Options Available		No
RSP Eligibility		100%

Distributions

	Income	Cap. Gains
Frequency	Qtrly	Yr-End

History (per unit)

	2001YTD
Dividends	$0.05
Return of Capital	$0
Capital Gains	$0
Total	$0.05

Sector Exposure (%)   June 29/01

Financials	30.8
Energy	12.2
Materials	12.1
Information Technology	11.6
Industrials	11.0
Telecommunications Srvcs.	7.6
Consumer Discretionary	6.3
Utilities	4.5
Health Care	2.0
Consumer Staples	1.4

Top Ten Holdings (%)

Nortel Networks	8.0
Royal Bank of Canada	6.3
BCE	6.0
Bombardier B	4.6
Toronto Dominion Bank	4.6
Bank of Nova Scotia	4.3
Bank of Montréal	3.7
Manulife Financial	3.9
CIBC	3.6
Alcan	3.8
Top Ten Total %	48.8

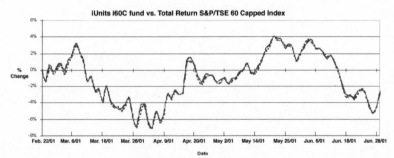

iUnits i60C fund vs. Total Return S&P/TSE 60 Capped Index

Performance %   June 29/01

	1 Mo	3 Mo	YTD	1Yr	3 Yr	5 Yr	10 Yr
Market Price	-4.65	1.53	-2.76	-	-	-	-
Benchmark Index	-4.42	2.49	-2.58	1.87	11.26	17.86	14.88

Fund Description

The iUnits S&P/TSE 60 Capped Index Fund (i60C) is an open-ended mutual fund trust, listed and traded on the Toronto Stock Exchange (TSE) designed to replicate the S&P/TSE 60 Capped Index. The Index consists of 60 large cap, liquid stocks balanced across 10 industry sectors and represents approximately 60% of the whole market. The Index is a constrained market capitalized weighted, float adjusted and rebalanced quarterly or when single company exposure exceeds a weighting of 10%.

Source: BGI Canada

iUnits™S&P®/TSE™ Canadian MidCap Index Fund　　　Mid Cap

Pricing and Fund Data

	June 29/01	52 Week Range
Price	$48.40	H $53.40
		L $45.30
Fund Ticker Symbol		XMD
Benchmark Ticker		SPTSEM
MER		0.55%
Fund Manager		BGI Canada
Inception Date		Mar. 19/01
Net Assets		$73.8MM
Shares Outstanding (000)		1,511
Avg. Daily Trading Vol. (Jun/01)		$412M
Underlying Securities		60
Original Index Divisor		1/4
Options Available		No
RSP Eligibility		100%

Distributions

	Income	Cap. Gains
Frequency	Qtrly	Yr-End

History (per unit) 2001YTD

Dividends	$0.20
Return of Capital	$0
Capital Gains	$0
Total	$0.20

Sector Exposure (%)　June 29/01

Financials	32.7
Information Technology	16.8
Energy	10.5
Industrials	8.9
Consumer Discretionary	8.5
Materials	7.6
Telecommunications Srvcs.	5.4
Consumer Staples	3.9
Utilities	3.5
Healthcare	1.8

Top Ten Holdings (%)

Canada Life Financial	6.3
Ballard Power Systems	5.6
Clarica Life Insurance	5.5
Power Corp.	4.9
George Weston	4.1
Power Financial	3.3
C-Mac Industries	3.2
Trizec Hahn	2.7
Fairfax Financial	2.6
Onex	2.5
Top Ten Total %	40.7

iUnits IMidCap fund vs. Total Return S&P/TSE Canadian MidCap Index

—— XMD　- - - - Total Return S&P/TSE Canadian MidCap Index

Performance %　　　　　　　　　　　　　　　　　　　　June 29/01

	1 Mo	3 Mo	YTD	1Yr	3 Yr	5 Yr	10 Yr
Market Price	-5.92	2.43	-6.29	-	-	-	-
Benchmark Index	-4.57	3.66	-4.72	-18.31	-	-	-

Fund Description

The iUnits S&P/TSE 60 Canadian MidCap Index Fund (iMidCap) is an open-ended mutual fund trust, listed and traded on the Toronto Stock Exchange (TSE) designed to replicate the S&P/TSE Canadian MidCap Index. The Index consists of 60 mid cap stocks balanced across 10 industry sectors and represents the middle tier of Canadian companies listed on the TSE. The Index is market capitalized weighted, float adjusted and rebalanced quarterly.

Source: BGI Canada

Pricing and Fund Data

	June 29/01	52 Week Range
Price	$10.35	H $13.30
		L $8.30
Fund Ticker Symbol		XIT
Benchmark Ticker		SPTSET
MER		0.55%
Fund Manager		BGI Canada
Inception Date		Mar. 19/01
Net Assets		$18.79MM
Shares Outstanding (000)		1,948
Avg. Daily Trading Vol. (Jun/01)		$303M
Underlying Securities		25
Original Index Divisor		1/4
Options Available		No
RSP Eligibility		100%

Distributions

	Income	Cap. Gains
Frequency	Qtrly	Yr-End

History (per unit)   2001YTD

Dividends	$0
Return of Capital	$0
Capital Gains	$0
Total	$0

Sector Exposure (%)   June 29/01

Electronic Equipment & Instrmnts	34.6
Communications Equipmnt	27.5
Software	13.2
Semiconductor Equipment & Prod.	11.8
Computer & Peripherals	6.4
Internet Software & Services	3.6
IT Consulting & Services	2.4

Top Ten Holdings (%)

Nortel Networks	24.4
Celestica	24.0
C-MAC Industries	7.1
ATI Technologies	6.4
Onex	5.5
Research In Motion	5.0
Cognos	4.7
Mitel	3.7
Group CGI A	2.5
Descartes Systems	2.4
Top Ten Total %	85.7

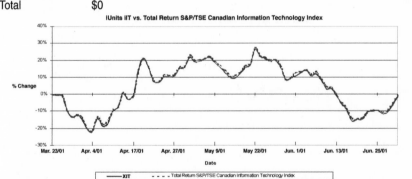

iUnits iIT vs. Total Return S&P/TSE Canadian Information Technology Index

Legend: —— XIT   - - - - Total Return S&P/TSE Canadian Information Technology Index

Performance %   June 29/01

	1 Mo	3 Mo	YTD	1Yr	3 Yr	5 Yr	10 Yr
Market Price	-10.00	12.50	-1.43	-	-	-	-
Benchmark Index	-9.6	13.09	-0.48	-53.69	-	-	-

Fund Description

The iUnits S&P/TSE Canadian Information Technology Index Fund (iIT) is an open-ended mutual fund trust, listed and traded on the Toronto Stock Exchange (TSE) designed to replicate the performance of the S&P/TSE Canadian Information Technology Index. The Index consists of Canadian IT sector companies selected using Standard & Poor's industrial classifications and guidelines for evaluating company capitalization, liquidity and fundamentals. The Index is constrained market capitalization weighted, float adjusted and is rebalanced quarterly or when a single company exposure exceeds a weighting of 25%.

Source: BGI Canada

iUnits™S&P®/TSE™ Canadian Gold Index Fund   Industry Sector

Pricing and Fund Data

	June 29/01	52 Week Range
Price	$30.10	H $35.10
		L $25.75
Fund Ticker Symbol		XGD
Benchmark Ticker		SPTSEG
MER		0.55%
Fund Manager		BGI Canada
Inception Date		Mar. 23/01
Net Assets		$51.00MM
Shares Outstanding (000)		1,698
Avg. Daily Trading Vol. (Jun/01)		$985M
Underlying Securities		7
Original Index Divisor		1/4
Options Available		No
RSP Eligibility		100%

Distributions

Distributions	Income	Cap. Gains
Frequency	Qtrly	Yr-End

History (per unit) 2001YTD

	2001YTD
Dividends	$0.01
Return of Capital	$0
Capital Gains	$0
Total	$0.01

Sector Exposure (%)   June 29/01

Gold	100.0

Holdings (%)

Franco-Nevada Mining	25.7
Placer Dome	24.4
Barrick Gold	23.5
Goldcorp New A	11.2
Meridian Gold	6.2
Agnico Eagle Mines	5.7
Kinross Gold	3.3
Top Ten Total %	100.0

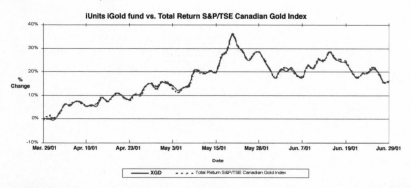

iUnits iGold fund vs. Total Return S&P/TSE Canadian Gold Index

Performance %   June 29/01

	1 Mo	3 Mo	YTD	1Yr	3 Yr	5 Yr	10 Yr
Market Price	-0.95	16.25	16.48	-	-	-	-
Benchmark Index	-0.99	14.71	16.32	10.45	-	-	-

Fund Description

The iUnits S&P/TSE Canadian Gold Index Fund (iGold) is an open-ended mutual fund trust, listed and traded on the Toronto Stock Exchange (TSE) designed to replicate the performance of the S&P/TSE Canadian Gold Index. The Index consists of Canadian Gold sector companies selected using Standard & Poor's industrial classifications and guidelines for evaluating company capitalization, liquidity and fundamentals. The Index is constrained market capitalization weighted, float adjusted and is rebalanced quarterly or when a single company exposure exceeds a weighting of 25%.

Source: BGI Canada

192 — Howard J. Atkinson

iUnits™S&P®/TSE™ Canadian Financials Index Fund   Industry Sector

Pricing and Fund Data

	June 29/01	52 Week Range
Price	$27.20	H $28.20
		L $25.05
Fund Ticker Symbol		XFN
Benchmark Ticker		SPTSEF
MER		0.55%
Fund Manager		BGI Canada
Inception Date		Mar. 23/01
Net Assets		$41.67MM
Shares Outstanding (000)		1,534
Avg. Daily Trading Vol. (Jun/01)		$1.4MM
Underlying Securities		26
Original Index Divisor		1/4
Options Available		No
RSP Eligibility		100%

Distributions

	Income	Cap. Gains
Frequency	Qtrly	Yr-End

History (per unit) 2001YTD

Dividends	$0.07
Return of Capital	$0
Capital Gains	$0
Total	$0.07

Sector Exposure (%)   June 29/01

Banks	60.2
Insurance	26.5
Diversified Financials	10.0
Real Estate	3.2

Top Ten Holdings (%)

Royal Bank of Canada	16.2
Toronto Dominion Bank	11.7
Bank of Nova Scotia	10.6
Bank of Montréal	9.7
Manulife Financial	9.6
CIBC	9.3
SunLife Financial	7.2
Canada Life Financial	3.2
Clarica Life Insurance	2.8
National Bank of Canada	2.6
Top Ten Total %	82.9

iUnits iFin fund vs. Total Return S&P/TSE Canadian Financials Index

—— XFN   - - - - Total Return S&P/TSE Canadian Financials Index

Performance %   June 29/01

	1 Mo	3 Mo	YTD	1Yr	3 Yr	5 Yr	10 Yr
Market Price	0.61	3.48	5.89	-	-	-	-
Benchmark Index	1.14	4.79	6.89	27.24	-	-	-

Fund Description

The iUnits S&P/TSE Canadian Financials Index Fund (iFin) is an open-ended mutual fund trust, listed and traded on the Toronto Stock Exchange (TSE) designed to replicate the performance of the S&P/TSE Canadian Financials Index. The Index consists of Canadian financial sector companies selected using Standard & Poor's industrial classifications and guidelines for evaluating company capitalization, liquidity and fundamentals. The Index is constrained market capitalization weighted, float adjusted and is rebalanced quarterly or when a single company exposure exceeds a weighting of 25%.

Source: BGI Canada

iUnits™S&P®/TSE™ Canadian Energy Index Fund   Industry Sector

Pricing and Fund Data

	June 29/01	52 Week Range
Price	$27.00	H $30.25
		L $25.15
Fund Ticker Symbol		XEG
Benchmark Ticker		SPTSEE
MER		0.55%
Fund Manager		BGI Canada
Inception Date		Mar. 19/01
Net Assets		$40.40MM
Shares Outstanding (000)		1,500
Avg. Daily Trading Vol. (Jun/01)		$427M
Underlying Securities		25
Original Index Divisor		1/4
Options Available		No
RSP Eligibility		100%

Distributions

	Income	Cap. Gains
Frequency	Qtrly	Yr-End

History (per unit)   2001YTD

Dividends	$0
Return of Capital	$0
Capital Gains	$0
Total	$0

Sector Exposure (%)   June 29/01

O&G Exploration & Production	59.0
Integrated Oil & Gas	34.5
O&G Drilling	4.4
O&G Equipment & Services	2.0

Top Ten Holdings (%)

Petro Canada	14.0
Suncor Energy	12.6
Alberta Energy	11.4
Talisman Energy	10.3
Canadian Natural Res.	7.4
Imperial Oil	6.8
Nexen	6.1
Anderson Exploration	4.7
Shell Canada	3.5
Precision Drilling	3.0
Top Ten Total %	79.8

iUnits iEnergy fund vs. Total Return S&P/TSE Canadian Energy Index

Performance %   June 29/01

	1 Mo	3 Mo	YTD	1Yr	3 Yr	5 Yr	10 Yr
Market Price	-9.09	0.33	2.23	-	-	-	-
Benchmark Index	-9.42	0.27	2.24	15.44	-	-	-

Fund Description

The iUnits S&P/TSE Canadian Energy Index Fund (iEnergy) is an open-ended mutual fund trust, listed and traded on the Toronto Stock Exchange (TSE) designed to replicate the performance of the S&P/TSE Canadian Energy Index. The Index consists of Canadian energy sector companies selected using Standard & Poor's industrial classifications and guidelines for evaluating company capitalization, liquidity and fundamentals. The Index is constrained market capitalization weighted, float adjusted and is rebalanced quarterly or when a single company exposure exceeds a weighting of 25%.

Source: BGI Canada

iUnits™ Government of Canada 10-year Bond Fund   Fixed Income

Pricing and Fund Data

	June 29/01	52 Week Range
Price	$25.30	H $27.30
		L $25.20
Fund Ticker Symbol		XGX
Benchmark Ticker		-
MER		0.25%
Fund Manager		BGI Canada
Inception Date		Nov. 20/00
Net Assets		$71.70MM
Shares Outstanding (000)		2,838
Avg. Daily Trading Vol. (Jun/01)		$253M
Underlying Securities		1
Options Available		No
RSP Eligibility		100%

Sector Exposure (%)   June 29/01

CAN 6% 06/01/11

Benchmark Bond Yield: 5.84%

Distributions

	Income	Cap. Gains
Frequency	Semi-annually	Yr-End

History (per unit)

	2000	2001YTD
Interest Income	$0.10	$0.79
Return of Capital	$0.64	$0
Capital Gains	$0	$0
Total	$0.74	$0.79

iUnits iG10 fund vs. Total Return on Benchmark Bond

Performance %   June 29/01

	1 Mo	3 Mo	YTD	1Yr	3 Yr	5 Yr	10 Yr
Market Price	0.30	-1.78	-1.41	-	-	-	-
Benchmark Index	-0.15	-2.14	-1.03	-	-	-	-
Mid Term Cdas Index	-0.04	-1.47	0.26	6.14	4.68	7.81	9.70

Fund Description

The iUnits Government of Canada 10-year Bond Fund (iG10) is an open-ended mutual fund trust, listed and traded on the Toronto Stock Exchange (TSE) designed to replicate the performance of a 10-year Government of Canada (GOC) bond. Approximately once a year, the fund will sell the existing holding and select a new 10-year bond to maintain the term to maturity.

* BGI Canada

iUnits™ Government of Canada 5-year Bond Fund　　　Fixed Income

Pricing and Fund Data

	June 29/01	52 Week Range
Price	$26.70	H $28.15 L $26.65
Fund Ticker Symbol		XGV
Benchmark Ticker		-
MER		0.25%
Fund Manager		BGI Canada
Inception Date		Nov. 20/00
Net Assets		$76.20MM
Shares Outstanding (000)		2,868
Avg. Daily Trading Vol. (Jun/01)		$434M
Underlying Securities		1
Options Available		No
RSP Eligibility		100%

Sector Exposure (%)　　　June 29/01

CAN 7% 12/01/06

Benchmark Bond Yield: 5.61%

Distributions

	Income	Cap. Gains
Frequency	Semi-annually	Yr-End

History (per unit)

	2000	2001YTD
Interest Income	$0.12	$0.92
Return of Capital	$0.75	$0
Capital Gains	$0	$0
Total	$0.87	$0.92

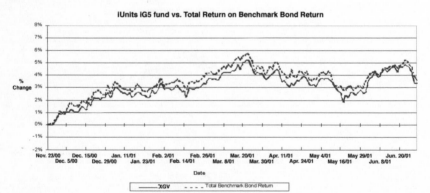

iUnits iG5 fund vs. Total Return on Benchmark Bond Return

Performance %　　　　　　　　　　　　　　　　June 29/01

	1 Mo	3 Mo	YTD	1Yr	3 Yr	5 Yr	10 Yr
Market Price	0.78	-0.67	1.15	-	-	-	-
Benchmark Index	0.08	-0.96	1.11				
*Mid Term Cdas Index	-0.04	-1.47	0.26	6.14	4.68	7.81	9.70

Fund Description

The iUnits Government of Canada 5-year Bond Fund (iG5) is an open-ended mutual fund trust, listed and traded on the Toronto Stock Exchange (TSE) designed to replicate the performance of a 5-year Government of Canada (GOC) bond. Approximately once a year, the fund will sell the existing holding and select a new 5-year bond to maintain the term to maturity.

Source: BGI Canada

iUnits™ S&P® 500 Index RSP Fund   U.S. Equity

Pricing and Fund Data

	July	52 Week
Price	$18.61	H $19.70
		L $18.05
Fund Ticker Symbol		XSP
Benchmark Ticker		SPX
MER		0.30%
Fund Manager		BGI Canada
Inception Date		May 24/01
Net Assets		$18.57MM
Shares Outstanding (000)		1,294
Avg. Daily Trading Vol. (MM)		$828M
Underlying Securities		500
Options Available		No
RSP Eligibility		100%

Distributions

	Income	Cap. Gains
Frequency	Yr-End	Yr-End

History (per unit) 2001YTD

Dividends	$0
Return of Capital	$0
Capital Gains	$0
Total	$0

Sector Exposure (%)   July 27/01

Consumer Discretionary	17.0
Information Technology	15.4
Health Care	14.2
Financials	14.0
Materials	8.2
Utilities	8.0
Industrials	8.0
Consumer Staples	7.4
Energy	5.2
Telecommunication Srvcs	2.6

Top Ten Index Holdings (%)

General Electric	3.9
Microsoft	3.3
Exxon	2.6
Pfizer	2.4
Citigroup	2.3
Wal-Mart	2.2
Intel	1.9
AOL	1.9
AIG	1.8
IBM	1.7
Top Ten Total %	24.0

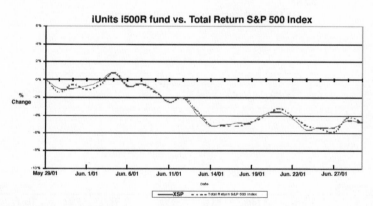

iUnits i500R fund vs. Total Return S&P 500 Index

Performance % (in CAD$)   June 29/01

	1 Mo	3 Mo	YTD	1Yr	3 Yr	5 Yr	10 Yr
Market Price	-3.82	-	-	-	-	-	-
Benchmark Index	-4.23	1.85	-5.61	-12.62	4.96	16.95	18.42

Fund Description

The iUnits S&P 500 Index RSP Fund (i500R) is an open-ended mutual fund trust, listed and traded on the Toronto Stock Exchange (TSE) designed to track the performance of the S&P 500 Index. The Index consists of 500 large cap, liquid stocks balanced across 10 industry sectors and is considered to be the leading barometer of U.S. market activity. The i500R maintains 100% RSP eligibility by investing primarily in S&P 500 Index futures and high quality money market instruments.

Source: BGI Canada

TD TSE 300 Index Fund

Broad Market

Pricing and Fund Data

	June 29/01	52 Week Range
Price	$25.80	H $28.15
		L $24.90
Fund Ticker Symbol		TTF
Benchmark Ticker		TS300
MER		0.25%
Fund Manager		TD Asset Management
Inception Date		Feb. 23/01
Net Assets		$175.53MM
Shares Outstanding		6.78MM
Avg. Daily Trading Vol.		$1.80MM
Underlying Securities		300
Original Index Divisor		1/300
Options Available		No
RSP Eligibility		100%

Distributions	**Income**	**Cap. Gains**
Frequency	Qtrly	Yr-End

History (per unit)	**2001YTD**
Dividends	$0.07
Return of Capital	$0
Capital Gains	$0
Total	$0.07

Sector Exposure (%)   June 29/01

Financials	29.4
Industries	12.1
Information Technology	11.9
Energy	11.8
Materials	11.5
Consumer Discretionary	7.3
Telecommunication Svcs	6.5
Utilities	4.2
Health Care	2.7
Consumer Staples	2.6

Top Ten Holdings (%)

Nortel Networks	6.1
Royal Bank of Canada	4.6
BCE	4.5
Bombardier B	3.4
Toronto Dominion Bank	3.3
Bank of Nova Scotia	3.1
Manulife Financial	2.8
Alcan	2.8
Bank of Montréal	2.7
CIBC	2.7
Top Ten Total %	36.0

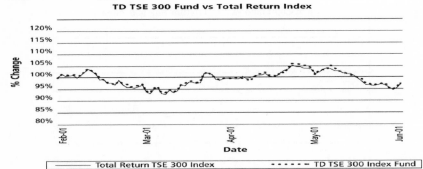

TD TSE 300 Fund vs Total Return Index

Legend: —— Total Return TSE 300 Index   - - - - - TD TSE 300 Index Fund

Performance %   June 29/01

	1 Mo	3 Mo	YTD	1Yr	3 Yr	5 Yr	10 Yr
Market Price	-5.60	1.90	-2.70	-	-	-	-
Benchmark Index	-4.99	2.10	-3.00	-23.11	3.12	10.63	10.69

Fund Description

The TD TSE 300 Index Fund is an open-ended mutual fund trust, listed and traded on the Toronto Stock Exchange (TSE), designed to replicate the performance of the TSE 300 Composite Index. The TSE 300 Composite Index comprises approximately 71% of market capitalization for Canadian-based, TSE listed companies. The broad economic sector coverage has made the TSE 300 the premier indicator of market activity for Canadian equity markets since its launch on January 1, 1977.

Source: TDAM

TD TSE 300 Capped Index Fund   Broad Market

Pricing and Fund Data

	June 29/01	52 Week Range
Price	$29.75	H $32.50
		L $28.65
Fund Ticker Symbol		TCF
Benchmark Ticker		TS300C
MER		0.25%
Fund Manager	TD Asset Management	
Inception Date		Feb. 23/01
Net Assets		$86.88MM
Shares Outstanding		2.90MM
Avg. Daily Trading Vol.		$0.77MM
Underlying Securities		300
Original Index Divisor		1/300
Options Available		No
RSP Eligibility		100%

Distributions	**Income**	**Capital Gains**
Frequency	Qtrly	Yr-End

History (per unit)	**2001YTD**
Dividends	$0.08
Return of Capital	$0
Capital Gains	$0
Total	$0.08

Sector Exposure (%)   June 29/01

Energy	11.8
Materials	11.5
Industries	12.1
Consumer Discretionary	7.3
Consumer Staples	2.6
Health Care	2.7
Financial	29.4
Information Technology	11.9
Telecommunication Svcs	6.5
Utilities	4.2

Top Ten Holdings (%)

Nortel Networks	6.1
Royal Bank of Canada	4.6
BCE Inc.	4.5
Bombardier B	3.4
Toronto Dominion Bank	3.3
Bank of Nova Scotia	3.1
Manulife Financial	2.8
Alcan	2.8
Bank of Montréal	2.7
CIBC	2.7
Top Ten Total %	36.0

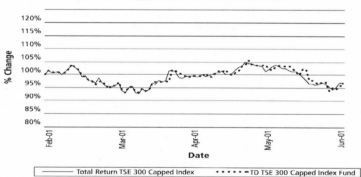

TD TSE 300 Capped Fund vs Total Return Index

Legend: Total Return TSE 300 Capped Index; TD TSE 300 Capped Index Fund

Performance %   June 29/01

	1 Mo	3 Mo	YTD	1Yr	3 Yr	5 Yr	10 Yr
Market Price	-4.80	1.60	-3.10	-	-	-	-
Benchmark Index	-4.84	2.39	-2.92	-6.59	8.03	13.77	12.25

Fund Description

The TD TSE 300 Capped Index Fund is an open-ended mutual fund trust, listed and traded on the Toronto Stock Exchange (TSE), designed to replicate the performance of the TSE 300 Capped Index. The TSE 300 Capped Index includes all of the constituents of the TSE 300 Composite Index. However, the relative weight of any single index constituent is capped at 10% and readjusted quarterly.

Source: TDAM

SSgA Dow Jones Canada 40 Index Participation Fund Large Cap

Pricing and Fund Data

	June 29/01	52 Week Range
Price	$47.00	H $73.40
		L $45.46
Fund Ticker Symbol		DJF
Benchmark Ticker		XLCAN
MER		0.08%
Fund Manager	State Street Global Advisors	
Inception Date		Sept. 25/00
Net Assets		$223MM
Shares Outstanding		4,738,084
Avg. Daily Trading Vol.		$5,501,441
Underlying Securities		40
Original Index Divisor		1/25
Options Available		No
RSP Eligibility		100%

Sector Exposure (%) June 29/01

Basic Materials	10.3
Consumer, Cyclical	4.7
Consumer, Non-Cyclical	1.1
Energy	12.9
Financial	35.7
Health Care	1.4
Industrial	15.9
Technology	10.0
Telecommunications	8.1
Utilities	0.0

Top Ten Holdings (%)

Nortel Networks Corp.	9.4
Royal Bank of Canada	7.0
BCE Inc.	6.5
Toronto-Dominion Bank	5.1
Bombardier Inc. Cl B	4.9
Bank of Nova Scotia	4.8
Manulife Financial Corp.	4.3
Alcan Inc.	4.3
Bank of Montréal	4.3
CIBC	4.1
Top Ten Total %	54.7

Distributions

	Income	Cap. Gains
Frequency	Qtrly	Yr-End

History ($)

	2000	2001YTD
Dividends	$0.07	$0.36
Return of Capital	$0.00	$0.02
Capital Gains	$0	$0
Total	$0.07	$0.38

DJ40 fund vs. DJ 40 Price Return Index

—— DJF closing price - - - - - DJ40 Index

Performance % June 29/01

	1 Mo	3 Mo	YTD	1Yr	3 Yr	5 Yr	10 Yr
Market Price	-7.02	-0.52	-19.10	-	-	-	-
Benchmark Index	-6.23	-0.93	-18.58	-34.02	1.70	10.71	-

Fund Description

The DJ40 Units are units of a trust known as the SSgA Dow Jones Canada 40 Index Participation Fund, whose goal is to track the Dow Jones Canada 40 Index returns. Managed by State Street Global Advisors Ltd, the DJ40 Units allow you to buy an entire portfolio of some of the 40 largest and most liquid Canadian stocks in a single security.

Source: SSgA

Appendix B
Making Sense of the Indices: A Reference Guide to Canadian, U.S., International and Global Indices Associated with ETFs

Buying an ETF is something like buying a house: you've got to decide what kind of house you want before you start looking around. If you need a bungalow there's no point in looking at a two-storey house. You've got to exercise some fundamental selectivity beforehand or you'll likely waste a lot of time and fall in love with a house that doesn't suit your basic needs. An ETF investment should work like that, too. You shouldn't necessarily want to buy the top performing ETF or the one you believe has the best prospects. Before you lay your money on the line, you've first got to decide which index or indices will best suit your portfolio. To do this, you've got to understand the indices the ETF universe is related to. Here, then, are some of the key points about the indices used for ETFs in Canada and the U.S. Find the kind of index you need. Look at the other indices like it, decide on the index you want and then chose an ETF related to it.

First let's clarify a few terms. Because indices reflect the market they are trying to measure, they need to be adjusted to market changes. A significant change in the market value of a stock will affect the weighting of that stock in a market capitalization weighted index. Adjusting for stock weightings is called "rebalancing" the index. Rebalancing is an adjustment to the proportion of the index a company's stock takes up. Deciding what stocks to add or delete from an index is sometimes referred to as "reconstitution," or "constituent rebalancing." Many index sponsors post regular dates for rebalancing and reconstitution along with the criteria for these changes, so money managers who are keenly interested in an index can anticipate changes and work to adjust their holdings in a systematic way. The fewer times an index is adjusted, the more tax efficient its associated ETF will be. The more times it is adjusted, the closer it will pace its market.

Some indices have more movement within than others. The S&P/Barra style indices, for example, bump their constituents around from value and growth generally more than the Dow Jones style indices. That is simply a function of the way the styles are defined. If you want a style-related ETF, take a look at how the styles are determined. This will give you an idea of how much adjustment within the indices might occur so you can weigh the anticipated taxable distributions against the style definition you like best if tax is an issue. Small cap indices graduate their holdings to mid cap indices frequently, too, so these also may have relatively more reconstitution changes than a large cap index, for instance.

Also, you will recall from our previous discussion of indexing, the percentage of outstanding shares available for investment (the "float") affects the investability of an index. Since investability is one of the desiderata of index construction, most contemporary indices are float-adjusted. In other words, the market capitalization weighting is adjusted to reflect the actual market value of the shares available for investment, not just the total number of shares issued by a company. The mechanics of this adjustment are not uniform among index sponsors. For instance, Dow Jones ignores block holdings less than 5% whereas the *Financial Times* index folks who run the FTSE indices will sometimes aggregate these small block holdings and adjust the free-float accordingly. The details of free-float calculation are too technical for our purposes here, but you can usually obtain this information from the index sponsor's Web site. We highly recommend a stroll through Dow Jones Indexes site, *www.djindexes.com* and S&P's Web site, *www.spglobal.com*. They are models of fulsome information on their indices and their maintenance methodology. That's especially handy because S&P administers the major Canadian equity indices.

U.S. Indices

Wilshire 5000 Total Market Index
www.wilshire.com

This is the broadest U.S. equity index with approximately 7,000 stocks and covering about 99% of the U.S. equity market capitalization. It is a market capitalization weighted index that does not adjust for free-floats.

Companies included must be headquartered in the U.S. and publicly traded. Stocks with no easily available price or shares outstanding data are excluded as are some illiquid stocks. Real Estate Investment Trusts (REITs) and limited partnerships are not excluded. Reconstitution is done when necessary. Rebalancing is usually done at the end of each month, but may also occur during the month.

ETF: Vanguard Total Stock Market VIPER* Fund
*This ETF is actually a separate class of the Vanguard Group's Total Stock Market Index Fund, a giant low-cost U.S. index mutual fund. The mutual fund is based on an optimized basket of about 3,400 stocks in the Wilshire 5000 Index. The ETF is a further optimized basket of approximately 1,800 stocks out of the 3,400 in the index fund.

Dow Jones U.S. Total Market Index
www.djindexes.com/jsp/giMethod.jsp

This index captures about 95% of the total U.S. market capitalization and has no fixed number of stocks. It was designed for investability and consists of roughly 1,800 liquid stocks. It excludes foreign stocks, thinly traded stocks, closed-end mutual funds, unit trusts, limited partnerships. REITs, however, are not excluded. It includes all large and mid cap publicly traded stocks, but to preserve the index's overall liquidity, only about half of the small cap market is included.

The overall index is divided into the following ten sectors:

- Consumer, noncyclical
- Consumer, cyclical
- Energy; Financial
- Health Care
- Technology
- Industrials
- Basic Materials
- Telecommunication Services
- Utilities.

Nestled within each of these sectors are various industry groups. For instance, financials includes banks, insurance, real estate and specialty finance. Specialty finance encompasses sub-groups, savings and loans, brokerages, and others.

These indices are free-float adjusted and market cap weighted. They are reconstitued quarterly and when extraordinary corporate events occur.

Rebalancing occurs quarterly unless the number of a company's outstanding shares changes more than 10%, in which case the rebalancing is immediate. Delisted stocks are not replaced until a reconstitution date.

ETFs: iShares DJ U.S. Total Market Index Fund

There is also an iShares ETF for each of the ten DJ U.S. Total Market sectors. A few select industry groups also sport iShare ETFs. For example, *iShares DJ U.S. Chemical Index Fund; iShares DJ U.S. Financial Services Composite Index Fund; iShares DJ U.S. Real Estate Index Fund; iShares DJ U.S. Internet Index Fund.*

Dow Jones U.S. Total Market Style Indices
www.djindexes.com/jsp/tmsmethod.jsp

All the stocks in the DJ U.S. Total Market Index are first separated by class size. As with all Dow Jones country indices, classifying an index component as large, mid or small cap is based on a survey of the country's cummulative capitalization. The top 70% of that total capitalization is automatically classified as large cap. The next 20% is midcap, and the remaining 10% is screened for trading volume and market capitalization to select a final 5% that comprises the small cap segment. After that basic division, the components are ranked on the basis of six factors: projected price-to-earnings, projected earnings growth, trailing price-to-earnings, trailing earnings growth, price-to-book value and dividend yield. After some statistical work, each stock emerges identified either as growth, value or neutral, and the style indices are formed. Neutral stocks are excluded, so the resulting indices are a purer representation of growth and value styles than either the Russell or the S&P/Barra style indices (see below).

The style indices are reviewed at the end of each March and September. Capitalization is reviewed quarterly with immediate changes for extraordinary events.

ETFs: streetTRACKS DJ US Large Cap Growth Index Fund
streetTRACKS DJ US Large Cap Value Index Fund
streetTRACKS DJ US Small Cap Growth Index Fund
streetTRACKS DJ US Small Cap Value Index Fund

Russell 3000, 2000 and 1000 Indices
www.russell.com/US/Indexes/USMethodology.asp

This index is constructed by the Frank Russell Company, an investment management firm based in Tacoma, Washington and owned by Northwestern Mutual Life Insurance Company. The index is market capitalization weighted and holds the 3,000 largest stocks in the U.S. It represents around 90% of the U.S. market capitalization and is adjusted for free-float. It excludes stocks under $1, stocks of companies not domiciled in the U.S., and publicly traded entities that are not the stock of an operating company such as Berkshire Hathaway, royalty trusts, limited partnerships, closed-end funds, et cetera. The index is reconstituted on June 30 and changes are announced in advance. Capitalization rebalancing is done at the end of every month and when corporate activities, such as mergers and acquisitions, occur. Spin-off stocks may be added to the index when they are issued, but deleted stocks are not replaced between reconstitution dates so the number of stocks in the index may fluctuate. Oddly, bankruptcy is not a reason for being dropped from the index.

The largest 1,000 stocks in the Russell 3000 become the Russell 1000. The next 2,000 stocks become the Russell 2000 Index.

ETFs: iShares Russell 1000
iShares Russell 2000
iShares Russell 3000

The Russell Style Indices
www.russell.com/US/Indexes/US/default.asp*

The stocks in the Russell 3000, 2000 and 1000 indices are divided into growth and value styles. There is a Russell 3000 Growth Index, a Russell 3000 Value Index and so on for the thousand-series indices. The style decision is based on two variables: the price-to-book ratio (as with the S&P style indices) and the I/B/E/S forecasted long-term growth rate relative to its peers. (I/B/E/S International Inc. is a Thomson Corporation company well known for its concensus earnings estimates.) The results of these two variables are combined into a score for each stock, which, with more fiddling, determines style membership. A total of 70% of the stocks in each index are classified as all value or all growth and 30% are assigned proportionately to value and growth. Growth and value determinations, then, are not mutually exclusive. Some stocks have a little of both. Although this method actively identifies growth stocks as opposed to the S&P/Barra method that characterizes growth stocks as simply those that aren't value stocks, purists should know the Russell value and growth indices can cause a company's market cap to be divided between both growth and value.

ETFs: iShares Russell 3000 Growth
iShares Russell 3000 Value
iShares Russell 1000 Growth
iShares Russell 1000 Value
iShares Russell 2000 Growth
iShares Russell 2000 Value

*You must select "U.S. Resident" to access this page.

Russell Midcap Indices
www.russell.com/US/Indexes/US/default.asp

The Russell Midcap indices are a subset of the Russell 1000 indices. The Russell Midcap Index itself is a capitalization weighted index consisting of 800 of the smallest companies in the Russell 1000. These 800 companies make up about 25% of the market cap of the 1000 index. Russell's Web site reported as of July, 2001 that the latest reconstitution determined the index's average market capitalization was approximately $4 billion and its median market capitalization was approximately $2.9 billion. The largest company in the index was worth $12 billion in market cap.

The Russell Midcap Growth Index is a subset of the Russell 1000 Growth Index and consists of those companies with higher price-to-book ratios and higher forecasted growth values. Similarly, the Russell Midcap Value Index is also a subset of the Russell 1000 Value Index. It contains companies with lower price-to-book ratios and lower forecasted growth values.

ETFs: iShares Russell Midcap Index Fund
iShares Russell Midcap Growth Index Fund
iShares Russell Midcap Value Index Fund

S&P 500 Composite Index
www.spglobal.com/ssindexmain500.html

This is the most widely followed U.S. stock index for U.S. money managers. The index is constructed by the New York-based firm, Standard & Poor's which is owned by McGraw-Hill, Inc. It is a market capitalization weighted index consisting of 500 large U.S. companies. Contrary to popular belief, the S&P 500 does not contain the 500 largest stocks; rather it contains leading companies from leading industries which may include relatively small companies. S&P identifies industry sectors within the U.S. equity market, approximates the relative importance of these sectors in terms of market capitalization and then allocates a representative sample of stocks within each sector. No strict criteria are published. Closely held companies are typically screened out. The index is rebalanced quarterly for changes to shares outstanding, though share changes in excess of 5% are implemented when they happen. It covers about 79% of the U.S. market. With a selection of 500 companies from the U.S. equity market, the S&P 500 is not a broad market index. It is not free-float adjusted.

Deletions from the index occur due to company mergers, financial operating failure, lack of representation or company restructuring. Inclusion, though, is somewhat more subjective and involves the judgement of seven committee members. As a result, changes in index holdings cannot necessarily be forecast and they may happen at any time. There are no fixed reconstitution dates. In 2000, the S&P index committee added 57 stocks to the respected index, 26 of them high-tech. By mid-April 2001, the 57 stocks were down on average 12.9%. The 23 stocks expelled for reasons other than mergers or acquisitions clocked an average gain of 38.6% (see Ken Hoover "Did S&P Get Caught Up In Internet Mania?" *Investor's Business Daily*, April 24, 2001). This has lead to some criticism that perhaps the S&P 500 is more actively managed than other indices.

ETFs: SPDR
iShares S&P 500 Fund
iUnits S&P 500 Index RSP Fund

S&P Sector Indices
www.spglobal.com/indexmain500sector_description.html

Standard & Poor's uses the Global Industry Classification Standard which subdivides the S&P 500 into ten economic sectors. Separate from this, there are sector ETFs which split the S&P 500 into nine sectors, as determined by the ETF provider. The following are the sectors for the Select Sector SPDRs.

• Basic Industries
• Consumer Services
• Consumer Staples
• Transportation Sector/Consumer Cyclical
• Energy
• Financial
• Industrial
• Technology
• Utilities.

Together the stocks in these nine sectors make up the entirety of the S&P 500 Index so what holds for the S&P 500 Index holds for the corresponding sector ETFs.

ETF: Nine Select Sector SPDRs

S&P MidCap 400 Index
www.spglobal.com/ssindexmain.400.html

This index is intended to measure the performance of the mid-sized company segment of the U.S. market. It holds the stock of 400 U.S. mid cap companies selected by market cap, liquidity and industry representation. The median market capitalization of companies in the index as of July 2001 was US$1.8 billion. It is a market capitalization weighted index.

ETFs: MidCap SPDR
iShares S&P MidCap 400 Fund

S&P SmallCap 600 Index
www.spglobal.com/indexmain600.html

This index is intended to track the performance of the small cap segment of the U.S. market. It holds 600 U.S. small cap stocks. These stocks must be higher than $1 a share. Their annual trading must exceed 20% of shares outstanding and the company must not be majority owned by another entity. A few other requirements apply. The index is rebalanced quarterly although any share changes greater than 5% are implemented when they happen.

The S&P 500, 400 and 600 together make up the S&P SuperComposite 1500 Index.

ETF: iShares S&P SmallCap 600 Fund

S&P/ Barra Style Indices
www.spglobal.com/indexmain500growth_description.html

These indices include the S&P 500/Barra Growth, the S&P 400/Barra Growth, and the S&P 600/ Barra Growth and the corresponding S&P/Barra Value Indices.

These style indices divide the respective index holdings into value or growth companies by examining their price-to-book (P/B) ratio, a standard yardstick for evaluating the value of a stock. Stocks with a low P/B ratio are designated value stocks and stocks with a high P/B ratio are designated as growth stocks. These divisions are treated as mutually exclusive and the indices are split in half by market capitalization and sorted by price-to-book. Taken together the value and growth stocks always equal the total of their respective index be it the 500, 400 or 600.

This is a pretty simple system. A stock is either value or growth with nothing in between. Critics point out that price-to-book value may be a good indication of a value play, but it doesn't say much about a growth stock except to point out the obvious; namely, that it isn't a value stock.

Reconstitution happens twice a year on January 1 and July 1.

ETFs: iShares S&P 500/Barra Growth
iShares S&P 500/Barra Value
iShares S&P 400/Barra Growth
iShares S&P 400/Barra Value
iShares S&P 600/Barra Growth
iShares S&P 600/Barra Value

S&P 100 Index
www.spglobal.com/indexmain100_description.html

This index is a subset of the S&P 500 Index. One hundred large stocks are selected from the S&P 500 Index. Option contracts are also available on this index.

ETF: iShares S&P 100 Index Fund

Nasdaq-100 Index
www.nasdaq.com/indexshares/n100_index.stm

Nasdaq was the world's first electronic stock market, and according to their Web site, it's home to "over half of the companies traded on the primary U.S. markets." The Nasdaq-100 Index is made up of the largest 100 non-financial companies in the Nasdaq Composite Index. (The Nasdaq Composite Index tracks all the common stocks listed on the Nasdaq Stock Market, of which there are more than 5,000.) Major industry groups currently represented include computer hardware and software, telecommunications, retail/wholesale trade and biotechnology. The 100 Index is a modified market capitalization weighted index, which means that it caps the market weightings of its constituents to meet U.S. diversification requirements. No one company's weighting will represent more than 24% of the index, and all the companies with weightings of 4.5% or more cannot together add up to more than 48% of the index. This is a technology heavy index.

The index is reconstituted on the third Friday of December every year, with quarterly reviews for weighting changes.

ETF: Nasdaq-100 Index Tracking Stock, otherwise known as QUBES (QQQ)

Dow Jones Industrial Average
www.djindexes.com/jsp/avgMethod.jsp

This is the oldest continuously published stock index in the world (established in 1896) and is unusual in that it is a price weighted index. It has another peculiarity, too. Its 30 blue-chip constituents are selected by the editors of the *Wall Street Journal*. Rebalancing and reconstitution happen when corporate events require them. Because it is not a market cap weighted index, it does not need to take into account free floats.

ETF: Diamond Trust Series 1 (Diamonds)

Fortune 500 Index
www.cgi.fortune.com/cgi-bin/fortune/dex/dex.cgi

Fortune is an American business magazine that compiles a list every year ranking the 500 U.S.-based and incorporated companies with the biggest revenue. The Fortune 500 Index takes those companies, adds some additional eligibility criteria—such as minimum market capitalization, minimum share price, minimum trading volume and being exchange traded—and ranks them according to market capitalization (not free-float adjusted). As a result, the index ranking is different from the list ranking. Since some Fortune 500 companies are private, the index has fewer than 500 companies.

The index was launched on December 31, 1999. Its constituents are updated the third Friday in April, naturally after the publication of the Fortune 500 list in *Fortune* magazine, though additions and deletions can happen any time due to corporate actions. Rebalancing is done quarterly or as soon as is practicable after a share change of 5% or more.

ETF: streetTRACKS Fortune 500 Index Fund

Goldman Sachs Technology Index
www.ishares.com

Goldman Sachs is a global investment bank and securities firm. The index is made up of U.S. technology companies across every major sub-sector of technology. It is a modified cap weighted index to limit dominance by a few stocks. All stocks must trade on either the NYSE, AMEX or Nasdaq and have an annual trading volume of 30% of float to qualify in the index. If volume falls to less than 15%, the company is removed. Foreign companies, American Depositary Receipts (ADRs), limited partnerships and closed-end funds are excluded. Companies with free-float below 20% are not eligible and companies whose free-float falls below 10% will be removed. Rebalancing takes place semi-annually to reduce portfolio turnover. There is no fixed number of constituents.

ETF: iShares Goldman Sachs Technology Index Fund *www.ishares.com*

There are now three ETFs based on corresponding Goldman Sachs Technology sub-sector indices: *iShares Goldman Sachs Networking Index Fund; iShares Goldman Sachs Semiconductor Index Fund; iShares Goldman Sachs Software Index Fund.*

Fortune e-50 Index
www.timeinc.net/fortune/dex/e50/desc.html

This index is made up of 50 publicly traded Internet companies. A company must have at least 10% of its revenues from Internet activities. A company must alsohave minimum share price, trading volume and market value as well as being principally based in the U.S. The index is a modified capitalized weighted index where weights are modified based on a company's Internet revenue. Weightings are rebalanced quarterly and components are managed so that the index meets diversification requirements: no stock will exceed 10% of the index and no stocks over 4.5% will together add up to more than 50% of the index.

ETF: streetTRACKS Fortune e-50 Index Tracking Stock

Morgan Stanley Internet Index
www.morganstanlet.com/mox/index.html

Launched on December 31, 1999 this index comprises American companies involved in Internet usage.

Morgan Stanley's Web site says the companies are selected based on "liquidity, borrowability, a demonstration of current leadership, business momentum and market share." There is no fixed number of companies in the index. As of July 2001, it included 30 companies. The index is owned and maintained by Morgan Stanley, a U.S. financial services company. It is equal-dollar weighted and rebalanced quarterly.

ETF: streetTRACKS Morgan Stanley Internet Index Fund

Nasdaq Biotechnology Index
http://dynamic.nasdaq.com/dynamic/nasdaqbiotech_activity.stm

This capitalization weighted index includes the largest and most actively traded biotechnology companies listed on Nasdaq. According to the Nasdaq Web site, the companies "are primarily engaged in using biomedical research for the discovery or development of novel treatments or cures for human disease." Inclusion requirements include a market cap of at least US$200 million and a price of $10 or more, good daily trading volume (at least 100,000 shares a day on average) and have been publicly traded for at least six months, except for spin-offs. Securities are reviewed semi-annually and take effect on the third Friday in May and November. There were 66 companies in the index as of July 2001.

ETF: iShares Nasdaq Biotechnology Index Fund

Morgan Stanley High-Tech 35 Index
www.morganstanley.com/msh/structure.html

This index is made up exclusively of 35 publicly traded electronics-based U.S. technology companies. It was launched on December 16, 1994. It is equal-dollar weighted and adjustments are made annually on the third Friday of December. The American Stock Exchange calculates this index and Morgan Stanley acts as consultant to AMEX.

ETF: streetTRACKS Morgan Stanley High-Tech 35 Index Fund

Wilshire REIT Index
www.wilshire.com/Indexes/RealEstate/REIT/

This index tracks the performance of publicly traded US real estate investment trusts. The index requires the REITs it includes to have a book value of real estate assets of $100 million or more, and a market capitalization of at least $100 million, and that 75% or more of the company's revenue is from real eastate assets. Mortgage REITs, Health Care REITs, real estate finance companies, home builders, companies with more than 25% of their assets in direct mortgages, large land owners and subdividers are not included. Additions are made at quarterly intervals; deletions are done at year-end. The index is a subset of the Wilshire Real Estate Securities Index.

ETF: streetTRACKS Wilshire REIT Index Fund

Cohen & Steers Realty Majors Index
www.cohenandsteers.com

This index tracks the market in large, actively traded U.S. REITs, Real Estate Investment Trusts. There are REITs in many sectors of U.S. real estate. As of the end of March, 2001 the Cohen & Steers Index had REITS in office property, apartments, regional malls, warehouse/industrial, shopping centres, health care facilities, manufactured homes and others.

ETF: iShares Cohen & Steers Realty Majors Index Fund.

Global and International Indices

MSCI Indices
www.msci.com

Morgan Stanley Capital International, Inc. (MSCI), majority-owned by global financial services firm Morgan Stanley, runs a large series of international indices from broad global indices like MSCI World Index, to regional indices like MSCI Europe Index, right down to country-specific indices like MSCI South Korea Index. MSCI is in the process of revamping their international indices to full free-float weightings and a greater market coverage from 60% to about 85%. On May 19, 2001 they announced provisional indices which are revised in accordance with their free-float calculations. On May 31, 2002 the provisional indices will be discontinued as the permanent indices will have been completely converted to their enhanced free-float methodology. It is believed that the free-float changes will result in a lower weighting for Telecommunication and Utility stocks (commonly owned in some part by governments or with foreign ownership restrictions) and a heavier weighting for Energy and Technology stocks.

Stocks within each country are sorted by industry and by size in descending order with screens for free-float and liquidity. Rebalancing and reconstitution is done quarterly one region at a time. All indices are reviewed every 18 months. Extraordinary corporate events affecting weightings and industry representation are addressed as they happen. Changes are announced two weeks in advance.

ETFs: iShares MSCI EAFE Index Fund

The ETFs on MSCI country indices are extensive, 21 iShares as of spring 2001 (see Appendix C for a full list).

Note: Barclays Global Investors Canada Limited is expected to be launching a fully RRSP eligible ETF tracking one of MSCI's most well-known indices, the MSCI EAFE Index which covers Europe, Australasia and the Far East.

S&P Global 100 Index
www.spglobal.com/ssindexmainglobal100.html

The S&P Global 100 Index tracks the performance of 100 large multi-national companies. After determining that a company's activities are truly global in nature, each stock is screened for liquidity, sector representation, size and fundamentals. The index is free-float adjusted. Companies are removed from this S&P index for the same four reasons they would be removed from any S&P index: going broke, being bought-out or mergied, corporate restructuring or lack of industry representation. Rebalancing is quarterly or when a change greater than 5% occurs in the outstanding shares. Companies from the S&P Global 100 index are derived from the S&P Global 1200 Index.

ETF: iShares S&P Global 100 Index Fund

Dow Jones Global Titans 50 Index
www.djindexes.com/jsp/gtiMethod.jsp

Calling 50 of the world's largest multinational companies "Titans" is almost as poetic as it is descriptive.

These companies are selected from the Dow Jones Global Index and are sorted in descending order by weighted average market value for the last four quarters, with most emphasis on the last quarter. The top 100 companies that survive this screening are then ranked according to fundamental measures that look at assets, profit, foreign sales, book value, sales to revenue and their free-float market capitalization ranking. The top 50 finalists make it into the index. Reconstitution takes place annually, rebalancing quarterly or with a change of more than 10% in the number of a company's outstanding shares.

ETF: streetTRACKS DJ Global Titans Index Fund

S&P Europe 350 Index
www.spglobal.com/indexmaineuro350_method.html

This index is designed to track the performance of stocks in 15 pan-European markets. It has three sub-indices: the S&P Euro (holding stocks from the ten EuroZone countries); the S&P Euro Plus which adds Denmark, Norway, Sweden and Switzerland, and the S&P United Kingdom. It is intended to cover about 70% of the market capitalization of its target markets. Inclusion depends on liquidity, sector representation, fundamental analysis and market capitalization. It has 350 stocks adjusted for free-float.

Additions to the index generally occur when there is a vacancy arising from an index deletion. Float weights are reviewed annually, in the third week of June, or as soon as a change of 5% or greater occurs due to a major corporate event.

ETF: iShares S&P Europe 350 Index Fund

Canadian Indices

TSE 300 Composite Index
www.spglobal.com/indexmaintse300_method.html

This index is the broadest measure of the Canadian equity market and covers about 86% of the market capitalization of Canadian-based companies listed on the Toronto Stock Exchange. It is the primary benchmark for Canadian money managers. To be included in the index, companies must have been listed on the TSE for at least 12 months or six months in certain cases of large market value. It is float adjusted for companies with purchase restrictions on 20% or more of outstanding shares. Generally only stocks of operating companies are allowed on the index, which means limited partnerships, royalty trusts, REITs, preferred shares and exchangeable shares are excluded. Stocks are ranked on a "float quoted market value" (QMV) basis. The S&P's Web site defines QMV as "the close price of that security on that day multiplied by the number of float shares."

Reconstitution happens annually effective the third Friday of March, though deletions and a subsequent replacement can occur at any time. Rebalancings occur as soon as possible with a capitalization change of .05% or more of relative weight.

ETF: TD TSE 300 Index Fund

TSE 300 Capped Index
www.spglobal.com/indexmaintse300cap_method.html

This index holds all the stocks of the TSE 300 but their weights are limited (capped) to 10% of the index.

This ensures diversification and was a response to the heavy weighting of Nortel Networks Corp. in early 2000. The index was launched in April 2000. Weights are adjusted quarterly unless a company exceeds 15% of the total index in which case the component is capped at 10% "on the first practical date." If a previously capped component falls below 5%, its float will be adjust to 10% or to full float, whichever is less, again "on the first practical date." Share capitalization changes are announced one business day before being included in the index.

ETF: TD TSE 300 Capped Index Fund

S&P/TSE 60 Index
www.spglobal.com/indexmaintse_method.html

This index comprises 60 of Canada's largest companies by market capitalization and is selected from the TSE 300 Composite Index. The 60 Index is balanced across 10 sectors and float adjusted. Stocks are selected based on liquidity, size, sector representation and their stability. Because this is an S&P index, the same four reasons for deleting a company from the index apply: acquisition by another company, bankruptcy, company restructuring and lack of industry representation. Additions are made to replace deleted companies as required. Index rebalancing is quarterly and market cap adjustments are made to exclude block holdings of 20% or more. Stock weight changes greater than .05% are implemented when they occur. Index changes are announced three days in advance. This large cap index was launched December 31, 1998 and covers about 64% of the total Canadian market capitalization. The S&P/TSE 60 is included in the S&P Global 1200, a world equity index covering 29 countries.

ETF: iUnits S&P/TSE 60 Index Participation Fund

S&P/TSE 60 Capped Index
www.spglobal.com/indexmaintse6ocap_method.html

This index is a capped version of the S&P/TSE 60. No one company in the index will be greater than 10%. Weights are adjusted quarterly unless components go above 15% or capped components fall below 5% (see S&P/TSE Capped 60 for rules).

ETF: iUnits S&P/TSE 60 Capped Index Fund

S&P/TSE Canadian MidCap Index
www.spglobal.com/indexmaintsemc_method.html

Mid-sized Canadian companies are on this index with their weights adjusted across economic sectors. Capitalization, liquidity and fundamentals determine inclusion. Being bought by another company, bankruptcy, restructuring or lack of sector representation can knock a component. Additions will be made to fill deletions. Float is adjusted for changes of 20% or more. Stock weightings are updated quarterly or with a change of .05% or more on the basis of the TSE 300. Reconstitution changes are announced one month in advance. Other changes are announced three days ahead of time. This index was launched in May 1999.

ETF: iUnits S&P/TSE Canadian MidCap Index Fund

S&P/TSE Sector Indices
www.spglobal.com/indexmaintsesector_description.html

Stocks included in these sector indices are drawn from the pool of stocks listed in TSE 300 Composite Index. It has the same inclusion and ranking criteria as the S&P/TSE 60, but the weighting of any one component stock is capped at 25% of the index. The sector indices currently are

• Canadian Financials

- Canadian Information Technology
- Canadian Energy
- Canadian Gold

ETFs: iUnits S&P/TSE Canadian Energy Index Fund
iUnits S&P/TSE Canadian Financials Index Fund
iUnits S&P/TSE Canadian Gold Index Fund
iUnits S&P/TSE Canadian Information Technology Index Fund

Dow Jones Canada 40 Index *www.djindexes.com/jsp/xlbcMethod.jsp*

This is the Canadian part of the Dow Jones Country Titan Index family, country specific large cap indices. The country Titan indices are designed, according to Dow Jones' Web site, to "maximize liquidity and replicability and to minimize turnover and transaction costs, while maintaining acceptable levels of market coverage, sector representation and tracking error relative to broader benchmarks." The number of stocks included in each country Titan varies from index to index. Canada's Titans amount to 40 and cover approximately 58% of Canada's (free-float) market capitalization. The index is a free-float market capitalization weighted index and was designed for use as the basis of investment products like ETFs. The constituents are reviewed annually in March.

ETF: SSgA Dow Jones Canada 40 Index Participation Fund

Appendix C
ETF Directory:
Vital Statistics on International ETFs, both Existing and Pending

U.S. ETFs: classified by market cap and style

Trading Symbol Exchange Traded Funds	Intraday NAV Symbol	Approx # of Stocks in Fund	Original Index Divisor	Inception Date	Expense Ratio (%)	Total Assets ($ Mil)	Avg Daily Volume (1000/shrs)	†Listed Options Exchange	Options (O) LEAPS (L)
MAJOR MARKET FUNDS									
Broad Market									
IYY iShares DJ US Total Market Index Fd	NLA	1,786	1/5	06/12/00	0.20	66	25		
IVV iShares Russell 3000 Index Fd	NMV	2,797	1/10	05/22/00	0.20	760	69		
VTI Total Stock Market VIPERs	TSJ	1,800	1/100	05/31/01	0.15	17	31	A	O
Large Cap									
DIA Diamond Trust Series 1	DXA	30	1/100	01/20/98	0.18	2,626	3,211		
QQQ Nasdaq-100 Index Tracking Stock	QXV	100	1/40	03/10/99	0.18	25,900	70,544	A,C,PS,P	O,L
OEF iShares S&P 100 Index Fd	OEL	99	1/10	10/23/00	0.20	98	7	C	O
IVV iShares S&P 500 Index Fd	NNV	500	1/10	05/15/00	0.09	2,576	310		
SPY Standard & Poor's Depository Receipts	SXV	500	1/10	01/29/93	0.12	28,130	11,343		
IWB iShares Russell 1000 Index Fd	NJB	934	1/10	05/15/00	0.15	282	45	A	O
FFF streetTRACKS Fortune 500 Index Fd	FFY	441	1/10	10/10/00	0.20	48	7	A	O
Mid Cap									
IWR iShares Russell Midcap Index Fd	NIZ	800	1/25	07/16/01	0.20	51	-		
IJH iShares S&P MidCap 400 Index Fd	NJH	401	1/5	05/22/00	0.20	295	56		
MDY Standard & Poor's MidCap 400 Dep Rec	MXV	400	1/5	05/04/95	0.25	3,970	1,079	A	O,L
Small Cap									
IJR iShares S&P SmallCap 600 Index Fd	NIR	599	1/2	05/22/00	0.20	437	71		
IWM iShares Russell 2000 Index Fd	NJM	1,806	1/5	05/22/00	0.20	981	346	A	O

Trading Symbol Exchange Traded Funds	Intraday NAV Symbol	Approx # of Stocks in Fund	Original Index Divisor	Inception Date	Expense Ratio (%)	Total Assets ($ Mil)	Avg Daily Volume (1000/shrs)	†Listed Options Exchange	Options (O) LEAPS (L)
STYLE FUNDS									
Broad Market Growth									
IWZ iShares Russell 3000 Growth Index Fd	NBE	1,708	1/10	07/24/00	0.25	22	17		
Broad Market Value									
IWW iShares Russell 3000 Value Index Fd	NNW	1,807	1/10	07/20/00	0.25	34	4		
Large Cap Growth									
IVW iShares S&P 500/Barra Gr Idx Fd	NJG	124	1/10	05/22/00	0.18	228	52		
IWF iShares Russell 1000 Gr Idx Fd	NBF	525	1/5	05/22/00	0.20	354	86		
ELG streetTRACKS DJ U.S. Large Cap Gr Idx Fd	FLG	106	1/20	09/29/00	0.20	25	0.7		
Large Cap Value									
IVE iShares S&P 500/Barra Val Idx Fd	NME	378	1/5	05/22/00	0.18	475	102		
IWD iShares Russell 1000 Val Idx Fd	NJU	691	1/5	05/22/00	0.20	323	134		
ELV streetTRACKS DJ U.S. Large Cap Val Idx Fd	FLV	108	1/20	09/29/00	0.20	39	2		
Mid Cap Growth									
IWP Russell Midcap Growth Index Fd	NIW	422	1/8	07/16/01	0.25	15	-		
IJK iShares S&P MidCap 400/Barra Gr Idx Fd	NNK	151	1/2	07/24/00	0.25	111	45		
Mid Cap Value									
IWS Russell Midcap Value Index Fund	NIV	578	1/8	07/16/01	0.25	8	-		
IJJ iShares S&P MidCap 400/Barra Val Idx Fd	NJJ	252	1/2	07/24/00	0.25	155	21		

Trading Symbol Exchange Traded Funds	Intraday NAV Symbol	Approx # of Stocks in Fund	Original Index Divisor	Inception Date	Expense Ratio (%)	Total Assets ($ Mil)	Avg Daily Volume (1000/shrs)	†Listed Options Exchange	Options (O) LEAPS (L)
Small Cap Growth									
IJT iShares S&P SmallCap 600/Barra Gr Idx Fd	NLT	191	1/2	07/24/00	0.25	50	9		
IWO iShares Russell 2000 Gr Index Fd	NLO	1,189	1/5	07/24/00	0.25	228	93	A	O
DSG streetTRACKS DJ U.S. Small Cap Gr Idx Fd	PSG	477	1/20	09/29/00	0.25	8	2		
Small Cap Value									
IJS iShares S&P SmallCap 600/BARRA Val IdxFd	NJS	411	1/2	07/24/00	0.25	145	27		
IWN iShares Russell 2000 Val Index Fd	NAJ	1,153	1/5	07/24/00	0.25	408	60	A	O
DSV streetTRACKS DJ U.S. Small Cap Val Idx Fd	PSV	370	1/10	09/29/00	0.25	25	2		
U.S. EQUITY ETFS CLASSIFIED BY SECTOR									
Basic Materials									
XLB Basic Industries Select Sector SPDR Fd	BXV	43	1/10	12/22/98	0.28	102	89	A	O,L
IYM iShares DJ U.S. Basic Mat Sector Index Fd	NLB	64	1/4	06/12/00	0.60	14	5		
IYD iShares DJ U.S. Chemical Index Fd	NNE	33	1/4	06/12/00	0.60	17	8		
Capital Goods									
XLI Industrial Select Sector SPDR Fd	TXV	43	1/10	12/22/98	0.28	68	39	A	O,L
IYJ iShares DJ U.S. Industrial Sector Index Fd	NIJ	251	1/5	06/12/00	0.60	50	3		
Consumer Cyclicals									
XLV Consumer Services Select Sector SPDR Fd	NXV	42	1/10	12/22/98	0.28	110	32	A	O,L
XLY Cyclical/Transportation Select Sector SPDR Fd	YXV	66	1/10	12/22/98	0.28	131	263	A	O
IYC iShares DJ U.S. Cons Cyc Sector Index Fd	NLL	274	1/5	06/12/00	0.60	36	9		
RTH Retail HOLDRS	IRH	20	-	05/02/01	*	N/A	73	A,C	O

Exchange Traded Funds

Trading Symbol	Exchange Traded Funds	Intraday NAV Symbol	Approx # of Stocks in Fund	Original Index Divisor	Inception Date	Expense Ratio (%)	Total Assets ($ Mil)	Avg Daily Volume (1000/shrs)	†Listed Options Exchange	Options (O) LEAPS (L)
Consumer Staples										
XLP	Consumer Staples Select Sector SPDR Fd	PXV	68	1/10	12/22/98	0.28	214	91	A	O,L
IYK	iShares DJ U.S. Cons Non-cyclical Sector Fd	NMJ	107	1/5	06/12/00	0.60	17	8		
Energy										
XLE	Energy Select Sector SPDR Fd	EXV	31	1/10	12/22/98	0.28	243	248	A	O,L
IYE	iShares DJ U.S. Energy Sector Index Fd	NLE	64	1/5	06/12/00	0.60	45	32		
OIH	Oil Service HOLDRS	OXH	19	-	02/07/01	*	167	144	A,PS	O
Financials										
XLF	Financial Select Sector SPDR Fd	FXV	70	1/10	12/22/98	0.28	810	881	A	O,L
IYF	iShares DJ U.S. Financial Sector Index Fd	NLF	284	1/5	05/22/00	0.60	68	28		
IYG	iShares DJ U.S. Financial Services Index Fd	NAG	158	1/5	06/12/00	0.60	39	8		
RKH	Regional Bank HOLDRS	XRH	20	-	06/23/00	*	66	50	A,C	O
Health Care										
BBH	Biotech HOLDRS	IBH	20	-	11/23/99	*	1,493	11	A,C,PS	O,L
IBB	iShares DJ Nasdaq Biotechnology Index Fd	IBF	77	1/10	02/08/01	0.50	119	25		
IYH	iShares DJ U.S. Health Care Sector Index Fd	NHG	182	1/5	06/12/00	0.60	134	30		
PPH	Pharmaceutical HOLDRS	IPH	17	-	02/01/00	*	523	318	A,C	O
Real Estate										
IYR	iShares DJ U.S. Real Estate Index Fd	NLR	71	1/2	06/12/00	0.60	74	17		
ICF	iShares Cohen & Steers Realty Majors Idx Fd	ICG	31	1/4	01/29/01	0.35	43	6		
RWR	streetTRACKS Wilshire REIT Index Fd	EWR	98	1/1	04/27/01	0.25	17	1		

Trading Symbol	Exchange Traded Funds	Intraday NAV Symbol	Approx # of Stocks in Fund	Original Index Divisor	Inception Date	Expense Ratio (%)	Total Assets ($ Mil)	Avg Daily Volume (1000/shrs)	†Listed Options Exchange	LEAPS (L) Options (O)
Technology-Broad Based										
IYW	iShares DJ U.S. Technology Sector Index Fd	NJW	344	1/10	05/15/00	0.60	107	49		
IGM	iShares Goldman Sachs Tech Index Fd	IPM	214	1/4	03/13/01	0.60	129	98		
MTK	streetTRACKS MS High-tech 35 Idx Fd	JMT	35	1/10	09/29/00	0.50	67	87		
XLK	Technology Select Sector SPDR Fd	KXV	97	1/10	12/28/98	0.28	1,275	951	A	O,L
Technology-Internet										
IYV	iShares DJ U.S. Internet Index Fd	NNU	41	1/4	05/15/00	0.60	20	32		
MII	streetTRACKS Morgan Stanley Int Idx Fd	MMI	28	1/1	09/29/00	0.50	5	4		
FEF	streetTRACKS Fortune e-50 Idx Tkg Stock	FEY	50	1/10	10/10/00	0.20	17	2	A	O
HHH	Internet HOLDRS	HHI	17	-	09/23/99	*	224	275	A,C,PS	O,L
BHH	B2B Internet HOLDRS	BUX	16	-	02/24/00	*	104	454	A,C	O
IAH	Internet Architecture HOLDRS	XAH	20	-	02/25/00	*	173	112	A,C	O
IIH	Internet Infrastructure HOLDRS	YIH	18	-	02/25/00	*	107	222	A,C	O
Technology-Other										
IGN	Goldman Sachs Networking Index Fund	NVK	33	1/4	07/10/01	0.50	24	1		
IGW	Goldman Sachs Semiconductor Index Fd	NVW	54	1/4	07/10/01	0.50	32	22		
IGV	Goldman Sachs Software Index Fd	NVV	55	1/4	07/10/01	0.50	27	51		
BDH	Broadband HOLDRS	XDH	19	-	04/06/00	*	231	341	A,C	O
SMH	Semiconductor HOLDRS	XSH	20	-	05/05/00	*	759	1,707	A,C	O
SWH	Software HOLDRS	XWH	20	-	09/27/00	*	115	122	A,C	O

Trading Symbol	Intraday NAV Symbol	Exchange Traded Funds	Approx # of Stocks in Fund	Original Index Divisor	Inception Date	Expense Ratio (%)	Total Assets ($ Mil)	Avg Daily Volume (1000/shrs)	†Listed Options Exchange	Options (O) LEAPS (L)
Telecommunications										
IYZ	NJZ	iShares DJ U.S. Telecom Sector Index Fd	51	1/5	02/01/00	0.60	53	17		
TTH	ITH	Telecom HOLDRS	18	-	02/01/00	*	343	104	A,C	O
WMH	IWH	Wireless HOLDRS	20	-	11/01/00	*	87	36	A,C	O
Utilities										
IDU	NLU	iShares DJ U.S. Utilities Sector Index Fd	77	1/2	06/12/00	0.60	43	23		
XLU	UXV	Utilities Select Sector SPDR Fd	40	1/10	12/22/98	0.28	92	32	A	O,L
UTH	XUH	Utilities HOLDRS	20	-	06/23/00	*	60	77	A,C	O

INTERNATIONAL EQUITY ETFS CLASSIFIED BY REGION

Trading Symbol	Intraday NAV Symbol	Exchange Traded Funds	Approx # of Stocks in Fund	Original Index Divisor	Inception Date	Expense Ratio (%)	Total Assets ($ Mil)	Avg Daily Volume (1000/shrs)	†Listed Options Exchange	Options (O) LEAPS (L)
Global/International										
DGT	UGT	streetTRACKS DJ Global Titans Index Fund	50	1/3	09/20/00	0.50	22	0		
IOO	OON	iShares S&P Global 100 Index Fund	101	1/20	12/05/00	0.40	119	30		
MKH	XKH	Market 2000+ HOLDRS	52	-	08/30/00	*	252	30	A	O
EFA	EFV	iShares MSCI EAFE	800	-	08/17/01	0.35	278	0		
Asia/Pacific										
EWA	WBJ	iShares MSCI Australia Index Fund	54	-	03/18/96	0.84	53	15		
EWH	INH	iShares MSCI Hong Kong Index Fund	29	-	03/18/96	0.84	59	57		
EWJ	INJ	iShares MSCI Japan Index Fund	214	-	03/18/96	0.84	584	662		
EWM	INM	iShares MSCI Malaysia (Free) Index Fd	61	-	03/18/96	0.84	70	69		
EWS	INR	iShares MSCI Singapore Index Fund	29	-	03/18/96	0.84	54	38		
EWY	WWK	iShares MSCI South Korea Index Fund	57	-	05/12/00	0.99	25	28		
EWT	WWM	iShares MSCI Taiwan Index Fund	61	-	06/23/00	0.99	100	56		

Trading Symbol	Exchange Traded Funds	Intraday NAV Symbol	Approx # of Stocks in Fund	Original Index Divisor	Inception Date	Expense Ratio (%)	Total Assets ($ Mil)	Avg Daily Volume (1000/shrs)	†Listed Options Exchange	Options (O) LEAPS (L)
Europe										
IEV	iShares S&P Europe 350 Index Fund	NJG	335	-	07/25/00	0.60	171	37		
EZU	iShares MSCI EMU Index Fund	WWE	239	-	07/14/00	0.84	80	19		
EKH	Europe 2001 HOLDRS	EKI	49	-	01/18/01	*	47	10	A	O
EWO	iShares MSCI Austria Index Fund	INY	16	-	03/18/96	0.84	11	7		
EWK	iShares MSCI Belgium Index Fund	INK	21	-	03/18/96	0.84	9	5		
EWQ	iShares MSCI France Index Fund	WBF	48	-	03/18/96	0.84	64	38		
EWG	iShares MSCI Germany Index Fund	WDG	45	-	03/18/96	0.84	129	75		
EWI	iShares MSCI Italy Index Fund	INE	38	-	03/18/96	0.84	35	19		
EWN	iShares MSCI Netherlands Index Fund	INN	29	-	03/18/96	0.84	25	9		
EWP	iShares MSCI Spain Index Fund	INP	31	-	03/18/96	0.84	27	19		
EWD	iShares MSCI Sweden Index Fund	WBQ	31	-	03/18/96	0.84	11	18		
EWL	iShares MSCI Switzerland Index Fund	INL	35	-	03/18/96	0.84	34	15		
EWU	iShares MSCI United Kingdom Index Fd	INU	109	-	03/18/96	0.84	122	66		
Americas										
EWC	iShares MSCI Canada Index Fund	WPB	65	-	03/18/96	0.84	31	17		
IKC	iShares S&P/TSE 60 Index Fund	NLJ	46	-	06/12/00	0.60	7	4		
EWZ	iShares MSCI Brazil Index Fund	WWC	40	-	07/14/00	0.99	18	44		
EWW	iShares MSCI Mexico (Free) Index Fd	INW	22	-	03/18/96	0.84	41	66		

Source: *Morgan Stanley, Barclays Global Investors, State Street Global Advisors, Bank of New York, Goldman Sachs, AMEX*

* Expenses for HOLDRS consist of a custody fee of $2 per round lot (100 shares) per quarter. However, according to the HOLDRS prospectus, the trustee will waive that portion of the fee, which exceeds the total cash dividends and other cash distributions.

** Source: Bloomberg

Δ Total Assets as of July 27, 2001

Pending ETFs[*]

Expected Trading Symbol	Exchange Traded Fund
	Mid Cap
	VIPERs Extended Market Index
	Small Cap
NAESX	VIPERs Small-Cap
	Style Funds
	Broad Market Growth
VIGRX	VIPERs Growth
	Broad Market Value
VIVAX	VIPERs Value
	Sector
	Americas Fastest Growing Companies
	iShares GS Health Care
	iShares GS Natural Resources
	TechIES (Pacific Exchange Tech 100)
	Fixed Income
	FITRs (Fixed Income Trust Receipts)
	iShares 1–3 Year Treasury Index
	iShares 7–10 Year Treasury Index
	iShares 20+ Year Treasury Index
	iShares Treasury Index
	iShares Government/Credit Bond Index
	International
	Bank of New York ADR Fund
GXN FP	DJ STOXX EX
GXE FP	DJ EuroStoxx 50 EX
	iShares Nikkei 225 Index
	iShares S&P International 700 Index
	iShares S&P Latin America 40 Index
	iShares S&P/Topix (Japan) 150 Index
XIN	iUnits MSCI EAFE RSP
	Sensex UTI Notional DRS
SMI EX	SMI EX
	streetTRACKS S&P/ASX 50
	streetTRACKS S&P/ASX 200
	StreetTRACKS Straits Times Index (Singapore)

Source: Managed Account Reports, LLC, Barclays Global Investors

[*] List of planned ETF products as of August 2001. Some or all of these ETFs may or may not be subsequently launched.

International ETFs

Trading Symbol	International Exchange Traded Fund	Sector/ Country	Inception Date	Expense Ratio (%)
Europe (Euro denominated unless otherwise specified)				
Australia (AUD denominated)				
AXSBAE AU	Access BNP Paribas AU Equity	Active Australia	Jul.01	1.90%
AXSMGE AU	Access BNP Paribas Global	Active Global	Jul.01	2.10%
AXSBMD AU	Access BNP Paribas Managed	Active Balanced	Jul.01	1.90%
AXSBSC AU	Access BNP Paribas Small Co.	Active Small Cap	Jul.01	2.15%
IDX AU	Indexshares Fund	Broad Market	Mar.01	0.95%
DeutscheBorse				
SX5E	DJ Euro Stoxx 50 Ex Anteile	EMU Large Cap	Dec.00	0.50%
SX5P	DJ Stoxx 50 Ex Anteile	Europe Large Cap	Dec.00	0.50%
EUN2 GR	DJ Euro Stoxx 50 LDRS	EMU Large Cap	Apr.00	0.50%
EUN1	DJ Stoxx 50 LDRS	Europe Large Cap	Apr.00	0.50%
SX7E	DJ Euro Stoxx Banks	EMU Financials	May.01	0.50%
SX7P	DJ Stoxx 600 Banks	Europe Financials	May.01	0.50%
SX8E	DJ Euro Stoxx Technology	EMU Technology	May.01	0.50%
SX8P	DJ Stoxx 600 Technology	Europe Technology	May.01	0.50%
SXDE	DJ Euro Stoxx Healthcare	EMU Healthcare	May.01	0.50%
SXDP	DJ Stoxx 600 Healthcare	Europe Healthcare	May.01	0.50%
SXKE	DJ Euro Stoxx Telecommunications	EMU Telecoms	May.01	0.50%
SXKP	DJ Stoxx 600 Telecommunications	Europe Telecoms	May.01	0.50%
DAXEX GR	DAXEX Anteile	German Large Cap	Dec.00	0.50%
MDAXEX	MDAX EX	German Mid Cap	Apr.01	0.50%
NDQ GR	NASDAQ 100 QQQ	U.S. Large Cap	Mar.99	0.18%
NMKXEX	NEMAX 50 EX	German Large Cap	Apr.01	0.50%
SMIEX	SMI EX Anteile	Swiss Large Cap	Mar.01	0.50%
SRD	SPDRs SPY	U.S. Large Cap	Jan.93	0.12%
Euronext (Amsterdam)				
AEXT	streetTRACKS AEX Index Fd	Netherlands Large Cap	May.01	0.30%
EUE	DJ Euro Stoxx 50 LDRS	EMU Large Cap	Apr.00	0.50%
EUN	DJ Stoxx 50 LDRS	Europe Large Cap	Apr.00	0.50%
IBQ	iBloomberg European Technology	European Technology	Feb.01	0.50%
IBF	iBloomberg European Financials	European Financials	Feb.01	0.50%
IBP	iBloomberg European Pharmaceuticals	European Pharmaceuticals	Feb.01	0.50%
IBT	iBloomberg European Telecoms	European Telecoms	Feb.01	0.50%
STUK	streetTRACKS MSCI UK Index	U.K. Cap Weighted	Jul.01	0.30%
Euronext (Paris)				
ERO FP	streetTRACKS MSCI Pan-Euro	Broad Market	Jun.01	0.30%
CAC FP	Master Share CAC 40	French Large Cap	Jan.00	0.30%
MSE FP	Master DJ Euro Stoxx 50	EMU Large Cap	Mar.01	0.40%
DJE FP	DJIA Master Unit	U.S. Industry	Apr.01	0.50%
EUE FP	DJ Euro STOXX 50 LDRS	EMU Large Cap	Apr.00	0.50%
EUN FP	DJ STOXX 50 LDRS	Europe Large Cap	Apr.00	0.50%
ETE FP	Easy ETF Euro STOXX 50	EMU Large Cap	Apr.01	1.00%
ETN FP	Easy ETF STOXX 50 Europe	Europe Large Cap	Apr.01	1.00%
ETT FP	Easy ETF Global Titans 50	Global Large Cap	Apr.01	1.00%

Trading Symbol	International Exchange Traded Fund	Sector/ Country	Inception Date	Expense Ratio (%)
Hong Kong (Asset & price values in USD)				
2800 HK	SSgA TraHK	Hong Kong Large Cap	Nov.99	0.10%
4363 HK	iShares MSCI-South Korea Index Fd	South Korea	May 00	0.99%
4362 HK	iShares MSCI-Taiwan Index Fd	Taiwan	Jun.00	0.99%
Israel				
TALI IT	TALI 25	Israeli Large Cap	May 00	0.80%
Japan (Tokyo) (U.S. denominated)				
1320 JP	Daiwa Nikkei 225	Broad Cap	Jul.01	0.23%
1305 JP	Daiwa TOPIX	Large Cap	Jul.01	0.20%
1307 JP	iShares TOPIX	Large Cap	Aug.01	0.22%
1330 JP	Nikko Nikkei 225	Broad Cap	Jul.01	0.23%
1321 JP	Nomura Nikkei 225	Broad Cap	Jul.01	0.24%
1306 JP	Nomura TOPIX	Large Cap	Jul.01	0.24%
New Zealand				
WIN NZ	AMP Investments World Index	Global	Aug.97	0.80%
OM Sweden (SEK denominated)				
XACT	XACTOMX	Swedish Large Cap	Oct.00	0.30%
Peru Stock Exchange				
QQQ PE	Nasdaq 100 QQQ	U.S. Large Cap	Mar.99	0.18%
Singapore				
DIA SP	DIAMONDS Trust Series 1	U.S. Large Cap	Jan.98	0.18%
IYW SP	iShares DJ US Technology Index Fd	U.S. Technology	May 00	0.60%
EWS SP	iShares MSCI-Singapore Index Fd	Singapore	Mar.96	0.84%
IVV SP	iShares S&P 500 Index Fd	U.S. Large Cap	May 00	0.09%
SPY SP	SPDRs	U.S. Large Cap	Jan.93	0.12%
South Africa (SAR denominated)				
STX40	SATRIX 40	South Africa Large Cap	Nov-00	0.30%
Switzerland				
EUN SW	DJ Stoxx 50 LDRS	Europe Large Cap	Apr.00	0.50%
EUNE SW	DJ Euro Stoxx 50 LDRS	EMU Large Cap	Apr.00	0.50%
XMSMI SW	SMI-XMTCH	Swiss Large Cap	Mar.01	0.35%
United Kingdom (GBP denominated)				
ISF LN	iShares iFTSE 100 Index	U.K. Large Cap	Apr.00	0.35%
ITMT LN	iShares iFTSE TMT	Tech/Media/Telecom	Oct.00	0.50%
IEUR LN	iShares iFTSE Ex-UK 100	Europe non-U.K.	Dec.00	0.50%
IBEC LN	iBloomberg European Cyclicals	European Cyclicals	Jul.01	0.55%
IBEI LN	iBloomberg European Industrials	European Industrials	Jul.01	0.55%
IBQQ LN	iBloomberg European Technology	European Technology	Feb.01	0.55%

Trading Symbol	International Exchange Traded Fund	Sector/ Country	Inception Date	Expense Ratio (%)
IBET LN	iBloomberg European Telecoms	European Telecoms	Feb.01	0.55%
IBEF LN	iBloomberg European Financials	European Financials	Feb.01	0.55%
IBEP LN	iBloomberg European Pharmaceuticals	European Pharmaceuticals	Feb.01	0.55%
IBER LN	iBloomberg European Resources	European Resources	Jul.01	0.55%
IBES LN	iBloomberg European Staples	Consumer Staples	Jul.01	0.55%
EUN LN	DJ Stoxx 50 LDRS	Europe Large Cap	Apr.00	0.50%
EUE LN	DJ Euro Stoxx 50 LDRS	EMU Large Cap	Apr.00	0.50%
QQQ LN	NASDAQ 100 QQQ	U.S. Large Cap	Mar.99	0.18%

Source: Managed Account Reports, LLC, Barclays Global Investors

Appendix D
Web Directory

For Canadian ETF products
www.iunits.com
>Describes Barclays Global Investors Canada Limited iUnits family of ETFs including daily NAV and related information.

www.tdassetmanagement.com
>Deals with ETFs,closed-end funds and pooled indexed and quantitative funds. Shows daily NAV and related information.

www.streettracks.com
>Information on State Street Global Advisors' offering of ETFs.

www.tse.com
>Toronto Stock Exchange site. All Canadian-based ETFs are traded on the TSE.

www.me.org
>Montréal Exchange site. Options on the i60s are traded at the Montréal Exchange. Outstanding explanation of options and futures in their "Derivatives Institute" section (see *http://www.derivatives-institute.com/accueil_en.htm*).

For U.S.-based ETF Products
www.amex.com
>Information on all AMEX-listed ETFs with quotes and graphing.

www.amextrader.com
>Outstanding ETF section with distribution history on all AMEX-listed ETFs from inception. Gives volumes, premiums/discounts last trade to NAV and arranges for delivery of paper or electronic

prospectus.

www.holdrs.com

Devoted to news and market information on HOLDRS, a Merrill Lynch exchange-traded basket security.

www.ishares.com

Information on Barclays Global Investors U.S.-based ETF offering iShares. Displays NAV information and tracking against the index.

www.spdrindex.com

Information and data on select Sector SPDRs.

www.nasdaq-100.com

Part of the nasdaq.com site devoted to the Nasdaq-100 Index tracking Stock, Qubes. Quotes, prospectus, holdings, etcetera. ETF section gives daily most active ETFs by trading volume.

General ETF and Indexing Sites

www.indexfunds.com

Excellent site for news, articles and information on index funds, indexing and ETFs. Very comprehensive listing of available ETFs.

www.exchangetradedfunds.com

This site is attempting to become the premier information source for ETFs. It has partnered with *ETFR*, the only industry newsletter devoted exclusively to ETFs.

www.marhedge.com

Site of *ETFR*, the ETF industry newsletter. News on alternative investments like ETFs, hedge funds, HOLDRs, etcetera.

www.bylo.org

Site run by a Canadian private investor about do-it-yourself mutual fund investing and indexing.

Index Providers

www.cgi.fortune.com

Information on *Fortune* indices.

www.djindexes.com

Revamped site full of information on methodology and maintenance of indices.

www.msci.com

Site specific to MSCI international indices.

www.morganstanley.com

Morgan Stanley indices site.

www.russell.com

Site for information on Russell indices.

www.spglobal.com

Site for extensive information on S&P indices, their methodology and maintenance.

www.wilshire.com

Wilshire index information.

Mutual Fund Sites

www.globefund.com

Exceptionally good site for information on all Canadian mutual funds; includesbenchmark comparisons.

www.ici.org

Provides a monthly assets report on ETFs not including HOL-DRS. This is the site of the Investment Companies Institute, the American trade organization for mutual fund companies

www.morningstar.ca

Canadian mutual fund site with the famous five-star rating system. Extensive articles commissioned for the site.

Miscellaneous

www.cef.com

Closed-end funds site.

www.financialengines.com

Nobel prize winning economist, William Sharpe's site.

www.in-the-money.com

Site run by Mark Rubenstein, inventor of portfolio insurance.

Appendix E
Recommended Reading

Why Smart People Make Big Money Mistakes-and How to Correct Them, Gary
    Belsky and Thomas Gilovich, Simon & Schuster, New York, 1999.
Against the Gods: The Remarkable Story of Risk, Peter L. Bernstein, John
    Wiley & Sons, New York, 1996.
Capital Ideas, Peter L. Bernstein, The Free Press, New York, 1993.
*The Intelligent Asset Allocator : How to Build Your Portfolio to Maximize
    Returns and Minimize Risk,* William J. Bernstein, McGraw-Hill,
    New York, 2000.
Bogle On Mutual Funds : New Perspectives for the Intelligent Investo, John
    Bogle, McGraw-Hill, New York, 1994.
Common Sense on Mutual Funds, John Bogle, John Wiley & Sons, New York,
    1999.
John Bogle on Investing, John Bogle, McGraw-Hill, New York, 2001.
The Power of Index Funds (revised edition), Ted Cadsby, Stoddart Publishing
    Co., Toronto, 2001.
*The Wealthy Boomer—Life After Mutual Funds -Low Cost Alternatives in
    Managed Money,* Jonathan Chevreau, Michael Ellis and S. Kelly
    Rodgers, Key Porter Books, Toronto, 1998.
Classics—An Investor's Anthology, Edited by Charles D. Ellis and James
    R.Vertin, Business One Irwin, Homewood, Illinois, 1989.
Classics II—Another Investor's Anthology, Edited by Charles D. Ellis and
    James R.Vertin, Business One Irwin, Homewood, Illinois, 1991.
Investment Policy- How to Win the Loser's Game, Charles D. Ellis, Irwin
    Professional Publishing, Chicago, 1993
The Handbook of Equity Derivatives (revised edition), Jack Clark

Francis, William Toy and J. Whittaker (eds), John Wiley and Sons, New York, 2000.

How to Be an Index Investor, Max Isaacman, McGraw-Hill, New York, 2000.

A Random Walk Down Wall Street (revised edition), Burton G. Malkiel, W.W. Norton & Company, New York, 1996.

Stocks for the Long Run, Jeremy J. Siegel, McGraw-Hill, New York, 1998.

The Only Guide to a Winning Investment Strategy You'll Ever Need, Larry Swedroe, Truman Talley Books/Dutton, New York, 1998.

Core and Explore: The Investing Rush Without the Ruin, Duff Young, Prentice Hall Canada, Toronto, 2000.

Glossary

Actively managed   Portfolios can be actively or passively managed. Actively managed portfolios employ an investment manager to make investment decisions according to investment objectives, usually with the goal of beating a benchmark index.

Asset allocation   The practice of dividing a portfolio into investment categories known as asset classes such as cash, fixed income, equities, real estate, tangibles, et cetera, is asset allocation. **Strategic** asset allocation places investment in asset classes for the long run. **Tactical** asset allocation positions some or all of the asset classes temporarily to capture expected short or intermediate term market movements.

Authorized participant   A U.S. term for large investors, institutions, exchange specialist and arbitrageurs who place creation/redemption unit orders with an exchange traded fund.

Basis point   One one-hundredth of a percentage point, or .01%. Also, 100 basis points equals 1 percentage point.

Benchmark   Something against which to measure performance. The S&P/TSE 60 Index, for instance, is a benchmark for the performance of large cap Canadian equity managers.

Cap or Capitalization   Refers to market capitalization, the value of a public corporation's outstanding shares. It is calculated by multiplying the current market price of a company's share by all its outstanding shares.

Capped   An index or a fund is capped when there is a limit to the concentration of its holdings. For instance, the TSE 300 Capped Index limits all constituents to no more than 10% of the index. This ensures diversification in a market situation in which a few large companies can dominate an index.

Cash drag   Underperformance due to cash in a portfolio.

Closed-end fund   A fund that has a fixed number of issued shares and is traded on a stock exchange. Often trades at a discount or premium. Is opposed to an open-end fund that continually issues shares or units and doesn't trade on a stock exchange.

Correlation   How the movement of two variables are related. When asset classes respond similarly to market conditions, they are said to be positively correlated. When they respond differently they are said to be negatively correlated.

Creation unit   The smallest number of securities that can be cashed in for exchange traded fund (ETF) shares. Correspondingly, a redemption unit is the smallest number of ETF units that can be cashed in for the underlying securities. Most ETFs require a minimum of 50,000 of their own shares in order to exchange them for the underlying securities.

Derivatives   Contracts whose value is based on the performance of another asset or index. Derivatives include forwards, futures and options.

Designated broker (CDN)   Registered brokers and dealers who enter into agreements with an exchange traded fund to perform certain brokerage related funtions.

Dividends   Earnings paid out to shareholders.

Diversification   In portfolio management, spreading investments among different asset classes to mitigate risk.

Distributions   Payment of earnings by a mutual fund to unitholders of the fund.

Enhanced index fund   An index fund that overweights or underweights index constituents with the goal of achieving returns superior to the index.

Efficient frontier   In Portfolio Theory, the curve that depicts the points which maximize expected return for a predetermined level of risk.

Exchange traded funds (ETFs)   A basket of securities that trades on a stock exchange.

Ex-dividend   A stock is said to be ex-dividend during the time a dividend is declared and the time it is issued. Anyone buying a stock during this ex-dividend period will not be entitled to the forthcoming dividend.

Forward contracts   A promise to buy or sell a specific investment at a set time in the future for the current price when the contract is made. This is different from a futures contract, which is a promise to buy or sell at the future price at a set time in the future.

Futures   A promise to buy or sell a specific investment at a set time in the future for the then current price.

HOLDRS A fixed and mostly unchanging basket of investments traded on a stock exchange. Issued by Merrill Lynch. Stands for "Holding Company Depositary Receipts." Some consider HOLDRS a kind of exchange traded fund (ETF), but they are more properly known as exchange traded baskets.

Index A collection of stocks designed to be reflective of a market.

Indexing An investment management strategy that tries to track an index.

Liquidity The ease and speed with which an investment can be sold without affecting the price of the investment.

Margining Borrowing money from a brokerage to buy securities. Done through a margin account that charges interest on borrowings, collateral must be kept in the account to cover some percentage of the margined stock.

Market timing The practice of darting into and out of investments with the aim of catching them during their upward movement and only then.

Marginal tax rate The tax rate at which your next dollar of income is taxed.

Management Expense Ratio (MER) Fees charged by a manager of a fund, and other expenses (excluding security commissions), divided by the assets of the fund to arrive at a percentage of costs to assets.

Modern Portfolio Theory A study of the relationship between investments and asset classes and their expected risk and return.

Mutual fund A pool of securities managed on behalf of unit holders that is bought or redeemed by the fund company. Units are continually offered (open-ended).

Net Asset Value (NAV) The value of an individual unit in a fund. It is calculated by taking the total value of the fund including cash and dividing it by the number of outstanding shares.

Optimization In index management, the practice of buying selected components of an index to as closely match the movement of the index as possible without actually buying all the index constituents. This is opposed to replication of the index.

Options Contracts granting the right to buy or sell an investment at a set price by a specified date.

Over-the-counter (OTC) A market for securities that is apart from a stock exchange. Bonds are sold OTC. Transactions are arranged over the phone or through computer networks connecting dealers.

Passively managed An investment style in which a portfolio is structured to track a specific index. (See *Actively managed*.)

Price limit order An order to buy a stock that specifies a price or better.

Rebalancing In portfolio management, adjusting back to ideal asset allocation.

REITs Real Estate Investment Trusts

Replication An indexing strategy that involves buying everything in the index. This is one of a few indexing strategies. (See *optimization*.)

Reversion to the mean The habit of investment manager performance to revert to the mean performance over time.

Secondary market The market in which shares are bought and sold after their initial public offering. All stock exchanges and over-the-counter markets are secondary markets.

Secular Long-term Not seasonal or cyclical.

Tracking error The deviation from the index's price or return of any investment whose purpose is to keep pace with an index.

Short selling Selling a stock without owning it. This is done by those who expect the price of the stock to fall before the borrowed shares must be returned.

Segregated 1) In mutual funds, a fund in which all or most of the principal is guaranteed. 2) With respect to investment accounts, this refers to keeping an investor's holdings separate from those of other investors as opposed to commingling them.

Stop loss An order to sell a stock when the price goes below a designated threshold.

Style drift In mutual funds, style drift occurs when a fund manager makes investments not completely in keeping with the fund's declared investment style or bias. A value fund loaded with a popular growth stock to boast returns would be an example of a fund experiencing style drift.

Underwriters Registered brokers and dealers who subscribe for and buy units of an exchange traded fund as they are issued.

Index